Merge

Linguistic Inquiry Monographs
Samuel Jay Keyser, general editor

A complete list of books published in the Linguistic Inquiry Monographs series appears at the back of this book.

Merge
Binarity in (Multidominant) Syntax

Barbara Citko and Martina Gračanin-Yuksek

The MIT Press
Cambridge, Massachusetts
London, England

This book was set in Times New Roman by New Best-set Typesetters Ltd. Printed and bound in the United States of America.

Library of Congress Cataloging-in-Publication Data

Names: Citko, Barbara, 1970– author. | Gračanin-Yuksek, Martina, author.
Title: Merge : binarity in (multidominant) syntax / Barbara Citko, Martina Gračanin-Yuksek.
Description: Cambridge : The MIT Press, 2020. | Series: Linguistic inquiry monographs ; 83 | Includes bibliographical references and index.
Identifiers: LCCN 2020004636 | ISBN 9780262044790 (hardcover) | ISBN 9780262539869 (paperback)
Subjects: LCSH: Grammar, Comparative and general—Syntax. | Parallelism (Linguistics)
Classification: LCC P291 .C563 2020 | DDC 415—dc23
LC record available at https://lccn.loc.gov/2020004636

10 9 8 7 6 5 4 3 2 1

Contents

Series Foreword

We are pleased to present the eighty-third volume in the series *Linguistic Inquiry Monographs*. These monographs present new and original research beyond the scope of the article. We hope they will benefit our field by bringing to it perspectives that will stimulate further research and insight.

Originally published in limited edition, the *Linguistic Inquiry Monographs* are now more widely available. This change is due to the great interest engendered by the series and by the needs of a growing readership. The editors thank the readers for their support and welcome suggestions about future directions for the series.

Samuel Jay Keyser
for the Editorial Board

Acknowledgments

It was in May 2016 that the two of us sat together in Ithaca, New York, and decided to extend the scope of our work and write a monograph. Since then, the research presented in the book has evolved enormously. In the process, versions of it have been presented in several venues and have profited from comments made by many people that we would like to thank for their support. We would like to start with our editor Marc Lowenthal. Marc was encouraging from the very start of our project and has been an invaluable guide through the entire process. We are also greatly indebted to the three MIT Press reviewers for their very thoughtful and detailed comments and suggestions, as well as for constructive criticisms that led to substantial improvements in the final version. Our special thanks go to the reviewer who we know as "Reviewer 3" for a meticulous evaluation of our work and for all the ideas included in the review, many of which are now part of the book. Finally, we would like to thank Anne Mark for being not only fantastically quick and thorough in her copyediting, but also extremely approachable and friendly during the whole process.

Between the inception of the monograph and its publication, we presented its content (or parts of it) to various audiences. We would like to acknowledge them here: the audience at NELS (North East Linguistic Society) 48, held at the University of Iceland (October 2017), where we first presented our Binarity Constraint on Merge; the audiences at colloquia at New York University (May 2017) and the University of Leipzig (January 2018); the audience who came to see our poster at the Crete Summer School in Linguistics (July 2018); the audience at the Morphology and Syntax Workshop at the University of Chicago (December 2018), where Barbara presented the core research ideas in this monograph; and finally, the audience at the colloquium series of the Department of Theoretical and Applied Linguistics at Lomonosov Moscow State University (September 2019), where Martina presented a postreview version of the monograph. We would like to particularly acknowledge the comments and questions of the following members of these audiences: Karlos Arregi, Benjamin Bruening, Ksenia Ershova, Stefan Keine, Julie Anne Legate, Jason Merchant, Gereon Müller, Andy Murphy, Eszter Ronai, Philippe Schlenker, Laura Stigliano, Sandhya Sundaresan, Anna Szabolcsi, Michelle Yuan, and Erik Zyman.

Besides these formal occasions on which we had an opportunity to present our work, we discussed it with a number of people in more informal settings; we would like to thank Kyle Johnson, Roni Katzir, and Umut Özge for discussion of various aspects of our proposal. We would like to thank David Pesetsky for his comments on the book prospectus, and Kyle Johnson for teaching a very inspiring course on movement and multidominance at the Crete Summer School, which Barbara attended. Special thanks go to colleagues who helped us with grammaticality judgments in Croatian, English, and Polish. We apologize to anyone we omitted, and we alone are responsible for any omissions, misrepresentations, or remaining mistakes.

Finally, we would each like to thank our families and home institutions for their support throughout this process. Barbara would like to thank her husband Randy for his unwavering support, her colleagues and students at the University of Washington for creating a collegial work atmosphere, the Helen Riaboff Whiteley Center on San Juan Island (where portions of the monograph were written) for providing occasional necessary respite from everyday life, and the University of Washington for granting her a sabbatical leave in 2018–2019.

Martina is grateful to her husband Eray, her son Jan, her mum Grozdana, and her dad Emil (who, unfortunately, is no longer here to witness the final product, but whose memory this book honors), for graciously accepting the long hours of Skyping with Barbara, endless writing, rewriting, editing, and more, and for cheering her on throughout this journey. Heartfelt thanks go to the people in the Department of English Language Teaching at Middle East Technical University for their friendship and support.

1 Introduction

Our main goal in this monograph is to explore properties of Merge against the backdrop of *multidominant syntax*. While research on multidominance to date has led to a number of important theoretical and empirical insights regarding the properties, linearization, and interpretation of multidominant structures (Moltmann 1992; Wilder 1999, 2008; Citko 2000, 2005, 2011a, b; Gračanin-Yuksek 2007, 2013; Bachrach and Katzir 2009, 2017; De Vries 2009, 2013b; Johnson 2012, 2018, among many others), there have been fewer attempts to capitalize on the specific properties of multidominant derivations and representations in order to advance the understanding of Merge itself. In this monograph, we aim to remedy this gap.

We assume the syntactic architecture whereby Merge, the basic structure-building operation in Minimalist syntax, has the ability to create multidominant structures. We also assume that the two types of Merge responsible for creating multidominant structures are Internal Merge and Parallel Merge. Following Chomsky (2004), we take Internal Merge to be a way to capture syntactic displacement/movement. However, we take the term *Internal Merge* quite literally and assume that the "moving" element (such as B in (1a–b)), instead of being "copied and pasted" into its new position, as shown in (1a), is simply remerged in a new position, as shown in (1b) (Engdahl 1980; Starke 2001; Gärtner 2002; Zhang 2004; Johnson 2012, 2018, among others).

(1) a.

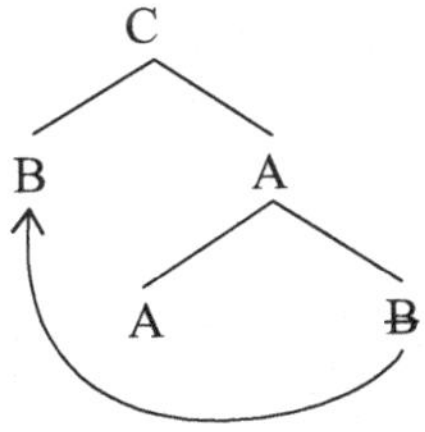

b.

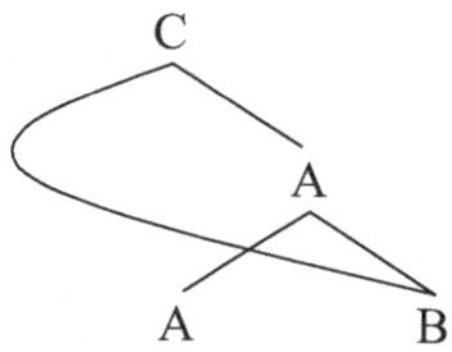

A concrete example is given in (2a–b).[1]

(2) a. **What**$_i$ did Pat read $\boldsymbol{t}_i$?

b.

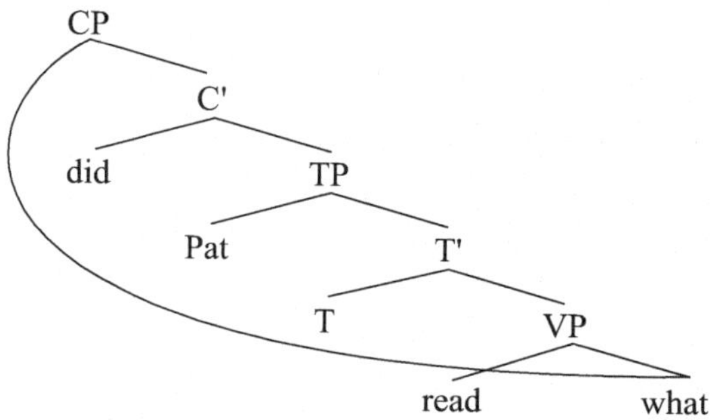

However, there also exists another type of multidominance, created by Parallel Merge (in Citko's [2000, 2005] terminology), illustrated in (3a–b). First, A (externally) merges with B; next, B parallel-merges with C. The result is a multidominant/multirooted structure in which neither mother of B dominates its other mother (McCawley 1982; Blevins 1990; Wilder 1999, 2008; Citko 2000, 2003, 2005, 2011a, b; Van Riemsdijk 2000, 2006b; Gärtner 2002; Gračanin-Yuksek 2007, 2013; Bachrach and Katzir 2009, 2017; Johnson 2012, 2018; Citko and Gračanin-Yuksek 2013, 2016; De Vries 2013a, b, among many others).[2]

(3) a.

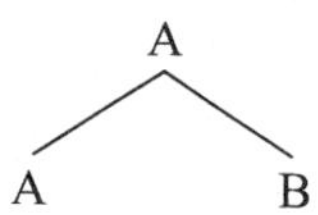

b.

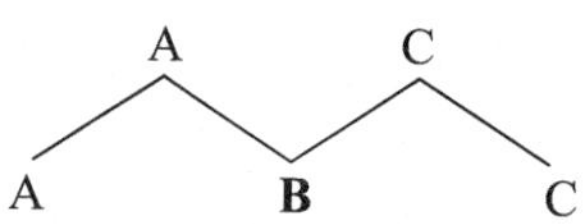

We take Right Node Raising (RNR) to be a representative example of Parallel Merge (McCawley 1982; Goodall 1987; Wilder 1999; Fox and Pesetsky 2007; Johnson 2007; Bachrach and Katzir 2009; Citko 2011b; De Vries 2013a, b, among others, and contra Postal 1998; Sabbagh 2007, among others).[3] For instance, in (4) the DP *a paper by a famous linguist* is merged with the verb *reviewed* in the first conjunct and the verb *edited* in the second conjunct.

(4) a. Pat reviewed __ and Chris edited __, **a paper by a famous linguist**.[4]

b.

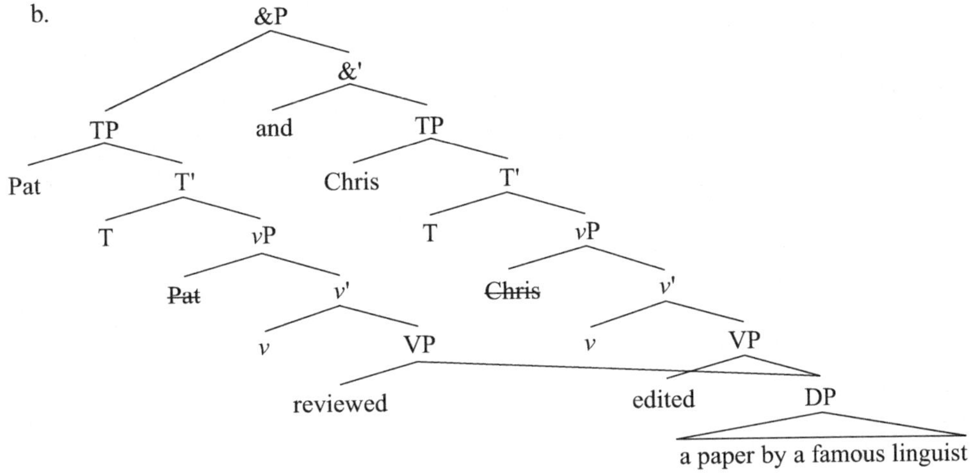

Furthermore, we assume that the same object may undergo both Parallel Merge and Internal Merge, as shown in (5), where B is first parallel-merged with A and C, and then internally merged with F.

(5)

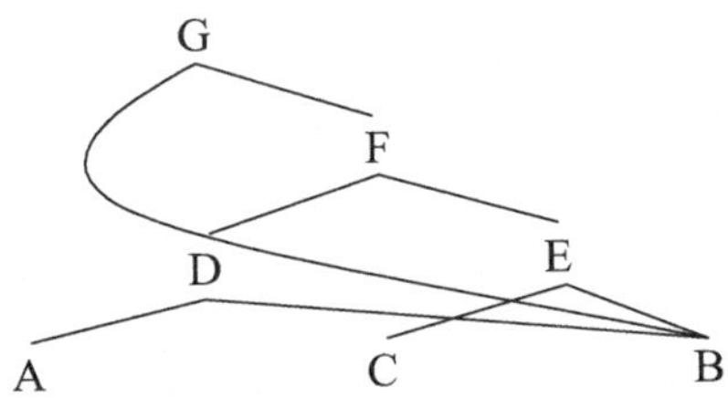

This is what we take to be the case in across-the-board (ATB) *wh*-questions, as shown in (6) (see Williams 1978; Goodall 1987; Muadz 1991; Moltmann 1992; Citko 2000, 2005, 2011b; Gračanin-Yuksek 2013; De Vries 2013b, 2017, among others, for various variants of multidominance approaches to ATB questions).[5]

(6) a. **What paper**$_i$ did Pat review t_i and Chris edit t_i?

b.

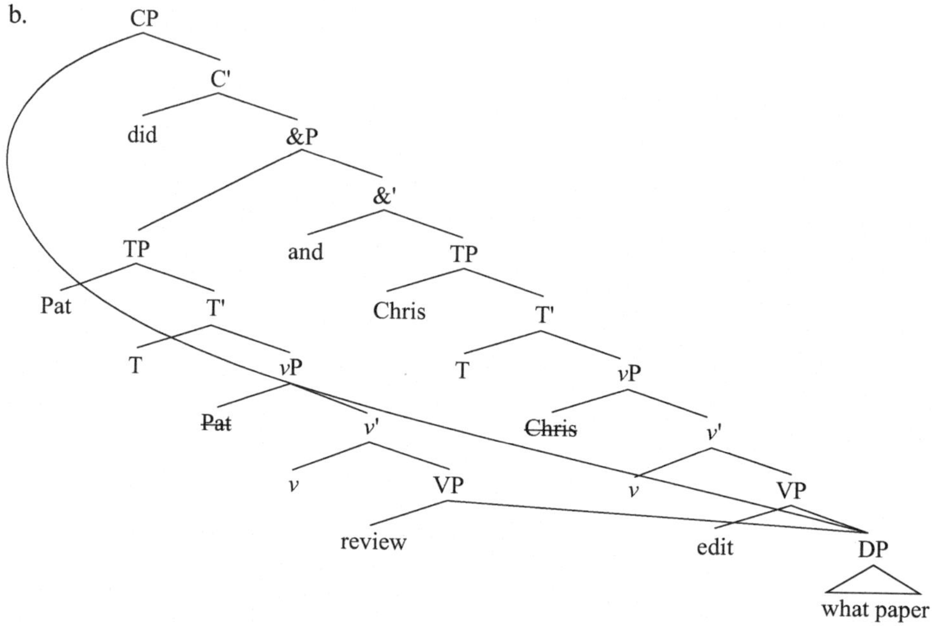

The fundamental question that we focus on throughout this monograph is what constraints emerge when Parallel Merge and Internal Merge apply to the same object, and what these constraints say about Merge itself. We show that the interaction between Parallel Merge and Internal Merge reveals constraints on Merge that are not detectable in configurations that do not involve multidominance.

We proceed as follows. In chapter 2, we spell out our assumptions about the computational system within which Merge operates. We outline the concepts that will be relevant for the analysis that we develop in subsequent chapters, the crucial ones being the concepts of a *workspace*, a *derivation*, and a *syntactic position*. While these concepts are intuitively well-understood, we provide formal definitions, following in some (but not all) respects the formal definitions given in Collins and Stabler 2016. What will be important to our proposal is that a workspace can contain more than a single derivation, which will allow us to relativize constraints to derivations in a system with multidominant structures.

In chapter 3, we lay out the empirical domain of our investigation. Since our focus is on the interaction between Parallel Merge and Internal Merge, we contrast ATB movement (where both Internal Merge and Parallel Merge apply to a single object) and RNR (where only Parallel Merge applies). The empirical insight that we explore is that certain violations of parallelism that are *disallowed* in ATB extraction are *allowed* in RNR. We start with Williams's (1978) observation that ATB extraction is ungrammatical if the fronted *wh*-phrase is extracted from nonparallel positions, as in (7a), which contrasts with the grammatical (7b), where the *wh*-phrase is extracted from parallel positions.[6]

(7) a. *I know a man **who**$_i$ Bill saw $\boldsymbol{t_i}$ and $\boldsymbol{t_i}$ likes Mary.

b. I know a man **who**$_i$ Bill saw $\boldsymbol{t_i}$ and Mary liked $\boldsymbol{t_i}$.

(Williams 1978: 34)

Interestingly, analogous lack of parallelism in RNR does not result in ungrammaticality once we control for independent constraints on RNR, as shown by the grammatical status of (8a–b).

(8) a. Everyone expected __, and into the room walked __, **a guy in a blue suit**.

b. Into the room walked __, and everyone's eyes turned to __, **the defendant's former wife**.

In this chapter, we also include data from Croatian and Polish, two Slavic languages that exhibit more word order flexibility than English, which enables us to test the differences between ATB extraction and RNR in a wider range of environments. Crucially though, these languages pattern with English in disallowing ATB extraction from nonparallel positions, but allowing analogous RNR constructions.[7]

In chapter 4, we derive the contrast between ATB extraction and RNR from an independent constraint on Merge, which we dub the *Binarity Constraint on Merge* (BiCoM) and give in (9).

(9) *Binarity Constraint on Merge* (first version, to be modified)

Merge cannot relate more than two positions at a time within a single derivation.

We argue that in ungrammatical examples of ATB extraction, illustrated by (7a) and (10a), Merge relates more than two positions in a derivation, as shown in (10b–c): the positions that the extracted *wh*-phrase (the circled *who*) occupies in the two conjuncts (Spec,vP in the first conjunct and Spec,TP in the second conjunct) and the position of the root with which it is merged (the circled CP in (10b), which becomes C' in (10c)).[8] Since this violates BiCoM, the outcome is ungrammatical. Our analysis thus derives the ungrammaticality of ATB extraction from nonparallel positions from a general constraint on Merge, rather than from the specifics of the construction in which it arises.

(10) a. *Tell me **who**$_i$ everyone expected $\boldsymbol{t}_i$ and $\boldsymbol{t}_i$ walked into the room.

b. *Tell me

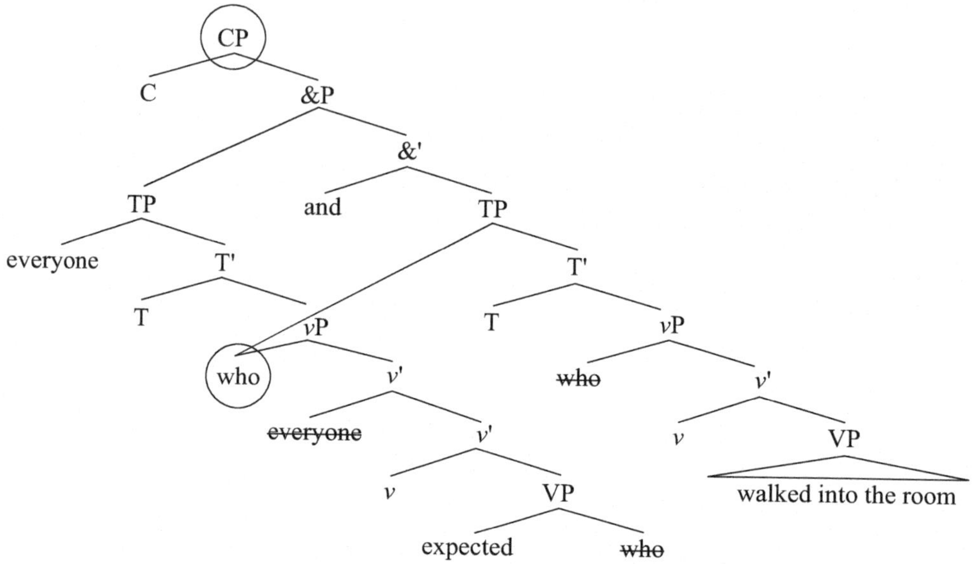

c. *Tell me

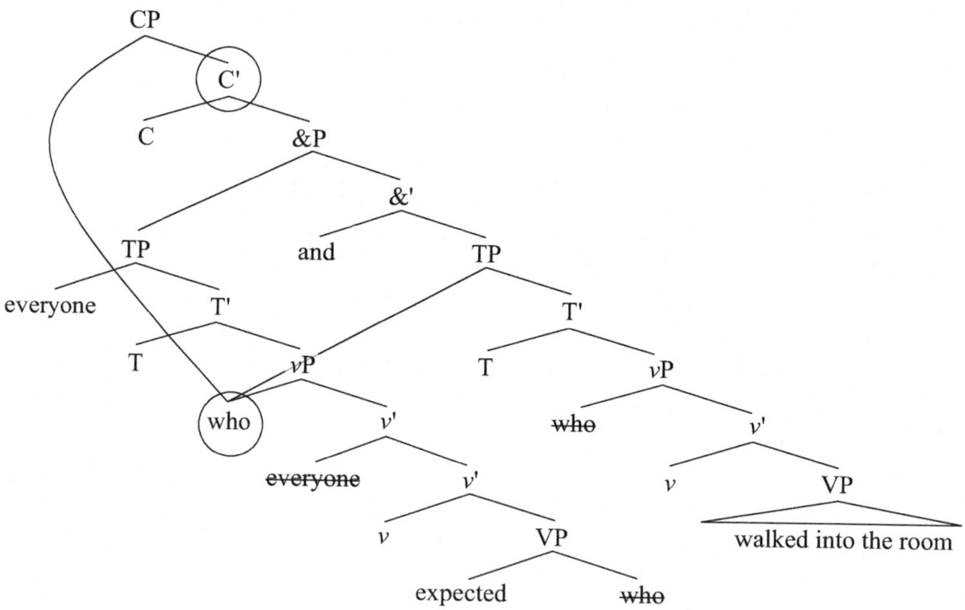

This proposal receives support from the fact that analogous examples of RNR, such as the one in (11a), are grammatical and therefore BiCoM-compliant. We argue that RNR does not violate BiCoM because the element that is shared between the conjuncts in RNR examples (the DP *a guy in a blue suit*) does not undergo further Merge operations after the two conjuncts have been "united" into a single derivation.

(11) a. Everyone expected __, and into the room walked __, **a guy in a blue suit**.

b.

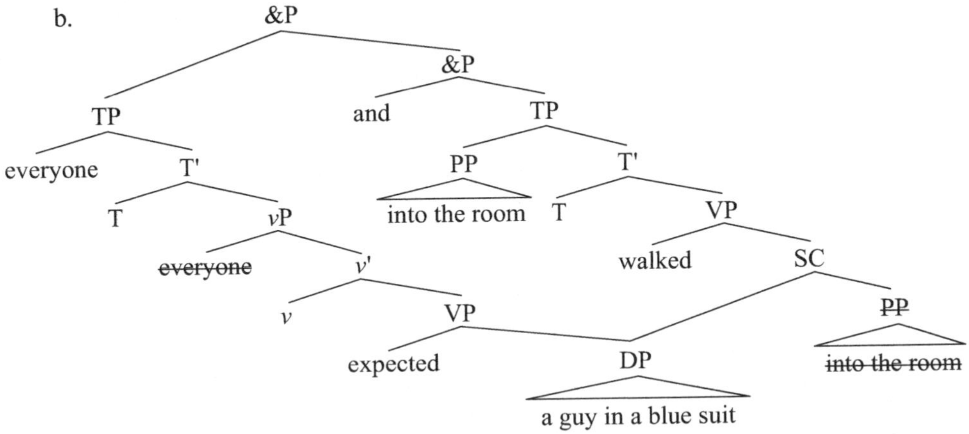

The proposal that Merge is subject to some kind of binarity constraint is by no means new (see, for example, Kayne's [1981, 1984] argument that syntactic representations are limited to binary branching—that is, Merge can only combine two objects at a time). However, since our discussion of Merge is couched in a multidominant system, it is possible for Merge to target two objects at a time but nevertheless violate BiCoM.

In chapter 5, we discuss two principled exceptions to BiCoM. The first involves grammatical cases of ATB extraction, such as the one in (12a). As shown in (12b), Internal Merge in this case violates BiCoM because *who* ends up occupying three positions: the complement of the verb *saw*, the complement of the verb *liked*, and the specifier of CP, and these three positions are related to the position of C′. Thus, Merge relates four positions in a single derivation.[9]

(12) a. I know a man **who**$_i$ Bill saw $\boldsymbol{t_i}$ and Mary liked $\boldsymbol{t_i}$.

b. I know a

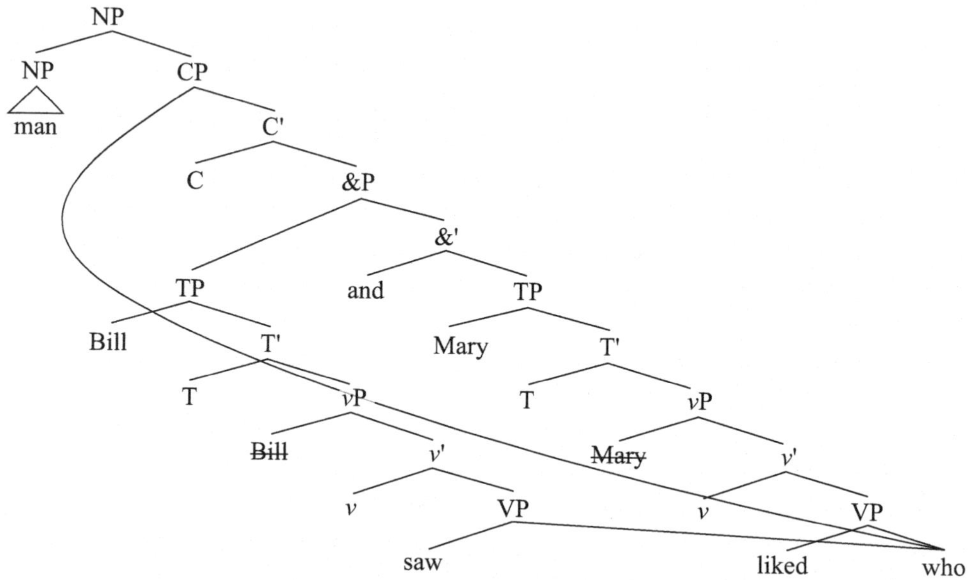

The second case where we would expect to find BiCoM violations, but we don't, involves successive-cyclic movement. In the run-of-the-mill long-distance *wh*-question in (13a), whose structure is given in (13b), all instances of Internal Merge except the first relate multiple positions in a single derivation. For example, when the *wh*-phrase *who* is merged in the specifier of the matrix vP, Merge relates five positions: all the positions of *who* (the complement of the verb *liked*, the specifier of the embedded vP, the specifier of the embedded CP, the specifier of the matrix vP) and the position of the matrix v′, with which *who* merges.

(13) a. $[_{CP}$ **Who**$_i$ did Bill $[_{vP}$ $\boldsymbol{t_i}$ say $[_{CP}$ $\boldsymbol{t_i}$ Mary $[_{vP}$ $\boldsymbol{t_i}$ liked $\boldsymbol{t_i}]]]]$?

b.

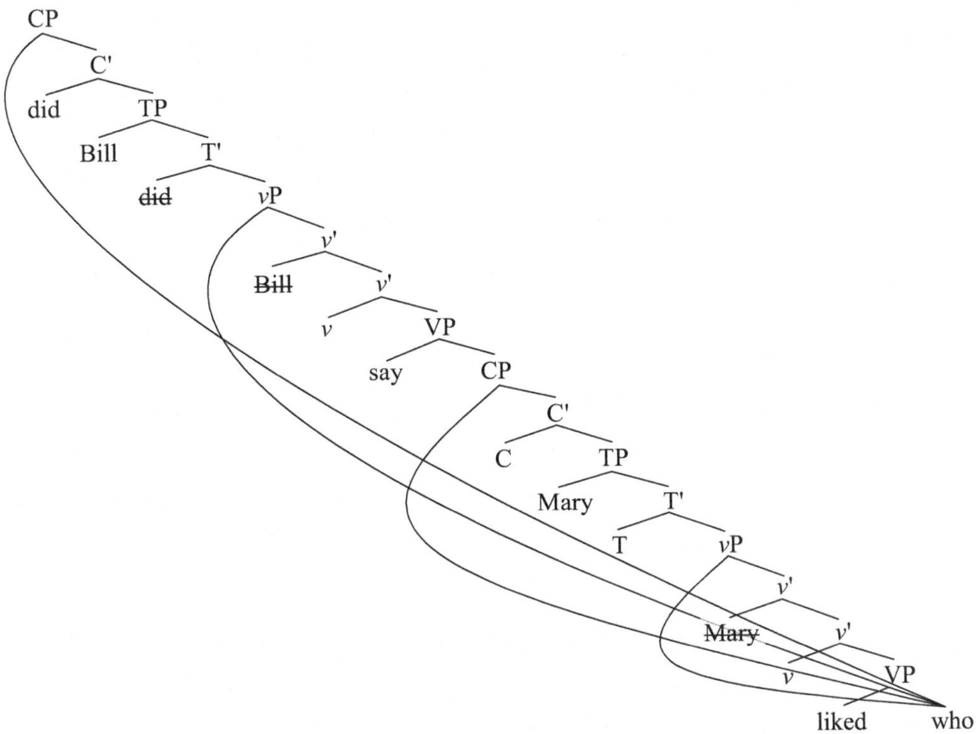

We argue in this chapter that BiCoM violations may be obviated in two principled ways. One is for two (or more) of the positions that Merge relates to be similar enough to count as one for the purposes of further Merge operations. We refer to this scenario as *structural syncretism*, building on the analogy with morphosyntactic syncretism. The other way is for Merge, due to locality considerations, to "see" only the highest position occupied by the shared constituent, and for other positions to be "forgotten/ignored" by the system. This is what happens in successive-cyclic movement.

In chapter 6, we examine consequences of our proposal, focusing on a variety of seemingly unconnected phenomena that are brought together under the umbrella of structural syncretism. First, we ask why certain cases of embedding improve ungrammatical ATB extraction, but others do not. We build on Williams's (1978) observation that embedding the subject gap improves cases of nonparallel extraction, as shown in (14a–b).

(14) a. *I know a man **who**$_i$ Bill saw ***t***$_i$ and ***t***$_i$ likes Mary.

b. I know the man **who**$_i$ John likes ***t***$_i$ and we hope ***t***$_i$ will win.

(Williams 1978: 34)

But sometimes embedding has the opposite effect; the grammatical (15a) becomes ungrammatical (for some speakers) when one conjunct is embedded, as shown in (15b).

(15) a. Tell me **who**$_i$ ***t***$_i$ nominated Mary and ***t***$_i$ will vote for her.

b. %Tell me **who**$_i$ ***t***$_i$ nominated Mary and we hope ***t***$_i$ will vote for her.

In our view, the effect of embedding depends on whether embedding creates new syncretic positions or not; in (14b) the added structure allows the *wh*-phrase to occupy syncretic positions in the two conjuncts, whereas in (15b) it does not. We also show in this chapter how structural syncretism can explain the so-called adverb effect in ATB constructions: the fact, discussed by Bruening (2010), that ungrammatical cases of ATB extraction from nonparallel positions become grammatical when an adverbial phrase is added in the conjunct containing the subject gap.

(16) a. *She is someone **OP**$_i$ that cooking amuses ***t***$_i$ and ***t***$_i$ hates jogging.

b. She is someone **OP**$_i$ that cooking amuses ***t***$_i$ and, according to her personal trainer, ***t***$_i$ hates jogging.

(Bruening 2010: 55)

On our analysis, the improvement in (16b) is a straightforward consequence of the fact that the presence of the adverb requires extra structure, which in turn allows the shared constituent to be extracted from syncretic positions.

Our investigation of Merge within the context of multidominance yields three major findings. First, the legitimacy of a syntactic operation is evaluated relative to a derivation—what is disallowed within a single derivation is often allowed across derivations. Second, within a single derivation, Merge can only relate two syntactic objects at a time, and it can only do so if these two objects do not end up occupying more than two syntactic positions. In other words, BiCoM operates on positions, not objects. And third, syncretism, which is known from morphology to alleviate mismatches that otherwise lead to ungrammaticality, also exists in syntax and yields grammatical outcomes in configurations that are ungrammatical in the absence of syncretic structures.

Before concluding this chapter, we would like to address the question of whether multidominance is necessary for our proposal that Merge is constrained by BiCoM.[10] This is a natural question to ask given that BiCoM makes reference to positions that syntactic objects occupy, and objects and positions are most easily distinguished in a system with multidominance: a multiply-dominated object occupies more than one position, which is not the case in a system without multidominance. In a system without multidominance, in which there is no Parallel Merge, and in which the effects of Parallel Merge, as well as the effects of Internal Merge, are captured by the Copy Theory of Movement (CTM), the distinction between objects and positions disappears: A multiply-dominated object in our system corresponds to multiple copies in the CTM system. Each copy is a distinct syntactic object and each occupies a single syntactic position. Thus, whenever one of the copies merges with another syntactic object, Merge relates two objects and two positions. In such a system, restricting Merge to positions is equivalent to restricting it to objects.

It is difficult to see how the CTM system could derive the differences between the constructions that we focus on. For example, if we assume the CTM, then ATB extraction from nonparallel positions, ATB extraction from parallel positions, and successive-cyclic movement would all involve Merge of two objects (each occupying a single position) at each step of the derivation. In both the grammatical and the ungrammatical cases of ATB extraction, shown in (17a–b) and (18a–b), the *wh*-phrase in the second conjunct is first copied and merged in a sideward manner with some element in the first conjunct, and then the copy of the *wh*-phrase in the first conjunct is copied again and merged with the C′ (Nunes 1995, 2001, 2004). Both configurations are BiCoM-compliant: each application of Merge relates two positions and two objects. Without extra assumptions, this system does not exclude ATB extraction from nonparallel positions, even if Merge is constrained by BiCoM.

(17) a. I know a man **who**$_i$ Bill saw $\boldsymbol{t_i}$ and Mary liked $\boldsymbol{t_i}$.

b. I know a man

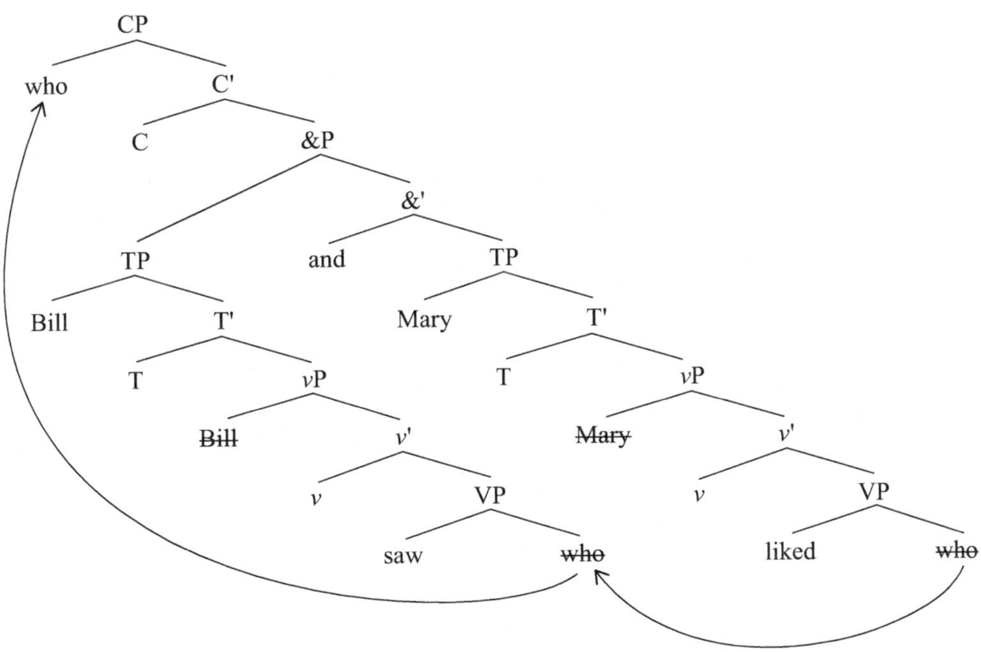

(18) a. *I know a man **who**$_i$ Bill saw $\boldsymbol{t_i}$ and $\boldsymbol{t_i}$ likes Mary.

b. *I know a man

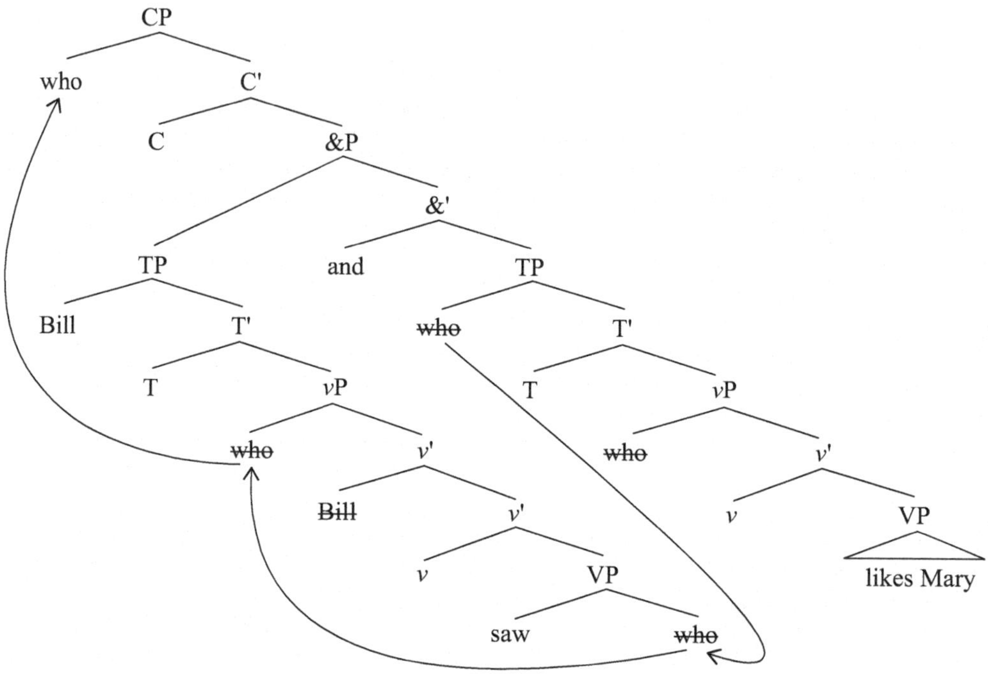

The difference in grammaticality between ATB extraction from parallel positions and ATB extraction from nonparallel positions could perhaps be derived by stipulating that cross-conjunct movement can only take place between parallel positions: for example, if the *wh*-phrase is an object in the second conjunct, it can move to the object position in the first conjunct, but not, for example, to the subject position. This restriction would, however, have to hold only of *sideward* Merge, so as not to exclude successive-cyclic movement, in which Merge typically relates nonparallel positions (e.g., Spec,vP and Spec,CP).[11] Thus, to the extent that the differences between the legitimate and the illegitimate instances of Merge could be derived at all in the CTM system, it seems to us that the explanation would require some stipulations and would hold of a narrower range of cases than it does in our system, in which both Parallel Merge and Internal Merge create multidominant structures. This, in our view, provides good evidence that syntax manipulates multidominant structures.

2 Theoretical Background

2.1 Properties of the Computational System

We assume, following Bobaljik (1995), Chomsky (1995), Zwart (2009), and Collins and Stabler (2016), among many others, that linguistic expressions—pairings of a PF representation and an LF representation—are derived in a syntactic *workspace* from elements contained in a *lexical array* by the application of a single operation, *Merge*. We adopt Collins and Stabler's definition of Merge, given in (1).

(1) *Merge*

Given any two distinct syntactic objects A, B, Merge (A, B) = {A, B}.

(Collins and Stabler 2016: 47)

In our view, only elements that have undergone Merge are part of a derivation. The very initial stage of a derivation (before Merge applies to the elements in a lexical array) is characterized by a workspace that is empty and a lexical array that contains *all* the lexical items necessary to build the current phase of the expression under construction.[1] Merge manipulates *syntactic objects*. We take these to be the elements contained in the lexical array (lexical items) as well as the elements in the workspace: complex syntactic objects already built.[2] Applied to two syntactic objects, A and B, Merge creates a set that contains A and B as its members—a new rooted syntactic object. The root in this new syntactic object immediately dominates both A and B. Every application of Merge constitutes a new *stage* in a derivation, defined as in (2), adapted from Chomsky 1995: 226.[3]

(2) *Stage*

A stage S in a derivation D is a set of syntactic objects created by an application of Merge in a workspace W.

Merge always creates a new set; thus, the number of sets in the workspace increases with every application of Merge—that is, at every stage. However, the number of sets that are *members of the workspace* (i.e., the number of roots, which we henceforth refer to as *sets^W*) does not necessarily increase with every application of Merge.[4] Merge may *increase* the number of sets^W, *decrease* the number of sets^W, or *leave the number of sets^W unchanged.* In what follows, we show how each of these possible outcomes arises.

Informally speaking, Merge increases the number of sets^W in the workspace if, after the application of Merge, the workspace contains more roots than it previously did. Put in more formal terms, Merge increases the number of sets^W at a stage S_i if the application of Merge at this stage (S_i) creates a set^W that does not contain as (an) element(s) any of the sets^W that were present in the workspace at S_{i-1}—that is, at the stage immediately preceding S_i. This situation arises, for example, if the workspace contains a syntactic object (say, a vP missing a subject) and Merge initiates the construction of a different syntactic object in the same workspace (say, a complex subject).

An application of Merge may also decrease the number of sets^W, and this happens if Merge applies to two roots that already exist in the workspace, combining them under a new, single root. Thus, the number of sets^W in the workspace decreases at a stage S_i if the application of Merge at S_i creates a set^W that contains as members two sets^W that were present in the workspace at the previous stage (S_{i-1}). The reduction of sets^W is exemplified by an application of Merge that combines, for instance, a vP missing a subject with a separately built, complex subject.

Finally, following an application of Merge, the number of sets^W may remain unchanged. This happens whenever one of the objects undergoing Merge is a complex syntactic object (a root) already present in the workspace, and the other is a lexical item taken from the lexical array. Lexical items contained in the lexical array are not part of the workspace and therefore are not roots. In such a situation, Merge simply "adds" a lexical item to a complex syntactic object and in doing so extends the structure, creating a new, single root. More formally, Merge preserves the number of sets^W in the workspace at S_i if the application of Merge at S_i creates a set^W that contains as a member *exactly* one of the sets^W that were present in the workspace at the previous stage (S_{i-1}).[5] For example, the number of sets^W is preserved when a head from the lexical array (say, T) is merged with a phrase that is already completed in the workspace (vP).

For our system, it matters how an application of Merge affects the number of sets^W. We propose that depending on how this number changes from one stage to the next, the number of derivations in the workspace may change. Specifically, every time the number of sets^W in the workspace *increases*, a new derivation is initiated. We provide a formal definition of a derivation in (3).

(3) *Derivation*

A derivation D is a sequence of stages $\langle S_0, S_1, S_2, \ldots, S_n \rangle$ in a workspace W, such that for every i, $0 \leq i \leq (n-1)$, S_{i+1} is created from S_i by an application of Merge, and the number of sets that are members of W (sets^W) at S_{i+1} does not exceed the number of sets that are members of W at S_i.

Informally speaking, this definition states that two stages belong to the same derivation if the number of sets^{W} in the workspace at a given stage does not exceed the number of sets^{W} at the previous stage. If the number of sets^{W} increases, a new derivation is initiated, as stated explicitly in (4).[6] This will be crucial to our account of the differences between ATB movement and RNR.

(4) *New derivation*

If the number of sets that are members of the workspace (sets^{W}) at the stage S_{i+1} exceeds the number of sets that are members of the workspace (sets^{W}) at the immediately preceding stage (S_i), a new derivation is initiated at S_{i+1}.

We thus depart from many previous authors who explicitly or implicitly assume that there can only be a single derivation per workspace (Nunes and Uriagereka 2000; Collins 2002; Nunes 2004; Stroik 2009; Jayaseelan 2017, among others) in that we allow a single workspace to host multiple derivations.

In what follows, we illustrate how our system works with a hypothetical derivation involving the lexical array in (5a).

(5) a. Lexical array = {A, B, C, D, E, F}

b. Workspace

The first application of Merge to the elements in the lexical array, shown in (6b), increases the number of sets^{W} in the workspace because the workspace in (5b) contains no sets, whereas in (6c) it contains one set: {A, B}.[7] Thus, Merge in this case initiates a new derivation; the number of sets^{W} in the workspace increases from zero to one. This instance of Merge is External Merge since neither A nor B has undergone Merge before.

(6) a. Lexical array = {A, B, C, D, E, F}

b. Merge A and B = {A, B}

c. Workspace

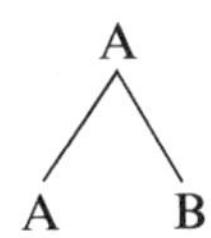

What happens if a given application of Merge does *not* increase the number of sets^{W} in the workspace and, instead, the set newly created by Merge contains the set(s) that already existed in the workspace? In this case, no new derivations are initiated: Merge simply advances the existing derivation, as in (7a–c). Here, Merge applies to the syntactic object already created in the workspace (the set {A, B}) and combines it with the lexical item C taken from the lexical array. The newly created set {C, {A, B}} contains the set {A, B} as a member, so the number of sets^{W} in the workspace remains the same. Thus, according to our definition of a derivation in (3), no new derivations are initiated.

(7) a. Lexical array = {C, D, E, F}

b. Merge C and {A, B} = {C, {A, B}}

c. 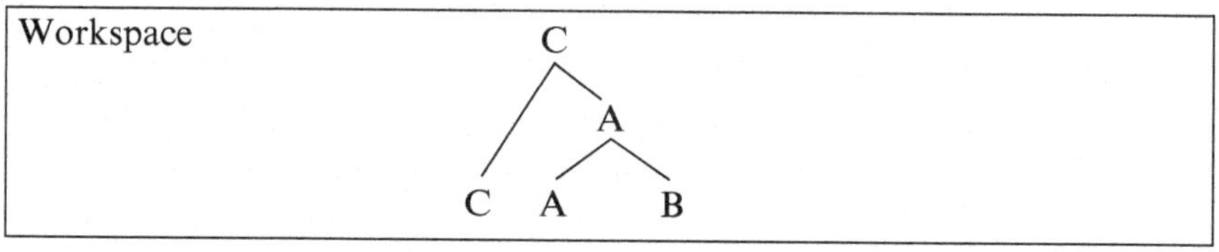

Internal Merge also preserves the number of sets^{W} in the workspace from one stage to the next; it advances the existing derivation. This is shown in (8a–c), where Merge targets the root (C) and a constituent dominated by that root (A). The set created by this instance of Internal Merge {A, {C, {A, B}}} contains the previously existing set {C, {A, B}} as one element, so the number of sets^{W} remains the same: no new derivations are initiated.

(8) a. Lexical array = {D, E, F}

b. Merge {C, {A, B}} and A = {A, {C, {A, B}}}

c. 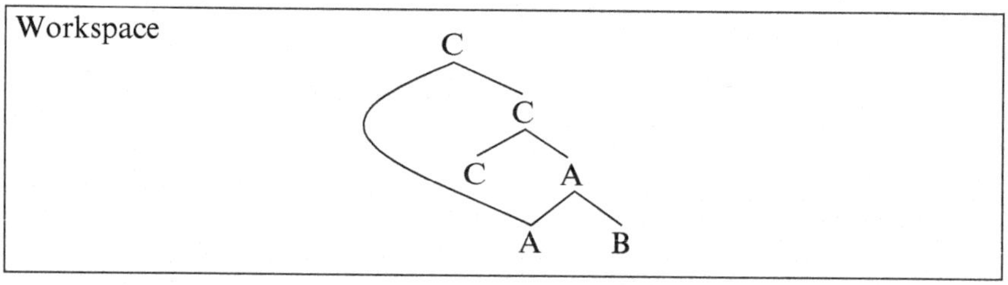

Now, suppose that the next application of Merge applies to two items taken directly from the lexical array—say, D and E—as shown in (9a–c). This is an instance of External Merge, but this time, the number of sets^{W} in the workspace increases by one, given that the new set {D, E} does not contain as its member the set {A, {C, {A, B}}} (i.e., the set already existing in the workspace). This means that a new derivation is initiated; this is the derivation that yielded the set {D, E}.

(9) a. Lexical array = {D, E, F}

b. Merge D and E = {D, E}

c. 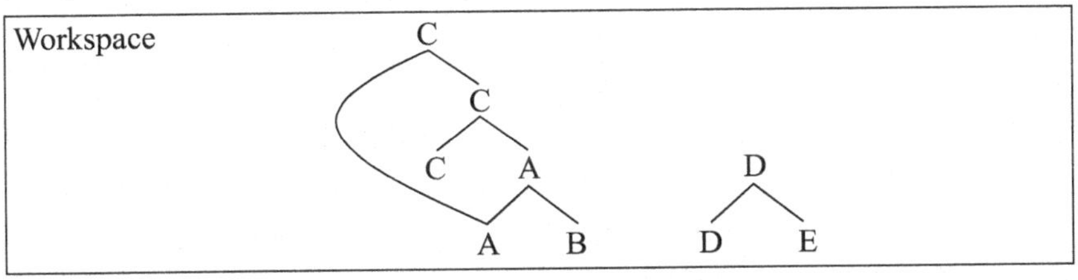

Next, Merge applies to the two sets^W in the workspace ({A, {C, {A, B}}} and {D, E}), as shown in (10a–c), decreasing the number of sets^W in the workspace by one. The newly created set {{A, {C, {A, B}}}, {D, E}} contains as its elements both sets^W previously existing in the workspace. Therefore, the workspace now again contains a single derivation.

(10) a. Lexical array = {F}

b. Merge {A, {C, {A, B}}} and {D, E} = {{A, {C, {A, B}}}, {D, E}}

c. 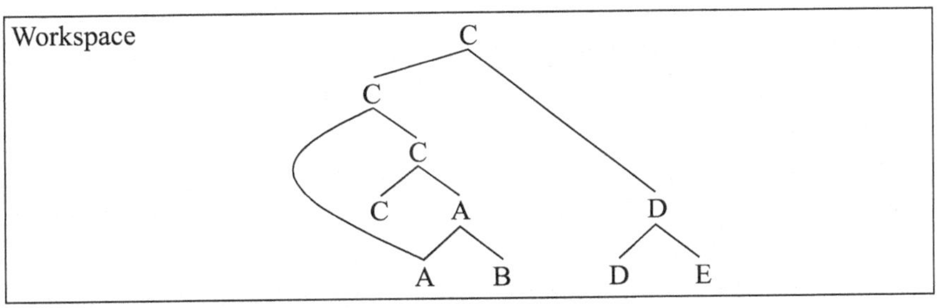

To sum up briefly, External Merge may *initiate a new derivation* by increasing the number of sets^W in the workspace, as in (6a–c) and (9a–c). Alternatively, it may *advance the existing derivation* either by keeping the number of sets^W in the workspace unchanged (as in (7a–c)) or by reducing the number of sets^W (as in (10a–c)). Internal Merge, as shown in (8a–c), always *advances the existing derivation*; it merges the root with a syntactic object included in it, creating a new *single* root, a new *single* set.

This brings us to Parallel Merge. Parallel Merge always increases the number of sets^W in the workspace, which means that it always initiates a new derivation. In order to discuss Parallel Merge, we will take (10c), repeated here, as a starting point.

(11) 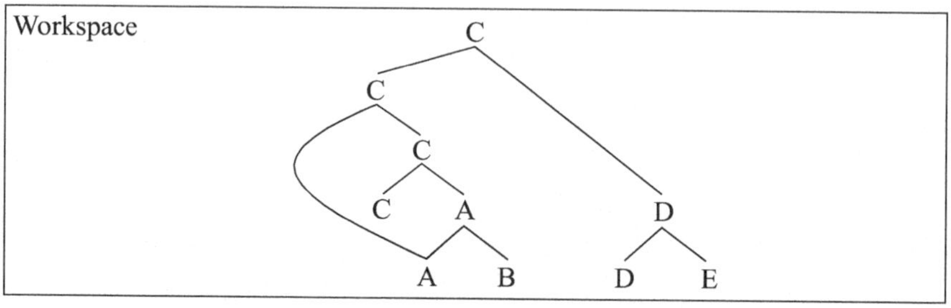

Suppose that this stage is followed by an application of Parallel Merge that combines E, a syntactic object in the workspace that has already undergone Merge, with F, the remaining lexical item in the lexical array. Nothing in our system prevents this: Merge, we said, has access to all syntactic objects in the lexical array as well as to all syntactic objects in the workspace—those that have and those that have not previously undergone Merge.[8] What Parallel Merge does is combine an object that has already undergone Merge with something other than the root that dominates it, as shown in (12a–c). In this sense, Parallel Merge combines the properties of Internal Merge and External Merge, the point made explicit by Citko (2005, 2011b), for example.

(12) a. Lexical array = {F}

b. Merge E and F = {E, F}

c. 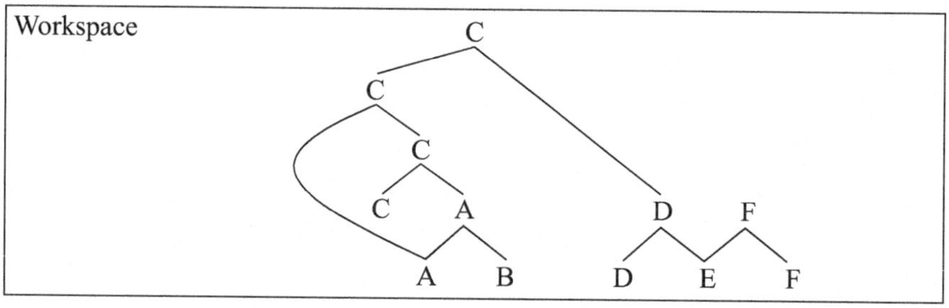

By our definitions, Parallel Merge applying to E and F initiates a new derivation because it increases the number of sets^W in the workspace: it creates the set {E, F}, which is a member of the workspace just like the set {{A, {C, {A, B}}}, {D, E}}, which was created at the previous stage. Although E is part of both sets, the new set {E, F} does not contain the set {{A, {C, {A, B}}}, {D, E}} (i.e., the set already existing in the workspace). The workspace illustrated in (12c) thus contains two different derivations. These two derivations may become part of a single derivation by a further application of Merge. This is shown in (13a–c), where the application of Merge reduces the number of sets^W from two to one. Since now the lexical array is empty and the workspace contains only one single-rooted structure, this step completes the derivation.[9]

(13) a. Lexical array = { }

b. Merge {{A, {C, {A, B}}}, {D, E}} and F = {{{A, {C, {A, B}}}, {D, E}}, {E, F}}

c. 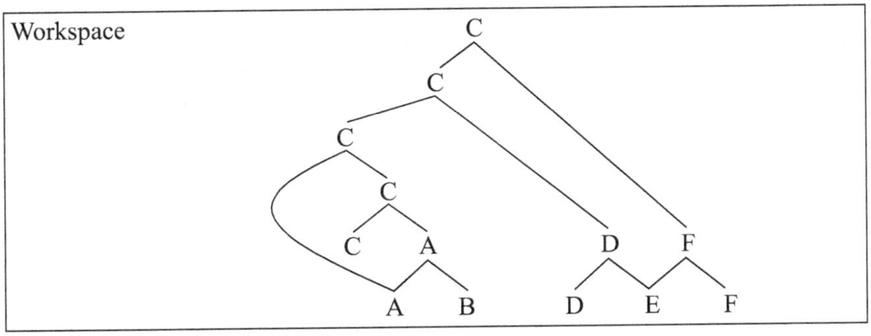

In our system, Merge is relatively unconstrained with respect to what elements it may target: they may be part of the lexical array or of the workspace. If they are part of the workspace, they may or may not have undergone a previous instance of Merge. Crucially, if a target of Merge has undergone a previous instance of Merge, it can be merged either with an object that contains it (Internal Merge) or with an object that does not contain it (Parallel Merge). The structures derived by Merge can thus violate the Single Mother Condition (Sampson 1975; McCawley 1982) and the No-Tangling Condition (Wall 1972; Higginbotham 1985; Zwicky 1985a, among others), given in (14a–b).[10]

(14) a. *Single Mother Condition*

A node has no more than one mother.

b. *No-Tangling Condition*[11]

If nodes M and N are sisters, then none of the descendent nodes of M is a sister of any of the descendent nodes of N.

(Zwicky 1985a: 207)

Internal Merge and Parallel Merge violate the No-Tangling Condition because both may result in configurations with crossing branches, and they violate the Single Mother Condition because any shared node necessarily has two mothers.[12] These violations are tolerable because the Single Mother Condition and the No-Tangling Condition were meant to prevent the generation of discontinuous constituents such as the VP *asked a difficult question* in (15a–b), where the verb in the first conjunct *asked* is separated from its object *a difficult question* by the material belonging to the second conjunct. Such discontinuous constituents cause linearization problems in a system where a phrase marker encodes both dominance and precedence relations among syntactic nodes. The discontinuous VP *asked a difficult question* in (15b) prevents the phrase marker from being linearized because, on one hand, the DP *a difficult question*, being the right sister of the verb *answered*, must follow it and, on the other, the No-Tangling Condition dictates that everything dominated by the first conjunct precedes everything dominated by the second conjunct, which places the DP *a difficult question* before the verb *answered*, causing a linearization problem.

(15) a. The judge asked and the defendant answered a difficult question.

b.

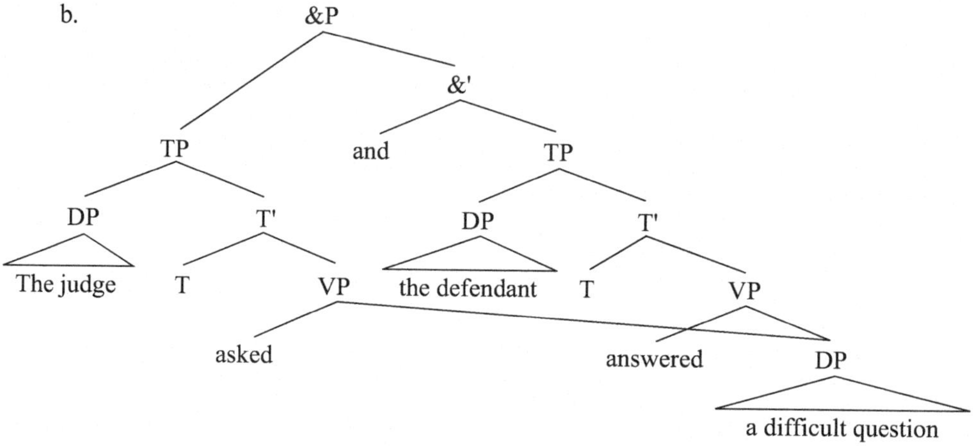

Nowadays, however, it is commonly assumed that the linear order of terminals in a syntactic tree is derived from a different (structural) relation (e.g., asymmetric c-command in Kayne 1994), removing the need for precedence to remain a primitive of the system. Furthermore, several algorithms have been developed to handle linearization of discontinuous constituents (Wilder 1999, 2008; De Vries 2009; Gračanin-Yuksek 2013, among others). For these reasons, we do not consider it problematic that Merge in our system violates the Single Mother Condition and the No-Tangling Condition.

Parallel Merge also violates the Extension Condition (Chomsky 1995; Collins and Stabler 2016), which requires that Merge always extend the objects already created in the course of a derivation. There are various formulations of the Extension Condition (also referred to as the Extension Requirement). For instance, Bobaljik (1995) gives two equivalent versions in (16a–b).[13]

(16) *Extension Requirement*

a. Syntactic operations must extend the phrase marker.

b. The input terms to syntactic operations must be root nodes.

We modify the Extension Condition as in (17) so that it requires Merge to extend *at least one* of the two objects it targets.

(17) *Extension Condition*

For any two syntactic objects to undergo Merge, one (or both) of them cannot have been input to a previous Merge operation.

This modification not only allows Parallel Merge, but also excludes a type of Merge we dub *Sub-Merge*, illustrated in (18a–b), where Merge targets two objects, both of which have undergone a previous Merge operation.[14]

(18) a.

b.

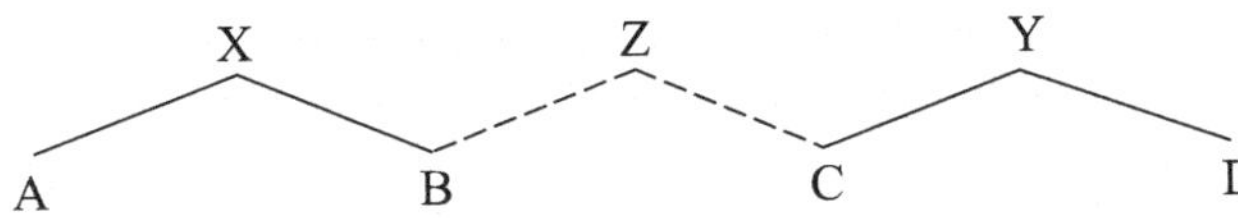

The definition of the Extension Condition in (17) completes the sketch of the computational system we are assuming in this work. This system admits three types of Merge: External Merge, Internal Merge, and Parallel Merge.[15] Every application of Merge generates a stage in a derivation; however, two consecutive stages belong to the same derivation only if the number of sets^W in the workspace does not increase from one stage to the next. If it does, Merge initiates a new derivation. A single workspace can thus contain multiple derivations. This is important for our proposal in chapter 4 that Merge is subject to a binarity constraint and that violations of this constraint are evaluated *relative to a derivation.*

The idea that violations of grammatical constraints are relativized to derivations, however trivial it may seem, offers an insight into the question of why Internal Merge and Parallel Merge structures are subject to different sets of constraints. While the relevant facts, summarized below, are well-known and often used to argue for a Parallel Merge derivation of a given construction, as opposed to a movement/Internal Merge derivation (see Citko 2011b, for example), the answer to the fundamental question of why Internal Merge and Parallel Merge should be different tends to be left implicit.

One difference between them involves case. The shared element in Internal Merge structures disallows multiple cases, as evidenced by the fact that movement from one case position to another is banned. In (19a), the DP *Maria* is assigned case in the finite embedded clause, so moving it to another case position (Spec,TP in the matrix clause) violates Last Resort (Chomsky 1991). By contrast, the shared DP *a paper by a famous linguist* in (19b), contained in a Parallel Merge structure, can be assigned two cases, one inside each conjunct. The assignment of case to the shared DP in the second conjunct is allowed because it does not violate Last Resort *in that derivation.*

(19) a. ***Maria**$_i$ seems t_i is smart. *(Internal Merge)*

b. Pat reviewed __, and Chris edited __, **a paper by a famous linguist**. *(Parallel Merge)*

Similarly, constituents that undergo the two types of Merge differ with respect to their ability to have multiple theta-roles. The shared element in Internal Merge structures resists multiple theta-roles in that movement from one theta-position to another is not allowed.[16] This is illustrated in the ungrammatical (20a), where *John* gets one theta-role inside the embedded clause (from the predicate *smart*) and another in the matrix clause (as the external argument of the verb *believe*). Similarly, in (20b), *John* gets one theta-role as an internal argument of the verb *see* and a different one as its external argument. If the movements schematized in (20a–b) were possible, both sentences should be grammatical; (20a) should mean 'John believes himself to be smart' and (20b) 'John saw himself in the mirror', contrary to fact.

(20) a. ***John**$_i$ believes $\boldsymbol{t_i}$ to be smart.

b. ***John**$_i$ saw $\boldsymbol{t_i}$ in the mirror.

Again, Parallel Merge is not constrained in this way. In example (19b), the shared constituent *a paper by a famous linguist* receives two theta-roles, one inside each conjunct, but this does not lead to ungrammaticality. On our view, this is because each theta-role is assigned within a separate derivation.

These differences between Internal Merge and Parallel Merge are expected once we allow multiple derivations per workspace and relativize constraints to derivations, which we take to be the null hypothesis. Once each derivation is considered separately, relevant constraints apply in the same way in Internal Merge and Parallel Merge structures.[17]

Since our core proposal (that Merge is constrained by a binarity constraint relativized to derivations) relies on the distinction between syntactic objects and syntactic positions, we now turn to this distinction.

2.2 Objects versus Positions

In a system with multidominance, *a single syntactic object* may simultaneously occupy *multiple syntactic positions*. Thus, combining two objects may relate more than two positions. In a system without multidominance, this is not the case: when Merge combines two objects, it necessarily relates two positions.

We begin by defining the position of a syntactic object. Chomsky (1995: 252), in his discussion of how to differentiate between identical copies in a movement chain, suggests that the position of a syntactic object (or its copy) be defined in terms of its sister. Thus, in (21), the position of the higher copy of A is defined as the pair ⟨A, C⟩, and the position of the lower copy is defined as the pair ⟨A, B⟩.

(21) 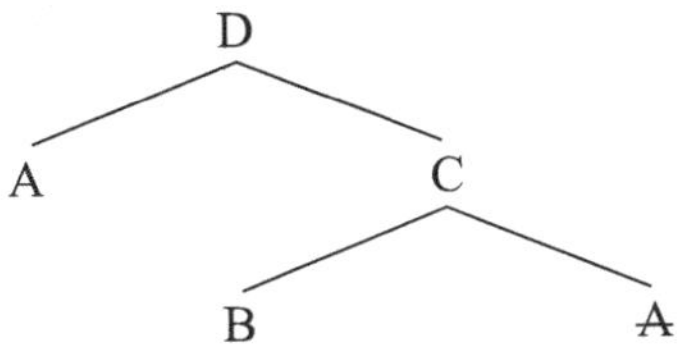

Collins and Stabler (2016: 51) point out that defining the position of a syntactic object in terms of its sister is problematic, given that the sister itself may occupy multiple positions. This is what happens when the sister has undergone displacement/Internal Merge, as in (22), where B, the sister of A, has moved. In (22), both the position of E and the position of A are defined as the sister of B.

(22) 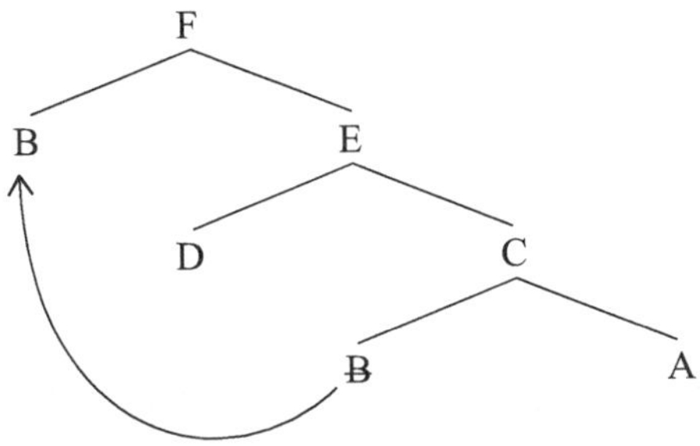

Collins and Stabler's solution is to identify the position of a syntactic object (SO_n) in terms of a path (a collection of nodes) from the root (SO_1) to the syntactic object in question.[18] Thus, according to their definition of a syntactic position, given in (23), the position of the higher copy of A in (21) is defined as the path ⟨D, A⟩, whereas the position of the lower copy of A is defined as the path ⟨D, C, A⟩. And in (22), the position of E (the sister of the higher copy of B) is the path ⟨F, E⟩, whereas the position of A (the sister of the lower copy of B) is the path ⟨F, E, C, A⟩.

(23) *Position of a syntactic object*

The position of SO_n in SO_1 is a path, a sequence of syntactic objects, $\langle SO_1, SO_2, \ldots, SO_n \rangle$ where for all $0 < i < n$, $SO_{i+1} \in SO_i$.

(Collins and Stabler 2016: 51)

Collins and Stabler's definition has the advantage of being able to unambiguously single out the specific position of a syntactic object irrespective of whether the sister of that object has undergone Internal Merge or not. At the same time, their definition makes it impossible to refer to the *position* of a syntactic object without referring to the *object* itself. This is because the final member in the sequence of nodes that define the position of a given object is the object itself. Intuitively, however, we would like the definition of a syntactic position to allow a given syntactic position to be the same position no matter what syntactic object occupies it. For example, we would like the position of the DP subject in (24a) to be the same as the position of the CP subject in (25a): both occupy Spec,TP positions. If a syntactic position is identified in terms of a path, we would like these two paths to be identical, but according to (23), they are not, as (24b) and (25b) show.

(24) a.

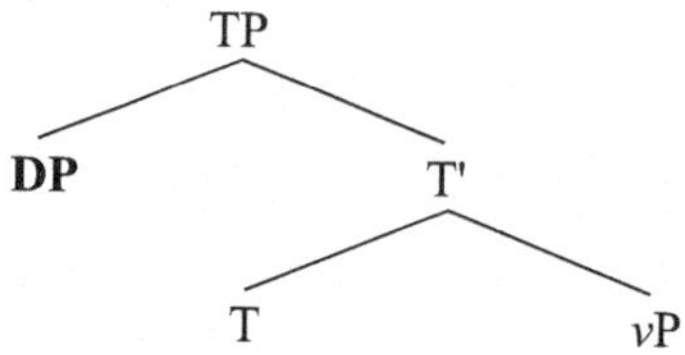

b. ⟨TP, DP⟩

(25) a.

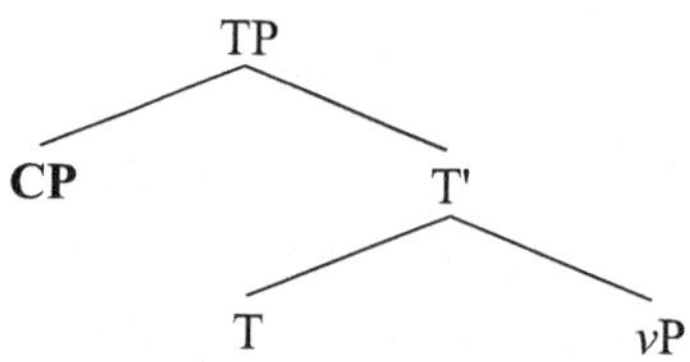

b. ⟨TP, CP⟩

To capture the intuition that the DP subject in (24a) and the CP subject in (25a) occupy the same syntactic position, we propose that the position of a syntactic object should be defined in terms of the path from the root of the tree to the *sister* of the object in question. This is done in (26).

(26) *Position of a syntactic object*

A position of SO_n in SO_1 is a path from SO_1 to SO_m, SO_1 the set^W formed by Merge, SO_m a sister of SO_n, where a path is a sequence of syntactic objects $\langle SO_1, SO_2, \ldots, SO_m \rangle$, and for all i, $0 < i < m$, $SO_{i+1} \in SO_i$.

According to the definition in (26), a syntactic object SO_n occupies as many syntactic positions as it has sisters. SO_n may have more than one sister in a single derivation (e.g., if it has undergone Internal Merge), or it may have more than one sister in multiple derivations (e.g., if it has undergone Parallel Merge). Since the definition of a position of SO_n in (26) makes reference to a path leading to a sister of SO_n rather than to SO_n itself, the positions of the DP subject in (24a) and the CP subject in (25a) are defined by the same path, ⟨TP, T′⟩, as desired.[19]

The definition of a syntactic position in (26) does not face the problem that Collins and Stabler (2016) point out for defining positions in terms of sisters (the problem concerning the situations in which the sister moves) because when the sister moves, it occupies multiple positions, and the paths from the root to each of these positions will be different. For example, in (22) the position of E (the higher sister of B) differs from the position of A (the lower sister of B): the position of E is the path ⟨F, B⟩, while the position of A is the path ⟨F, E, C, B⟩.

A potential question that this way of identifying positions raises is how (if at all) it can distinguish multiple specifiers from each other. This will become relevant in chapter 4, where we discuss whether the thematic Spec,vP position of the subject is the same as the intermediate landing site of a moving object (also Spec,vP). To put it in concrete terms, are the multiple Spec,vP positions occupied by DP_1 and DP_2 in (27) the same or different?[20]

(27)

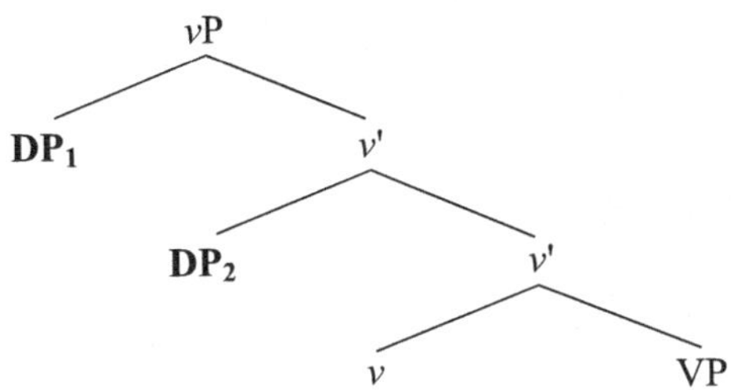

If positions are defined in terms of paths, multiple specifiers can be distinguished from one another. In (27), the position of DP_1 is the path ⟨vP, v′⟩, and the position of DP_2 is the path ⟨vP, v′, v′⟩. In Bare Phrase Structure (Chomsky 1994, 1995), (27) maps onto (28). The two positions can still be distinguished: the position of DP_1 in (28a) is the path ⟨v, v⟩, whereas the position of DP_2 is the longer path ⟨v, v, v⟩.

(28)

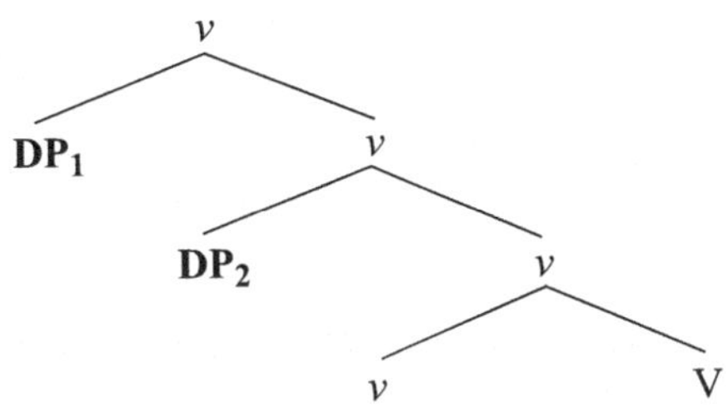

2.3 Conclusion

In the remainder of the monograph, we rely on the theoretical concepts that we have made explicit in this chapter. We have defined the concept of a derivation and of a syntactic position, and we have illustrated how Merge manipulates syntactic objects so as to either advance the existing derivation or initiate a new one. In the next two chapters, we present the phenomena leading to our proposal that Merge is subject to a binarity constraint that limits the number of positions (rather than objects) that can be related by a single application of Merge in a single derivation.

3 (Non)parallelism in Across-the-Board Extraction and Right Node Raising

We showed in chapter 1 that there are two types of multidominant structures—the ones generated by Internal Merge and the ones generated by Parallel Merge—and that the two have different properties. We took Internal Merge to represent movement, as shown in (1b) for the simple *wh*-question in (1a).[1] Crucially, in this case both positions of the multiply-dominated constituent belong to a single derivation: the structure within which the *wh*-phrase is remerged has a single root, and one of the two mothers of the *wh*-phrase dominates the other mother (i.e., CP dominates VP).

(1) a. **What**$_i$ did Pat read $\boldsymbol{t_i}$?

b.

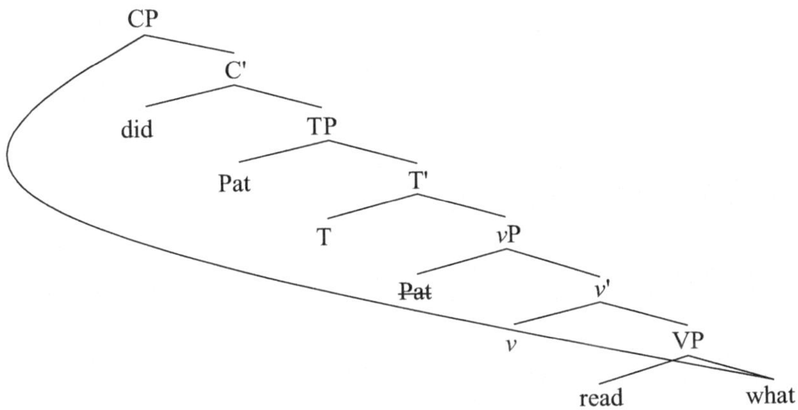

This is not the case with Parallel Merge. In a Parallel Merge structure, of which we took RNR to be a representative example, a multiply-dominated constituent (such as *a paper by a famous linguist* in (2a–c)) belongs simultaneously to two distinct derivations, indicated by the presence of two distinct TP roots (shown in (2b)). The two derivations become a single one at the point when the two TPs combine with the conjunction head, when one TP becomes its complement and the other its specifier. This is shown in (2c).

(2) a. Pat reviewed __, and Chris edited __, **a paper by a famous linguist.**

b.

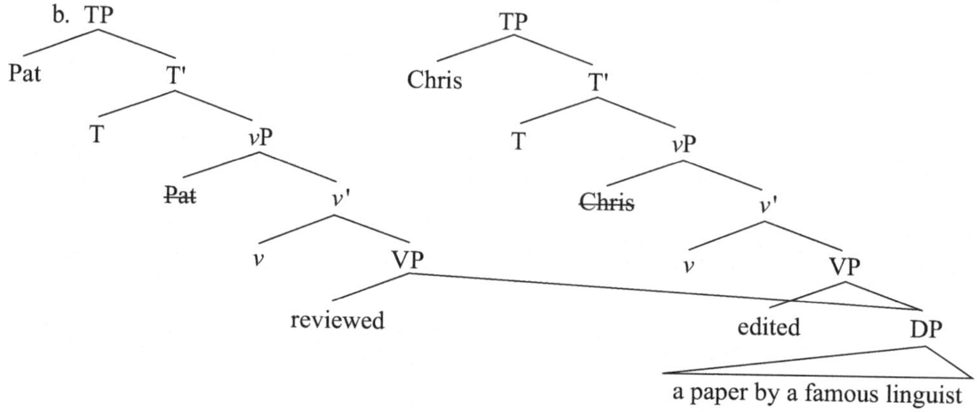

c.

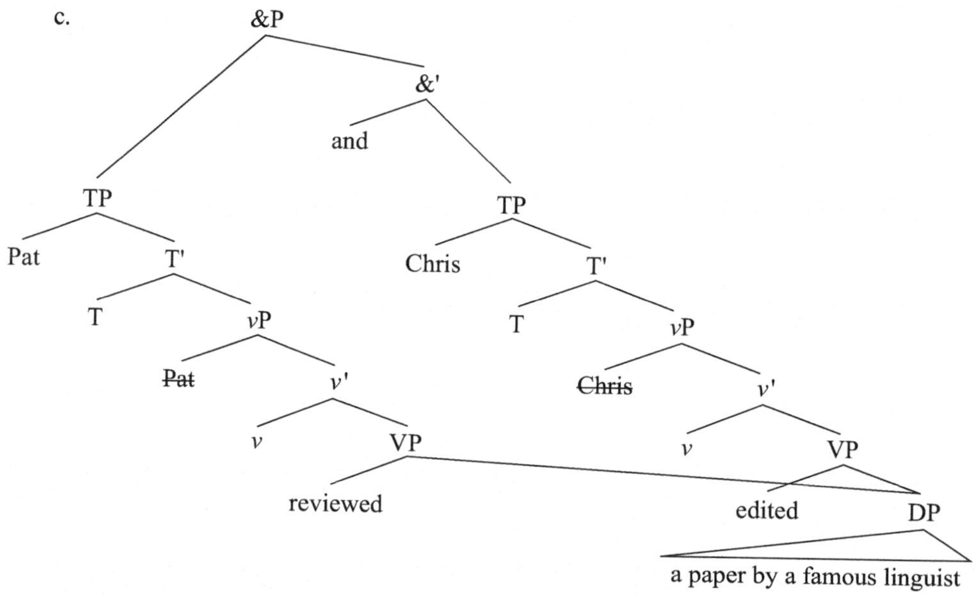

In this chapter, we set the stage for the discussion of how Internal Merge and Parallel Merge interact with each other. The question that we ultimately focus on is what constraints emerge when Parallel Merge and Internal Merge apply to a single object: when an element that has been parallel-merged undergoes subsequent Internal Merge. The central claim we defend is that Merge is subject to the Binarity Constraint on Merge (BiCoM), given in (3).

(3) *Binarity Constraint on Merge* (first version, to be modified)

Merge cannot relate more than two positions at a time within a single derivation.

BiCoM differs from the commonly assumed binarity requirement on Merge (Kayne 1981, 1984) in that it does not constrain the number of *syntactic objects* Merge combines, but the number of *syntactic positions* Merge relates.[2] Since Merge can create multidominant structures, it is possible for Merge to target only two objects at a time but nevertheless violate BiCoM. (4) schematically illustrates such a configuration. When the shared B in (4) is merged with F in the final step of the derivation, Merge relates *two objects* (B and F), but *four positions*: three positions of B (i.e, its positions as a sister of A, a sister of C, and a sister of F) and the position of F. Crucially, all of them are contained in a single derivation, with a single root (G), which is why (4) violates BiCoM.

(4)

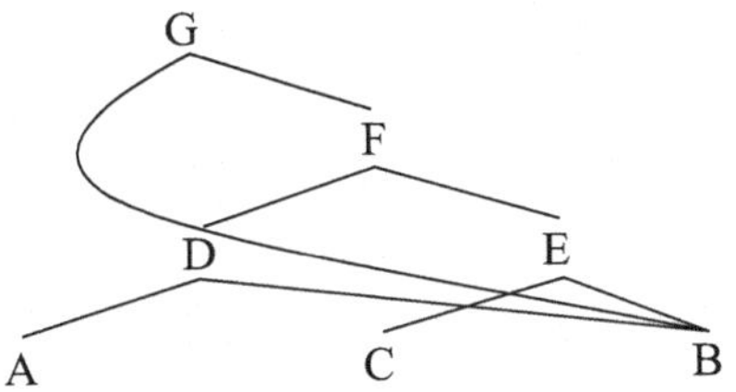

The abstract representation in (4) corresponds to what happens in cases of ATB extraction, illustrated in (5a–b). Internal Merge of *what paper* violates BiCoM; it happens *after* the two TPs have already been "united" into a single derivation, so it necessarily relates four positions.

(5) a. **What paper**$_i$ did Pat review $\boldsymbol{t_i}$ and Chris edit $\boldsymbol{t_i}$?

b.

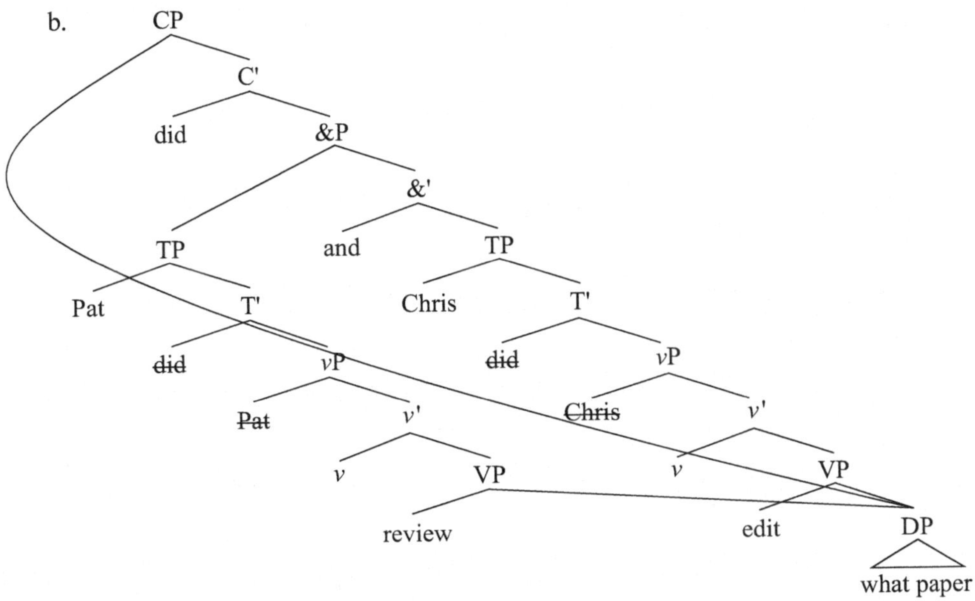

As it stands, then, our proposal that Merge is constrained by BiCoM excludes all ATB extraction, including grammatical examples like (5a). This is obviously not a welcome result. However, we do not believe that such cases are necessarily fatal counterexamples to the proposal that Merge is constrained by BiCoM. We defer a detailed discussion of grammatical ATB extraction until chapter 5, where we define circumstances under which BiCoM violations are allowed. We propose that there is something special about grammatical ATB extraction that allows it to escape BiCoM violations, on a par with, for instance, grammatical cases of agreement, shown in (6a), in a configuration that otherwise yields ungrammatical results, shown in (6b).[3]

(6) a. Either they or you are going to have to go.
(Pullum and Zwicky 1986: 754)
b. *Either they or I are/am/is going to have to go.
(Pullum and Zwicky 1986: 753)

In this chapter, we first examine ungrammatical cases of ATB extraction and show that they contrast with analogous but grammatical cases of RNR. More specifically, we compare ATB and RNR constructions in which the shared constituent occupies nonparallel positions in the two conjuncts: it is the subject in one and the object in the other. Since RNR is subject to an independent restriction that the shared constituent must be final in both or all conjuncts, our examples of RNR involve locative inversion in one conjunct, which allows the subject to occupy a clause-final position, satisfying this restriction. We then turn to Polish and Croatian, languages that allow postverbal subjects in a wider range of configurations, and show that RNR examples contrast with analogous ATB examples in these languages as well. In chapter 4, we explain how the contrast between ATB extraction and RNR follows from our proposal.

3.1 Parallelism in Across-the-Board Movement

We start with an observation, going back to Williams 1978, that ATB movement is ungrammatical if the fronted *wh*-phrase is extracted from nonparallel positions. This is shown by the contrast in (7a–b); in the ungrammatical (7a), the extracted element is the direct object in the first conjunct and the subject in the second conjunct, whereas in the grammatical (7b), it is the direct object in both conjuncts.

(7) a. *I know a man **who**$_i$ Bill saw $\boldsymbol{t_i}$ and $\boldsymbol{t_i}$ likes Mary.
(Williams 1978: 34)
b. I know a man **who**$_i$ Bill saw $\boldsymbol{t_i}$ and Mary liked $\boldsymbol{t_i}$.

This contrast is often attributed to a parallelism requirement on ATB movement, a representative formulation of which is given in (8) (Williams 1978; Gazdar 1981; Pesetsky

1982; Anderson 1983; Goodall 1987; Woolford 1987; Kasai 2004; Bruening 2010, among others).

(8) *Parallelism Condition on ATB Movement*

ATB movement must take place from syntactically parallel positions.

(Kasai 2004: 181)

Williams (1978) also notes that extraction from nonparallel positions improves if the subject gap is further embedded, as shown in (9a–b).

(9) a. *I know a man **who**$_i$ Bill saw $\boldsymbol{t_i}$ and $\boldsymbol{t_i}$ likes Mary.

b. I know the man **who**$_i$ John likes $\boldsymbol{t_i}$ and we hope $\boldsymbol{t_i}$ will win.

(Williams 1978: 34)

This effect has received considerable attention in the literature since the 1970s. Williams (1978) attributes the parallelism requirement (and the improvement with the embedding of the subject gap) to the constraint on factorization given in (10), which requires all conjuncts to be split by a factor line if one conjunct is split. The constraint also requires that all left conjunct brackets belong to the same factor.[4]

(10) If F is a factor and C a coordinate structure containing conjuncts $C_1 \ldots C_n$, then for F to be a well-formed factor the following must hold: if for any *i*, $[_{Ci} \in$ F and $]_{Ci} \notin$ F, then for all *i*, it must be the case that $[_{Ci} \in$ F and $]_{Ci} \notin$ F.

(Williams 1978: 32)

The nonparallel example in (9a) is ungrammatical because the left bracket in each conjunct (boldfaced in (11a)) belongs to a different factor. The improvement seen in (9b) (where the subject is embedded) is due to the fact that now the left brackets (boldfaced in (11b)) belong to the same factor.

(11)				
a.	C	[Bill saw	who]	
				and
			[who likes Mary]	
b.	C	[John likes	who]	
				and
		[we hope	[who will win]]	

Pesetsky (1982: 309) attributes the ungrammaticality of (9a) to a violation of the Path Containment Condition, stated informally in (12). The condition requires of any two paths between Ā-bound empty categories and their Ā-binders that one path contain the other if the paths interact with one another.

(12) *Path Containment Condition*

If two paths overlap, one must contain the other.

The ungrammatical example in (9a) contains three paths, represented schematically in (13a) and listed in (13b–d). They clearly overlap, yet the path in (13c) does not include one element of the path in (13d)—namely, VP_1. Conversely, the path in (13d) does not include one element of the path in (13c)—namely, $INFL'_2$. Thus, neither path contains the other. They both contain the path in (13b), so the problem is not with this path.

(13) a.

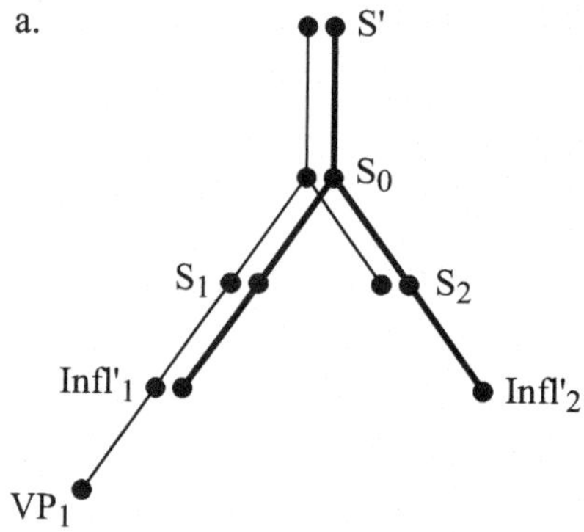

b. Path between the conjunction and the conjuncts: $\{S_1, S_2, S_0\}$

c. Path between $INFL_1$, $INFL_2$, and COMP: $\{INFL'_1, S_1, \mathbf{INFL'_2}, S_2, S_0, S'\}$

d. Path between e_1, e_2, and COMP: $\{\mathbf{VP_1}, INFL'_1, S_1, S_2, S_0, S'\}$

(Pesetsky 1982: 453–454, boldfacing ours)

Goodall (1987) attributes the ungrammaticality of examples like (9a) to a Principle C violation. He defines c-command in such a way that the trace in the matrix subject position of one conjunct c-commands the material in the other conjunct. Thus, in (14), the object trace in the first conjunct is c-commanded by, and coindexed with, the subject trace in the second conjunct and therefore bound by it, in violation of Principle C.

(14) *the man [$_S$ **who$_i$** < [$_S$ John [$_{VP}$ saw ***t$_i$***]]] / [$_S$ ***t$_i$*** [$_{VP}$ kissed Mary]]]

(Goodall 1987: 69)

Woolford (1987) derives the ungrammaticality of examples like (9a), illustrated in (15), from a violation of the Empty Category Principle: the subject trace in the second conjunct is not properly governed because the boldfaced S node that immediately dominates both conjuncts constitutes a barrier for government.

(15) $[_{CP}$ **who**$_i$ **[**$_S$ $[_S$ Bill saw $\boldsymbol{t_i}]$ and $[_S$ $\boldsymbol{t_i}$ likes Mary]]]

Franks (1995) derives the ungrammaticality of (9a) from a parallelism constraint on thematic roles given in (16).

(16) In any ATB construction, the gaps must pertain either to most prominent or to not most prominent arguments, consistently across all the conjuncts.
(Franks 1995: 67)

In the ungrammatical example (9a), the extracted *wh*-phrase is the Theme in one conjunct but the Experiencer in the other conjunct, as shown in (17a–b). Since the first conjunct also contains an Experiencer, the Theme is not the most prominent argument in this conjunct. The Experiencer, however, is the most prominent argument in the second conjunct. The improvement seen in (9b), where the gap is the embedded (rather than the matrix) subject, is due to the fact that the embedded subject is no longer the most prominent element in the second conjunct; the matrix subject *we* is, as shown in (17c).

(17)	a. **who**$_i$ Bill saw $\boldsymbol{t_i}$	(Experiencer, **Theme**)
	b. **who**$_i$ $\boldsymbol{t_i}$ likes Mary	(**Experiencer**, Theme)
	c. we hope $\boldsymbol{t_i}$ will win	(Experiencer, **Experiencer**, Theme)

Anderson (1983) proposes that the ungrammaticality of sentences like (9a), which contain nonparallel adjacent gaps, follows from the fact that such sentences are structurally ambiguous between the representation in which coordinated chunks are TPs, as in (18a), and the representation in which they are VPs, as in (18b).

(18) a. I know a man **who**$_i$ $[[_{TP}$ Bill saw $\boldsymbol{t_i}]$ and $[_{TP}$ $\boldsymbol{t_i}$ likes Mary]].
b. I know a man **who**$_i$ Bill $[[_{VP}$ saw $\boldsymbol{t_i}]$ and $[_{VP}$ likes Mary]].

In Anderson's system, the representation in (18a) does not violate any grammatical principles, but it is dispreferred by the parser, which favors low right attachment of small groups of words (Frazier and Fodor 1978). The representation in (18b), preferred by the parser, violates the prohibition against vacuous quantification and therefore yields an ungrammatical result.[5]

More recently, Kasai (2004) builds on a proposal by George (1980), who argues that sentences like (9a) do not involve ATB extraction at all; rather, the *wh*-phrase moves independently within each conjunct and is then deleted inside the second one. George proposes that this deletion can only happen if the *wh*-phrase occupies parallel positions in the two conjuncts. Kasai adopts this parallelism requirement and applies it not to deletion, but to movement, stipulating that ATB movement may only proceed from parallel positions, as stated in (19), repeated from (8).[6]

(19) *Parallelism Condition on ATB Movement*

ATB movement must take place from syntactically parallel positions.

(Kasai 2004: 181)

In chapter 4, we propose an alternative explanation for the parallelism requirement in ATB constructions, couched in terms of BiCoM. Our proposal shares with Kasai's the reference to parallelism of syntactic positions in ATB extraction, but departs from it in that it treats BiCoM as a constraint on Merge in general rather than as a condition on ATB extraction in particular. First, however, we show that RNR differs from ATB movement with respect to the parallelism requirement. This is the topic of section 3.2.

Before delving into RNR, we would like to briefly address (but ultimately reject) the possibility that the degradation of examples involving ATB extraction from nonparallel positions is due to a processing difficulty rather than a grammatical constraint.[7] On a processing view, Williams's (1978) original example, repeated in (20a), could be ungrammatical because it involves a garden path effect; that is, the two verbs (*saw* and *likes*) can be parsed as coordinated with each other, predicated of a single subject (*Bill*), as in (20b). On such a parse, the extracted *wh*-phrase *who* is initially construed as the object of both coordinated verbs. The disruption arises when the parser encounters the DP *Mary*, which is impossible to incorporate into the structure that the parser posited for the sentence.

(20) a. *I know a man **who**$_i$ Bill saw $\boldsymbol{t}_i$ and $\boldsymbol{t}_i$ likes Mary.

(Williams 1978: 34)

b. *I know a man **who**$_i$ Bill [saw and likes $\boldsymbol{t}_i$] Mary.

This account predicts that once we control for the garden path effect, the ungrammaticality should disappear.[8] While it is true that some cases of nonparallel extraction do improve once the garden path effect is controlled for, as shown by the grammaticality of (21a–c), crucially, not all of them do, as shown by the ungrammaticality of (22a–c).

(21) a. We went to see a movie **which**$_i$ the critics praised $\boldsymbol{t}_i$ but $\boldsymbol{t}_i$ was too violent for my taste.

(Anderson 1983: 3)

b. Here is a book **which**$_i$ I haven't read $\boldsymbol{t}_i$ but $\boldsymbol{t}_i$ was recommended by several professors.

(Anderson 1983: 3)

c. These are the medicines **OP**$_i$ that the government won't fund $\boldsymbol{t}_i$ but $\boldsymbol{t}_i$ are desperately needed.

(Jason Merchant, pers. comm.)

(22) a. *Tell me **which movie**$_i$ the critics praise t_i and t_i wins prizes.

b. *I wonder **which contestant**$_i$ all the viewers admire t_i and t_i wins all the prizes.

c. *The public would like to know **which medicines**$_i$ the government won't fund t_i but t_i cure all diseases.

The factors that might play a role are the choice of the conjunction (extraction tends to improve with *but*, as noted by Anderson [1983] and Franks [1995][9]), the choice of the verb (extraction improves when the extracted subject is the subject of a passive or an unaccusative verb, as noted by Valmala [2013] for Catalan and Spanish), or semantic relatedness between the conjuncts (Zhang 2010).[10] Relativization also sometimes improves ungrammatical examples: note that all the examples in (21a–c) involve relative clauses.[11]

There is also experimental evidence that the parallelism effect cannot be reduced to processing constraints. Sturt and Martin (2016) compared ATB examples involving *wh*-extraction from nonparallel positions with corresponding examples in which *wh*-extraction did not proceed in an ATB manner, but rather involved conjunct-internal movement of the *wh*-phrase. The types of sentences they tested are given in (23a–d). The results showed that ATB examples were judged worse than non-ATB examples.

(23) a. The surgeon **who** James tricked __, and Richard annoyed __, scrubbed up for surgery. (+PARALLEL, +ATB)

b. The surgeon **who** __ tricked James, and Richard annoyed __, scrubbed up for surgery. (–PARALLEL, +ATB)

c. The surgeon **who** James tricked __, and **who** Richard annoyed __, scrubbed up for surgery. (+PARALLEL, –ATB)

d. The surgeon **who** __ tricked James, and **who** Richard annoyed __, scrubbed up for surgery. (–PARALLEL, –ATB)

(Sturt and Martin 2016)

The processing preference for parallelism, generally operative in coordinate structures (as shown by Frazier, Munn, and Clifton [2000], for example), would predict no difference between nonparallel examples with ATB movement and nonparallel examples without ATB movement, as on this view parallelism has to do with coordination, not the presence or absence of ATB movement. Using a similar experimental design, Parker (2017) also concluded that there is an "extra" effect of parallelism in ATB examples, absent in their non-ATB counterparts.[12] We thus leave the processing explanation aside and proceed on the assumption that the reported ungrammaticality of ATB examples with extraction from nonparallel positions is the result of a grammatical constraint rather than of a parsing preference.

We next turn to parallelism in RNR.

3.2 Absence of Parallelism in Right Node Raising

At first, it appears that RNR examples in which the shared constituent occupies nonparallel positions in the two conjuncts are also ungrammatical. Consider the RNR example in (24a); its intended structure is (24b), where the shared DP *Bill* is the object in the first conjunct and the subject in the second one.[13]

(24) a. *John saw __, and **Bill** told a joke.

b.

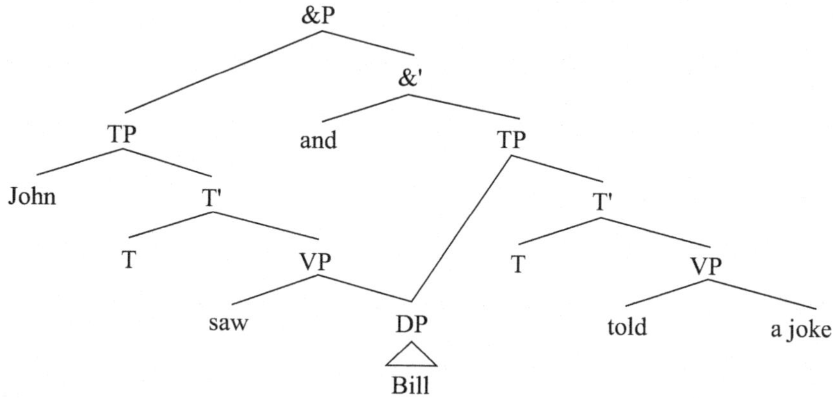

This might be deceiving, however, since such examples are independently ruled out by the so-called Right Edge Restriction on RNR, which requires the shared element to be right-peripheral in each conjunct (see Wilder 1999; Sabbagh 2007, among others). An explicit formulation of this requirement, due to Sabbagh, is given in (25).[14]

(25) In the configuration: $[[_A \ldots X \ldots]$ Conj $[_B \ldots X \ldots]]$ X must be rightmost within A and B before either (i) X can be deleted from A; (ii) X can be rightward ATB-moved; or (iii) X can be multiply dominated by A and B.

(Sabbagh 2007: 356)

In (24b), the shared constituent, the DP *Bill*, is not right-peripheral in the second conjunct, in violation of the Right Edge Restriction. The ungrammaticality of this example is thus unrelated to the parallelism requirement. The independence of the Right Edge Restriction from the parallelism requirement is illustrated in (26), where the shared element occupies parallel positions, but the sentence is nevertheless ungrammatical because it violates the Right Edge Restriction.

(26) *Joss will donate __ to the library, and Maria will donate **several old novels** to the museum.

(Sabbagh 2007: 354)

To examine whether RNR is subject to the parallelism requirement, we need examples in which the shared constituent is the subject in one conjunct and the object in the other, and, crucially, it is final in both conjuncts. Since subjects in English typically appear preverbally and objects postverbally, such examples are difficult to come by. However, postverbal subjects are not categorically banned in English: they are allowed in locative inversion (see Emonds 1976; Bresnan 1994; Collins 1997; Culicover and Levine 2001; Postal 2004; Bruening 2010, among many others), as shown in (27a–c) with the subjects boldfaced.[15]

(27) a. Down the hill rolled **John.**
(Collins 1997: 10)
b. Into the room walked **Robin**.
(Culicover and Levine 2001: 292)
c. From this observation will emerge **a new understanding of natural language**.
(Bruening 2010: 45)

Interestingly, as long as the Right Edge Restriction is not violated (which is what locative inversion controls for), the shared constituent in RNR does not need to occupy parallel positions in both conjuncts: it can be the subject in one and the object in the other. This is shown in (28a–b) and (29a–b); in (28a–b) the boldfaced shared element is the object in the first conjunct and the subject in the second conjunct, whereas in (29a–b) it is a subject in the first conjunct and an object (of a preposition) in the second conjunct.

(28) *RNR: Object/Subject*
a. Everyone expected __, and into the room walked __, **a guy in a blue suit**.
b. Bill pushed __, and down the hill rolled __, **the guy in a blue jacket**.

(29) *RNR: Subject/Object*
a. Into the room walked __, and everyone's eyes turned to __, **the defendant's former wife**.
b. From this data set emerged __, and everyone was surprised by __, **a new generalization about climate change**.

Either way, the result is grammatical, which shows that *RNR is not subject to the parallelism requirement.*[16] This is a crucial difference between RNR and ATB extraction; the latter is ungrammatical if extraction proceeds from nonparallel positions. ATB counterparts of the grammatical RNR examples in (28a–b) and (29a–b) are given in (30a–b) and (31a–b).

(30) *ATB: Object/Subject*

a. *This is the guy **OP**$_i$ that everyone expected t_i, and into the room walked t_i.

b. *This is the guy **OP**$_i$ that Bill pushed t_i, and down the hill rolled t_i.

(31) *ATB: Subject/Object*

a. *She is the person **OP**$_i$ that into the room walked t_i and everyone's eyes turned to t_i.

b. *This is the generalization about climate change **OP**$_i$ that from this data set emerged t_i and everyone was surprised by t_i.

As expected, these examples are ungrammatical. However, their ungrammaticality cannot be attributed to ATB extraction because *wh*-fronting and relativization of postverbal subjects in locative inversion are generally disallowed (see Coopmans 1989; Bresnan 1994; Diercks 2017, among others), as shown in (32a–b).

(32) a. ***Which horse**$_i$ out of the barn ran t_i?
(Coopmans 1989: 732)

b. *This is the horse **OP**$_i$ that out of the barn ran t_i.

Thus, the ATB examples in (30a–b) and (31a–b) are independently ruled out; in (30a–b), the second conjunct involves impossible subject extraction, and in (31a–b), the first one does. However, extraction of the postverbal subject in locative inversion is not banned in all languages. In Polish and Croatian, for example, locative inversion allows subject extraction, as shown in (33b) and (34b). Locative inversion also allows only a part of the subject to be extracted, as shown in (33c) and (34c). This is the process known as Left Branch Extraction (see Ross 1967 and much later work).

(33) a. Do portu wpłynął **nowy statek pasażerski.** *Polish*
into port sailed new ship passenger
'Into the port sailed a new passenger ship.'

b. **Ile statków**$_i$ do portu wpłynęło t_i?
how.many ships to port sailed
'How many ships sailed into the port?'

c. **Ile**$_i$ do portu wpłynęło t_i **statków**?
how.many to port sailed ships
'How many ships sailed into the port?'

(34) a. Svake godine u luku uplovi **američki ratni brod**. *Croatian*

Svake	godine	u	luku	uplovi	**američki**	**ratni**	**brod**.
every	year	into	port	sails	**American**	**war**	**ship**

'Every year into the port sails an American warship.'

b.

Čiji	**ratni**	**brod**$_i$	svake	godine	u	luku	uplovi	t_i?
whose	war	ship	every	year	into	port	sails	

'Whose warship sails into the port every year?'

c.

Čiji$_i$	svake	godine	u	luku	uplovi	t_i	**ratni**	**brod**?
whose	every	year	into	port	sails		war	ship

'Whose warship sails into the port every year?'

The difference between English, on the one hand, and Polish and Croatian, on the other, with respect to whether the postverbal nominative subject can be extracted in locative inversion raises the question of whether we are dealing with the same construction in the two types of languages. If so, this construction should be subject to the same restrictions.

One often-discussed restriction on locative inversion in English concerns unaccusativity: only unaccusative verbs are possible in locative inversion (however, see the discussion and references in section 4.3). Babyonyshev (1996) argues that the Locative Inversion operation in Russian is restricted in a similar way, and that it is only possible with unaccusative verbs (see also Harves 2002; Glushan and Calabrese 2014, among others).[17] However, as Babyonyshev also points out, unergative verbs are possible in what looks like the same construction (see (35c), for example). What distinguishes the two types of inversion is whether they are possible in discourse-neutral environments. While (35b), which contains an unaccusative verb and which Babyonyshev takes to be a true locative inversion construction, is possible in a discourse-neutral context, (35c), which contains an unergative verb, is not. Babyonyshev takes the infelicity of examples like (35c) in discourse-neutral contexts to be indicative of Focus or Topic movement of the postverbal subject and proposes that such sentences do not involve true Locative Inversion.

(35) a. What happened?

b. *Russian*

Na	stole	stojala	pepel'nica	i	pustoj	stakan.
on	table	stood.SG	ashtray.NOM	and	empty	glass.NOM

c.

#Na	večere	igrali	Vanja	i	Kolja.
at	party	played.PL	Vanja.NOM	and	Kolya.NOM

(Babyonyshev 1996: 82)

In what follows, we consider both types of inversion and contrast examples of ATB extraction from nonparallel positions with examples of RNR in which the shared constituent occupies nonparallel positions. We start with ATB and RNR examples in which one conjunct involves true Locative Inversion with an unaccusative verb. We turn to other inversion constructions in section 3.3. Crucially, in Polish and Croatian, just as in English, nonparallel RNR examples, where the shared element is the subject of an unaccusative verb in one conjunct and the direct object of a transitive verb in the other conjunct, are grammatical, while analogous examples of ATB extraction are not. This is shown by the contrast between the grammatical (a) and ungrammatical (b) examples in (36)–(39). This contrast holds regardless of whether the shared constituent is the subject in the first conjunct, as in (36a–b) and (38a–b), or in the second conjunct, as in (37a–b) and (39a–b).[18]

(36) a. *RNR: Subject/Object*

Do portu wpłynął __, i wszyscy chcieli *Polish*
into port sailed and all wanted
zobaczyć __, **nowy statek kontenerowy**.
see new.ACC/NOM ship.ACC/NOM cargo.ACC/NOM
'Into the port sailed and everyone wanted to see a new cargo ship.'

b. *ATB: Subject/Object*

??**Który statek**$_i$ do portu wpłynął $\boldsymbol{t_i}$
which.ACC/NOM ship.ACC/NOM into port sailed
i wszyscy chcieli zobaczyć $\boldsymbol{t_i}$?
and all wanted see
Int. 'Which ship into the port sailed and everyone wanted to see?'

(37) a. *RNR: Object/Subject*

Jan zrecenzował __, i w ostatnim numerze się ukazał __,
Jan reviewed and in last issue REFL appeared
nowy artykuł Chomskiego.
new.ACC/NOM article.ACC/NOM Chomsky.GEN
'Jan reviewed and in the last issue appeared a new article by Chomsky.'

b. *ATB: Object/Subject*

??**Który artykuł**$_i$ Jan zrecenzował $\boldsymbol{t_i}$
which.ACC/NOM article.ACC/NOM Jan reviewed
i w ostatnim numerze się ukazał $\boldsymbol{t_i}$?
and in last issue REFL appeared
Int. 'Which article did Jan review and appeared in the last issue?'

(38) a. *RNR: Subject/Object*

Svake godine u luku uplovi __ i svi uvijek *Croatian*
every year into port sails and all always
posjete __ **američki** **ratni** **brod**.
visit American.ACC/NOM war.ACC/NOM ship.ACC/NOM
'Every year into the port sails and everyone always visits the American warship.'

b. *ATB: Subject/Object*

***Čiji** **ratni** **brod**$_i$ svake godine u luku
whose.ACC/NOM war.ACC/NOM ship.ACC/NOM every year into port
uplovi t_i i svi uvijek posjete t_i?
sails and all always visit
Int. 'Whose warship every year into the port sails and everyone always visits?'

(39) a. *RNR: Object/Subject*

Jan je recenzirao __ i u sljedećem broju izlazi __
Jan AUX reviewed and in next issue comes.out
novi **članak** **Noama** **Chomskog**.
new.ACC/NOM article.ACC/NOM Noam.GEN Chomsky.GEN
'Jan reviewed and in the next issue will appear a new article by Noam Chomsky.'

b. *ATB: Object/Subject*

***Koji** **članak**$_i$ je Jan recenzirao t_i
which.ACC/NOM article.ACC/NOM AUX Jan reviewed
i u sljedećem broju izlazi t_i?
and in next issue comes.out
Int. 'Which article did Jan review and will appear in the next issue?'

If both ATB and RNR constructions contain a constituent that is shared between the conjuncts, as we have been assuming, the contrast between ATB extraction and RNR suggests that some principle of grammar prevents this constituent from occupying nonparallel positions in ATB examples, but not in RNR examples. In chapter 4, we will show that this principle is BiCoM: ATB extraction of the shared constituent from nonparallel positions causes Merge to relate more than two different positions within a single derivation, in violation of BiCoM. We take the absence of degradation in analogous RNR examples to argue for the analysis of RNR on which the shared constituent remains in situ and does not undergo rightward movement (McCawley 1982; Goodall 1987; Wilder 1999; Fox and Pesetsky 2007; Johnson 2007; Bachrach and Katzir 2009; Citko 2011b; De Vries 2013a, b, among many others).

In the remainder of this chapter, we turn to inversion constructions in Polish and Croatian that might not be instances of locative inversion; for example, they contain an unergative or transitive verb and/or a nonnominative subject. We show that RNR examples in which the shared element occupies nonparallel (subject/object) positions in the two conjuncts are grammatical as long as the shared constituent is conjunct-final, regardless of what process places the shared subject in a sentence-final position—that is, whether it is Locative Inversion (which we have been discussing so far), or some other type of inversion. We also show that in Polish and Croatian, just as in English, degraded examples of ATB extraction improve when the subject gap is embedded.

3.3 Widening the Perspective

Polish and Croatian allow a variety of constructions with postverbal subjects, illustrated in (40a–c) and (41a–c); (40a)/(41a) is an O(bject) V(erb) S(ubject) construction with a nominative subject (see Sekerina 1997; Bailyn 2003, 2004, 2018; Erechko 2003; Tajsner 2008; Witkoś 2008b; Wiland 2009, 2016; Slioussar 2011; Antonyuk 2015, under review; Perelts-vaig under review, among others, for a discussion of postverbal subjects in Polish and Russian), (40b)/(41b) is an existential construction with a genitive subject, and (40c)/(41c) is a psychological predicate construction with a dative subject.[19]

(40) a. Egzamin zdał **Piotr**. *Polish*
exam passed Peter.NOM
'Peter passed the exam.'

b. Na zajęciach nie było **Piotra**.
in class not was Piotr.GEN
'Peter wasn't in class.'

c. Zimno było **Piotrowi**.
cold was Piotr.DAT
'Peter was cold.'

(41) a. Ispit je položio **Petar**. *Croatian*

exam AUX passed Peter.NOM

'Peter passed the exam.'

b. U razredu nije bilo **Petra**.

in class not.AUX been Peter.GEN

'Peter wasn't in class.'

c. Hladno je bilo **Petru**.

cold AUX been Peter.DAT

'Peter was cold.'

Crucially, just as in the cases of locative inversion discussed in the previous section, these postverbal subjects can be extracted without incurring ungrammaticality. This is shown in (42)–(43).

(42) a. **Kto**$_i$ egzamin zdał $\boldsymbol{t_i}$? *Polish*

who.NOM exam passed

'Who passed the exam?'

b. **Kogo**$_i$ na zajęciach nie było $\boldsymbol{t_i}$?

who.GEN in class not was

'Who wasn't in class?'

c. **Komu**$_i$ zimno było $\boldsymbol{t_i}$?

who.DAT cold was

'Who was cold?'

(43) a. **Tko**$_i$ je ispit položio $\boldsymbol{t_i}$? *Croatian*

who.NOM AUX exam passed

'Who passed the exam?'

b. **Koga**$_i$ u razredu nije bilo $\boldsymbol{t_i}$?

who.GEN in class not.AUX been

'Who wasn't in class?'

c. **Kome**$_i$ je hladno bilo $\boldsymbol{t_i}$?

who.DAT AUX cold been

'Who was cold?'

One way to tell that the *wh*-subjects in (42a–c) and (43a–c) are extracted from postverbal positions is by looking at their word order: the verb is preceded by another phrase (direct object, locative PP, or adverbial). This word order is typical of sentences with postverbal subjects, as shown by the noninterrogative subject-final counterparts of these examples, given in (40a–c) and (41a–c). Further support comes from examples (44a–c) and (45a–c), which involve Left Branch Extraction stranding a nominal in a postverbal position.[20]

(44) a. **Ilu**$_i$ egzamin zdało t_i **studentów**? *Polish*
how.many exam passed students.GEN
'How many students passed the exam?'

b. **Którego**$_i$ na zajęciach nie było t_i **studenta**?
who.GEN in class not be student.GEN
'Which student wasn't in class?'

c. **Któremu**$_i$ na straży było zimno t_i **żołnierzowi**?
who.DAT on watch was cold soldier.DAT
'Which soldier on guard duty was cold?'

(45) a. **Koliko**$_i$ je ispit položilo t_i studenata? *Croatian*
how.many.NOM AUX exam passed students.GEN
'How many students passed the exam?'

b. **Kojeg**$_i$ u razredu nije bilo t_i učenika?
which.GEN in class not.AUX been student.GEN
'Which student wasn't in class?'

c. **Kojem**$_i$ je na straži hladno bilo t_i vojniku?
which.DAT AUX on watch cold been soldier.DAT
'Which soldier was cold on guard duty?'

Now that we have shown that Polish and Croatian allow extraction of the subject from a postverbal position in various configurations, we return to ATB and RNR constructions in which the shared constituent occupies nonparallel positions. Such examples involve a noninverted word order in one conjunct (with the shared constituent acting as its conjunct-final object) and an inverted order in the other conjunct (with the shared constituent acting as its conjunct-final subject). Examples (46)–(52), which involve this configuration, show that in Polish and Croatian, the shared constituent in RNR, unlike in ATB constructions, may occupy nonparallel positions. However, the RNR configurations are only grammatical if the Right Edge Restriction is not violated and if the shared constituent appears in the case form that satisfies the requirements of both verbs. This is possible if the verbs in the two conjuncts assign the same case (e.g., both assign dative or genitive, as in (49)–(52)) or if they assign different cases, but the two cases are identical in form, as in (46a–b) and (47a–b), where the shared constituent is syncretic between nominative and accusative forms. The latter is the case of "repair by syncretism" (Borsley 1983; Dyła 1984; Pullum and Zwicky 1986; Franks 1995; Asarina 2011, 2013, among others; however, see Hartmann, Konietzko, and Salzmann 2016, where it is shown that German ATB constructions require strict case identity). The contrast between the grammatical RNR examples and the ungrammatical ATB examples in (46)–(52) is the same contrast that we illustrated in section 3.2 with English, Croatian, and Polish locative inversion.

(46) *RNR: Object$_{ACC}$/Subject$_{NOM(NOM=ACC)}$*

a. Wykładowca przepytał __, i egzamin końcowy *Polish*
lecturer quizzed and exam final
zdały __, **najmłodsze studentki na roku**.
passed youngest.F.NOM/ACC students.F.NOM/ACC on year
Int. 'The lecturer quizzed (the youngest students in this cohort) and the youngest students in this cohort passed the final exam.'

b. Organizatori su pozvali __, a jučer su dolazak *Croatian*
organizers AUX invited and yesterday AUX arrival
potvrdile __, **političarke svih europskih zemalja**.
confirmed politicians.F.NOM/ACC all.GEN European.GEN countries.GEN
Int. 'The organizers invited (female politicians from all European countries) and the female politicians from all European countries yesterday confirmed their arrival.'

(47) *ATB: Object$_{ACC}$/Subject$_{NOM(NOM=ACC)}$*

a. ***Które studentki$_i$*** wykładowca przepytał t_i *Polish*
which.F.NOM/ACC students.F.NOM/ACC lecturer quizzed
i t_i zdały egzamin końcowy?
and passed exam final
Int. 'Which students did the lecturer quiz and (which students) passed the final exam?'

b. ***Koje političarke$_i$*** su organizatori *Croatian*
which.F.NOM/ACC politicians.F.NOM/ACC AUX organizers
pozvali t_i a t_i jučer su potvrdile dolazak?
invited and yesterday AUX confirmed arrival
Int. 'Which female politicians did the organizers invite and (which female politicians) yesterday confirmed their arrival?'

In (47a–b), the word order in the second conjunct—namely, the fact that the object follows the verb—suggests that the subject is ATB-extracted from its canonical, preverbal Spec,TP position. The word order in (48a–b), where the object precedes the verb, suggests that the subject here is extracted from a postverbal position. These examples are also degraded.

(48) *ATB: Object$_{ACC}$/Subject$_{NOM\ (NOM=ACC)}$*

a. *?**Które** **studentki$_i$** wykładowca przepytał ***t$_i$*** *Polish*
which.F.NOM/ACC students.F.NOM/ACC lecturer quizzed
i egzamin końcowy zdały ***t$_i$***?
and exam final passed
Int. 'Which students did the lecturer quiz and (which students) passed the final exam?'

b. ***Koje** **političarke$_i$** su organizatori *Croatian*
which.F.NOM/ACC politicians.F.NOM/ACC AUX organizers
pozvali ***t$_i$*** a jučer su dolazak potvrdile ***t$_i$***?
invited and yesterday AUX arrival confirmed
Int. 'Which female politicians did the organizers invite and (which female politicians) yesterday confirmed their arrival?'

The same contrasts hold in sentences with dative and genitive subjects, as shown in (49)–(50) and (51)–(52), respectively: RNR constructions where the shared element occupies nonparallel positions are fine, whereas corresponding ATB constructions are not.

(49) *RNR: Indirect Object$_{DAT}$/Subject$_{DAT}$*

a. Jan dał swoją marynarkę __, a mimo tego *Polish*
Jan gave his jacket and in.spite.of this
było zimno __, **nowej dziewczynie w naszej klasie.**
was cold new.DAT girl.DAT in our class
Int. 'Jan gave his jacket to (a new girl in our class) and a new girl in our class was cold in spite of this.'

b. Jan je dao jaknu __, a svejedno je bilo *Croatian*
Jan AUX given jacket and in.spite.of.this AUX been
hladno __, **novoj curici u našem razredu.**
cold new.DAT girl.DAT in our class
Int. 'Jan gave his jacket to (a new girl in our class) and a new girl in our class was cold in spite of this.'

(50) *ATB: Indirect Object$_{DAT}$/Subject$_{DAT}$*

a. *dziewczyna, **której$_i$** Janek dał t_i swoją marynarkę *Polish*
girl who.DAT Jan gave his jacket
a mimo tego t_i było zimno
and in.spite.of it was cold
Int. 'the girl who Jan gave his jacket and in spite of it was cold'
(Dyła 1984: 704)

b. *curica **kojoj$_i$** je Jan dao jaknu t_i a *Croatian*
girl.NOM which.DAT AUX Jan given jacket and
svejedno je t_i bilo hladno
in.spite.of.this AUX been cold
Int. 'the girl who Jan gave his jacket and was cold in spite of this'

(51) *RNR: Subject$_{GEN}$/Object$_{GEN}$*

a. Z powodu choroby na zajęciach nie *Polish*
from reason sickness in class not
było __, i Janowi było żal __, **nowego studenta lingwistyki**.
was and Jan was sorry new.GEN student.GEN linguistics.GEN
Int. 'Due to sickness wasn't in class and Jan felt sorry for the new student of linguistics.'

b. Zbog bolesti u razredu nije bilo __, *Croatian*
because.of sickness in class not.AUX been
i Janu je bilo žao __, **novog studenta lingvistike**.
and Jan AUX been sorry.for new.GEN student.GEN linguistics.GEN
Int. 'Due to sickness wasn't in class and Jan felt sorry for the new student of linguistics.'

(52) *ATB: Subject$_{GEN}$/Object$_{GEN}$*

a. *człowiek, **którego$_i$** t_i nie było na zajęciach *Polish*
man who.GEN not was in class
i Janowi jest żal t_i
and Jan is sorry.for
Int. 'the man who wasn't in class and Jan feels sorry for'
(Franks 1995: 71)

b. *student kojega$_i$ zbog bolesti t_i nije — *Croatian*
student.NOM who.ACC because.of sickness not.AUX
bilo u razredu i Janu je bilo žao t_i
been in class and Jan AUX been sorry.for
Int. 'the student who because of sickness wasn't in class and Jan felt sorry for'

The examples in (53a–b) further illustrate the same phenomenon; the extracted *wh*- or relative pronoun is the object in the first conjunct but the subject in the second one.

(53) a. ***Co**$_i$ Janek zrobił t_i a t_i zmartwiło Marię? — *Polish*
what.NOM/ACC John did and upset Mary
Int. 'What did John do and upset Mary?'
(Borsley 1983: 170)

b. *dziewczyna, **której**$_i$ Janek dał t_i swoją marynarkę
girl who.DAT Jan gave his jacket
a mimo tego t_i było zimno
and in.spite.of it was cold
Int. 'the girl who Jan gave his jacket and in spite of it was cold'
(Dyła 1984: 704)

Finally, in Polish and Croatian, just as in English, degraded examples of ATB extraction from nonparallel positions improve with the embedding of the subject, as discussed by Franks (1995) for Polish and shown in (54a–b) for Polish and in (55a–b) for Croatian.

(54) a. *dziecko, **które**$_i$ lubisz t_i i t_i było dobre — *Polish*
child who.ACC/NOM like and was good
Int. 'the child that you like and was good'

b. dziecko, **które**$_i$ lubisz t_i i chcesz, żeby t_i było dobre
child who.ACC/NOM like and want COMP was good
Int. 'the child that you like and want it to be good'
(Franks 1995: 76–77)

(55) a. *dijete **koje**$_i$ voliš t_i i t_i bilo je dobro — *Croatian*
child who.ACC/NOM like and been AUX good
Int. 'the child that you like and was good'

b. dijete **koje**$_i$ voliš t_i i želiš da t_i bude dobro
child who.ACC/NOM like and want that be good
Int. 'the child that you like and want it to be good'

3.4 Conclusion

In this chapter, we have shown that ATB and RNR constructions differ with respect to the parallelism requirement. ATB extraction requires the constituent that is shared between the conjuncts to occupy parallel positions prior to extraction, but RNR does not, as long as independent restrictions on RNR are satisfied: the shared constituent occupies a final position in each conjunct, and in languages with morphological case, it is assigned identical cases in each conjunct or is assigned different cases that are syncretic in form. Furthermore, we have shown that in Croatian and Polish this difference between ATB extraction and RNR holds in all constructions that allow postverbal subjects. This suggests that the parallelism requirement is independent of the exact process that places subjects in clause-final positions. What does matter, however, is the exact position that postverbal subjects end up occupying in these constructions; we discuss this in the next chapter. First, though, we discuss in detail how the contrast between ATB extraction and RNR follows from BiCoM.

4 The Binarity Constraint on Merge

We showed in the previous chapter that the shared constituent in RNR may occupy non-parallel positions in the two conjuncts, as long as independent conditions (Right Edge Restriction, case syncretism) are satisfied. However, as analogous ATB examples show, if the shared constituent undergoes extraction from nonparallel positions, the result is ungrammatical. In this chapter, we propose that such ATB examples are ungrammatical because they violate the Binarity Constraint on Merge: the shared constituent, parallel-merged in both conjuncts, undergoes Internal Merge, and this relates more than two positions in a single derivation. The grammaticality of RNR examples involving an analogous configuration suggests that in RNR the shared constituent does not undergo Internal Merge and therefore BiCoM is not violated.

4.1 Violations of the Binary Constraint on Merge

We first investigate whether each of the three types of Merge that our system allows (External Merge, Parallel Merge, and Internal Merge) obeys BiCoM, repeated in (1) from chapter 3.

(1) *Binarity Constraint on Merge* (first version, to be modified)

Merge cannot relate more than two positions at a time within a single derivation.

We show that BiCoM is not violated by External Merge or by Parallel Merge, but that it is violated by Internal Merge.[1] We then propose a modification of BiCoM in order to amend this problem. Next, we show that even this modified version of BiCoM is violated by certain combinations of Merge types. This will serve as our starting point for the explanation of the contrast that we established in chapter 3 between ungrammatical examples of ATB extraction from nonparallel positions and analogous but grammatical RNR examples.

We first examine External Merge and establish that it does not violate BiCoM. Recall that External Merge may initiate a new derivation if it increases the number of roots/

sets^W (i.e., sets that are members of the workspace), or it may advance an existing derivation if the number of sets^W in the workspace does not increase. External Merge results in a configuration in which there is a one-to-one relationship between the syntactic objects that Merge combines and the syntactic positions that these objects occupy.[2] Since the two objects related by External Merge occupy a single position each, Merge necessarily relates only two syntactic positions per derivation, in accordance with BiCoM. For example, in (2a), External Merge initiates a new derivation because it applies to the syntactic objects W and Q, creating the set^W {W, Q}, which was not part of the workspace prior to the application of Merge.[3] Having undergone Merge, W and Q come to occupy a single syntactic position each, and consequently, Merge ends up relating only two positions (in the derivation it initiated): the position of W, defined as the path ⟨H, Q⟩, and the position of Q, defined as the path ⟨H, W⟩. The next instance of External Merge, illustrated in (2b), advances the existing derivation: the previously built object H merges with a lexical item Y. As a result of this Merge, H and Y come to occupy a single position each, so this instance of Merge also relates only two positions: the position of H, defined as ⟨X, Y⟩, and the position of Y, defined as ⟨X, H⟩.

(2) a.

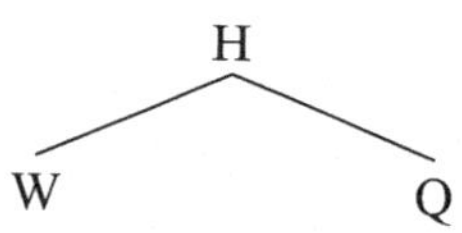

b.

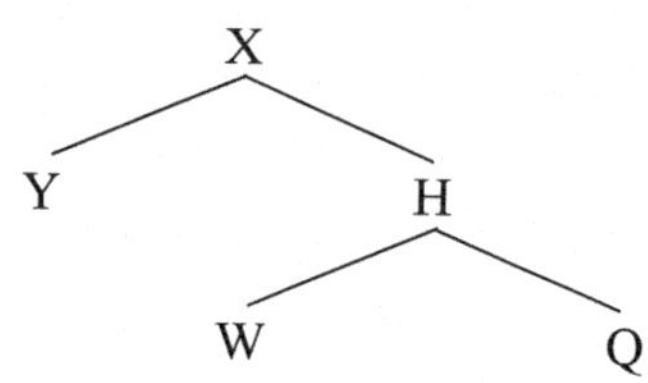

External Merge

BiCoM straightforwardly rules out ternary branching. Unlike the two situations in (2a–b), where each instance of Merge relates only two positions per derivation, the structure in (3), where Y, W, and Q are sisters (and daughters of X), is disallowed regardless of whether all three are merged simultaneously, as in (3), or two of them are merged first and a third one later, as in (4a–b).

(3)

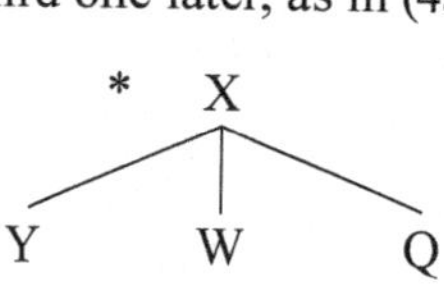

(4) a.

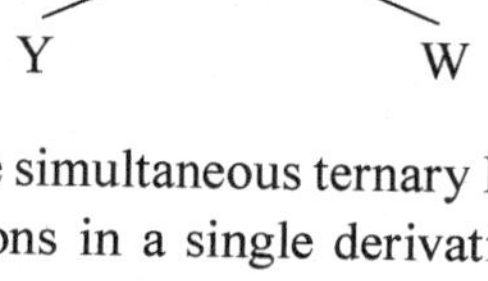

b.

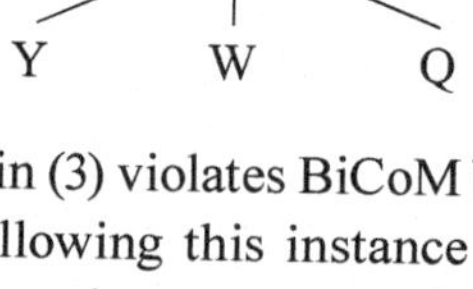

The simultaneous ternary Merge in (3) violates BiCoM because it relates *three* different positions in a single derivation. Following this instance of Merge, each of the merged objects—Y, W, and Q—ends up occupying *two* syntactic positions because each has two sisters, and a position of a syntactic object is the path from the root of the tree to a sister of the object itself. The positions of Y are defined by the paths ⟨X, W⟩ and ⟨X, Q⟩, the positions of W by the paths ⟨X, Y⟩ and ⟨X, Q⟩, and the positions of Q by the paths ⟨X, Y⟩ and ⟨X, W⟩. Nevertheless, the total number of positions occupied by Y, W, and Q is three, not six, because each two daughters of X share a sister, which in our system means that they share a position. For example, Y and W are both sisters of Q, so both occupy the position defined by the path ⟨X, Q⟩. In other words, the set of positions related by this instance of Merge is {⟨X, W⟩, ⟨X, Q⟩, ⟨X, Y⟩, ⟨X, Q⟩, ⟨X, Y⟩, ⟨X, W⟩}, which is equivalent to the set {⟨X, W⟩, ⟨X, Q⟩, ⟨X, Y⟩}. Thus, (3) violates BiCoM because Merge relates these three positions in a single derivation.

The situation in (4b) is no different: here too, Merge relates three positions in a single derivation. The first step, shown in (4a), is allowed by BiCoM because it is the same as the External Merge in (2a): following Merge, the position of Y (the path ⟨X, W⟩) is related to the position of W (the path ⟨X, Y⟩). However, if in the next step Q is merged as a sister of *both* Y and W (see (4b)), BiCoM is violated. Now, Y, W, and Q have two sisters each, which means that, as in (3), Merge in (4b) again illicitly relates three syntactic positions in a derivation.[4]

We next turn to Parallel Merge, illustrated in (5a–b), and show that a single element may undergo Parallel Merge without violating BiCoM. Here, the shared constituent Q is first merged with B, forming G, the set {B, Q}. This instance of Merge relates two positions: the position of Q (the path ⟨G, B⟩) and the position of B (the path ⟨G, Q⟩). Next, Q is merged with M, forming W, the set {M, Q}. Since the set {M, Q} does not contain as a member the set {B, Q}, this application of Merge (Parallel Merge) has increased the number of sets^{W} in the workspace; that is, it has initiated a new derivation. Crucially, within this new derivation Merge has again related only two positions: the position of Q (the path ⟨W, M⟩) and the position of M (the path ⟨W, Q⟩). Thus, each Merge operation applied to Q relates only two positions *per derivation*: the position of Q is related to the position of M in one derivation and to the position of B in the other derivation.

(5) a. b. *Parallel Merge*

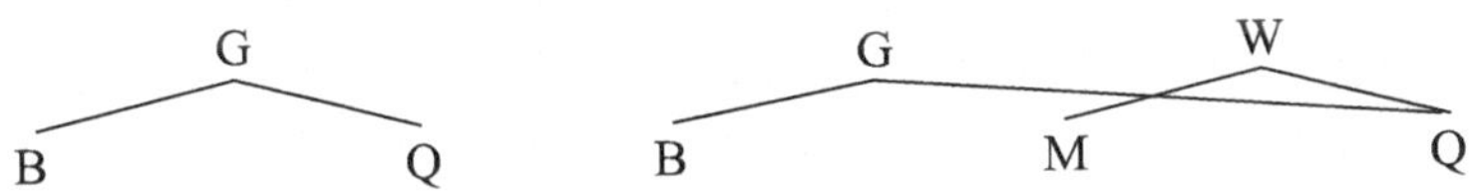

Following (5a–b), the workspace contains two distinct derivations until External Merge combines Y and H into a single derivation, as shown in (6).[5] Thus, given that Parallel Merge always operates transderivationally, it never violates BiCoM.

(6)

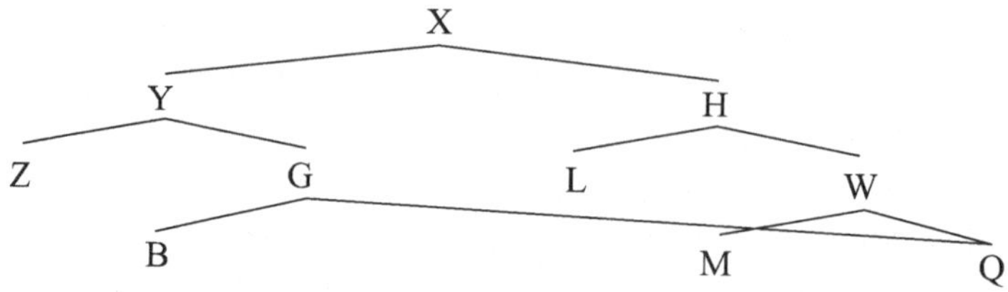

This brings us to Internal Merge, illustrated in (7), where Q, having undergone External Merge with W, undergoes Internal Merge with X. The External Merge of Q and W, shown in (2a), relates only two positions: the position of Q, defined by the path ⟨H, W⟩, and the position of W, defined by the path ⟨H, Q⟩. However, when Q undergoes Internal Merge with X, Merge relates *three* positions: the "new" position of Q, defined as the path ⟨R, X⟩, the "old" position of Q, defined as the path ⟨R, X, H, W⟩, and the position of X, defined as the path ⟨R, Q⟩. The workspace in which Merge operates while deriving R never contains more than a single derivation, so the domain in which BiCoM is evaluated is R itself. Thus, (7) violates BiCoM.

(7) *Internal Merge*

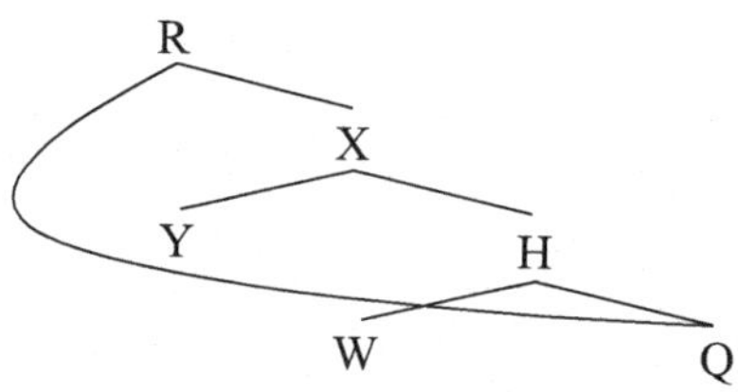

The violation arises because BiCoM "counts" positions that syntactic objects occupy *following* rather than *preceding* Merge and restricts this number to two. If, instead, BiCoM counted only those positions that existed prior to Merge, there would be no problem. However, counting syntactic positions prior to Merge would incorrectly admit ternary branching into the grammar: it would be impossible to limit the number of lexical items and/or roots that Merge operates on because such objects do not have a sister and therefore do not occupy a syntactic position. Since in our view excluding ternary branching is an important consequence of BiCoM, the positions that BiCoM operates on must be the positions that exist in the structure *after* Merge has applied. As a result, however, BiCoM excludes Internal Merge.

The instance of Internal Merge in (7) would satisfy BiCoM if BiCoM could somehow disregard one of the three positions occupied by the two objects that are input to Merge (two positions of Q: ⟨R, X⟩ and ⟨R, X, H, W⟩, and the position of X: ⟨R, Q⟩).[6] Since the position defined by the path ⟨R, Q⟩ is the only position of X, and X is one of the two objects that undergo Merge in (7), it stands to reason that BiCoM should have access to this position. This leaves us with the two positions of Q: the old position (defined by the path ⟨R, X, H, W⟩) and the new one (defined by the path ⟨R, X⟩). Unlike External Merge and Parallel Merge, Internal Merge is contingent on an Agree relation that holds between a probe and a goal (Chomsky 2000, 2001), and this relation is subject to locality: the probe (Y in (7)) searches for the goal (Q) and agrees with the goal in its *most local* position. Consequently, Internal Merge applies to the most local position of the goal, and no other.[7] Therefore, it seems to us that the "old" position of the goal (the one where the goal is accessed by the probe) should matter more than the "new" position of the goal; of the two positions of Q in (7), it is the old position of Q that must be "visible" to BiCoM, and the "new" position can be disregarded. Our next task involves modifying the definition of BiCoM in order to capture this insight and make the new position of Q (the one defined by the path ⟨R, X⟩) "not count" for the purposes of BiCoM.

The new position and the old position of Q differ in that the path defining the old (lower) position overlaps (shares at least one member) with the path that the search by the probe (Y) traverses while probing for the goal (Q). We refer to this path as a *search path.* We define a search path as the sequence of nodes from a sister of the probe to the goal, as in (8).

(8) A search path from the probe P to the goal G is a sequence of syntactic objects $\langle SO_1, SO_2, SO_3, \ldots, SO_n \rangle$ where SO_1 = a sister of P and SO_n = G, such that for every i, $0 < i < n$, $SO_{i+1} \in SO_i$.

The new/higher position of the goal (Q) is in no way implicated in the search by the probe and therefore does not count for the purposes of BiCoM in cases where Merge is contingent on Agree. In (9), we provide a modified definition of BiCoM, which reflects this difference between the old and new positions of the goal.

(9) *Binarity Constraint on Merge* (final version)

Merge cannot relate more than two positions at a time within a single derivation, where the position(s) of a syntactic object SO that Merge applies to must overlap with a search path for SO if there is a search path for SO.

This definition of BiCoM, together with the definition of a search path given in (8), allows Internal Merge and sets it apart from External Merge and Parallel Merge. Let us thus reconsider (7), repeated here as (10), in view of the new definition of BiCoM.

(10) *Internal Merge*

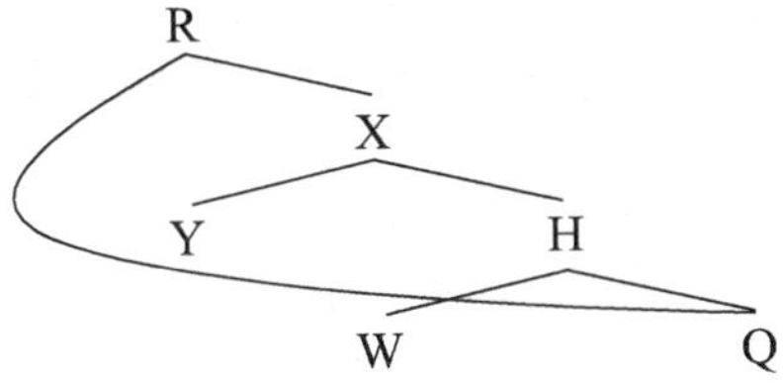

The two positions of Q in (10) are the paths ⟨R, X, H, W⟩ and ⟨R, X⟩, indicated in (11a–b) with boldfaced lines.

(11) a. *Lower position of Q*

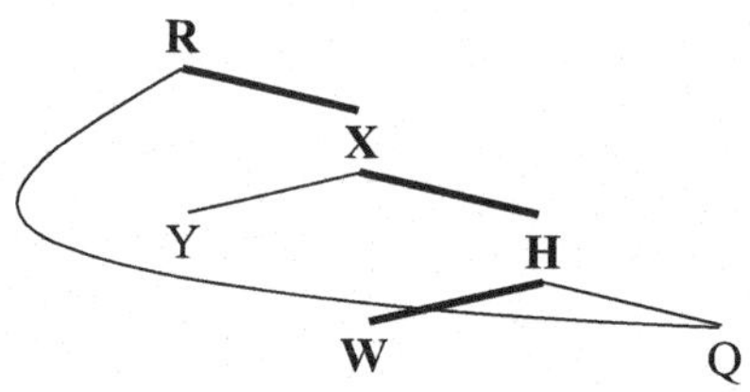

b. *Higher position of Q*

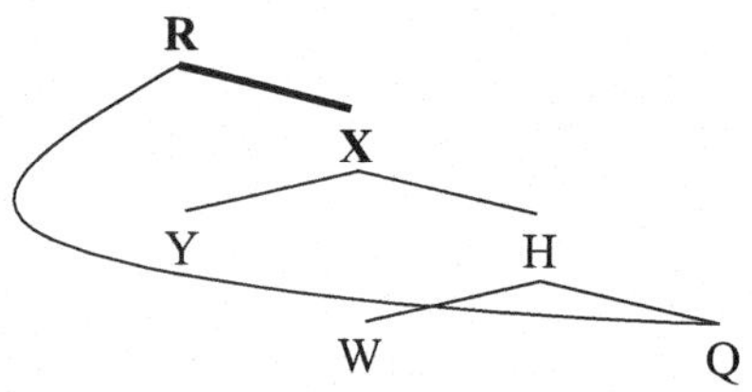

The instance of Internal Merge in (10) follows the Agree relationship that has been established between the probe Y and the goal Q. The search path between Y and Q is defined as the path ⟨H, Q⟩, shown in (12).

(12) *Search path from Y to Q*

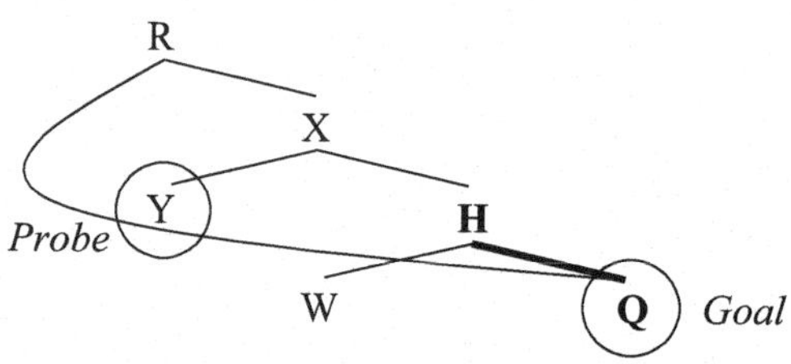

Of the two positions of Q, only the old one (the lower one) overlaps with the search path: the search path ⟨H, Q⟩ and the path ⟨R, X, H, W⟩ (i.e., the path to the lower position of Q) share one member (H). Therefore, this is the only one of the two positions occupied by Q that counts for the purposes of BiCoM. The path defining the new position of Q (⟨R, X⟩) does not share any members with the search path and therefore does not count for BiCoM. Thus, the total number of positions occupied by Q and X in (10) is two, and BiCoM is satisfied.

We next turn to situations in which the shared constituent undergoes both Parallel Merge and Internal Merge, and we show that even the modified version of BiCoM is violated if Internal Merge applies after Parallel Merge, and if this happens after the two derivations have been integrated into a single derivation. This is illustrated in (13), where, at the point when Q is internally merged with X, Merge relates *three positions in the same derivation*: the position of Q defined by the path ⟨R, X, S, H, W, M⟩; the position of Q defined by the path ⟨R, X, S, K, G, B⟩; and the position of X, defined by the path ⟨R, Q⟩. The new, most recently created position of Q does not enter the calculation because it does not overlap with any search path from the probe (Y) to the goal (Q). Nevertheless, the total number of positions occupied by the objects that have undergone Merge (X and Q) is three, which violates BiCoM. Since configurations like the one in (13) yield ungrammatical sentences, we argue that Merge is subject to binarity with respect to *positions* it relates rather than with respect to *objects* it combines.

(13) *Parallel Merge + Internal Merge*

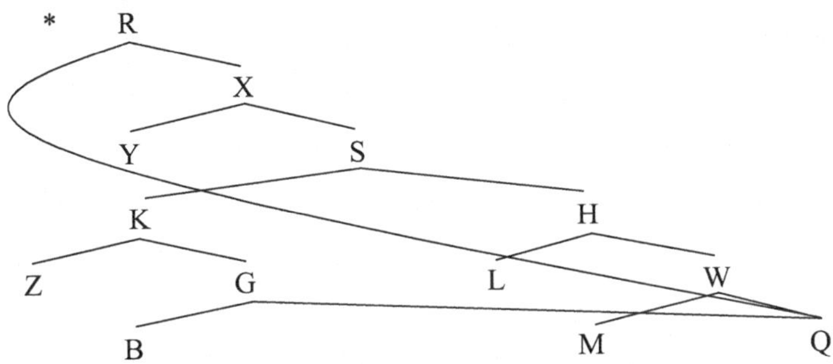

The structure in (13) represents ATB extraction and differs from the structure in (6), which obeys BiCoM and which is essentially the structure of RNR. The difference between these two structures with respect to BiCoM explains the contrast between RNR and ATB constructions with respect to parallelism. This is what we turn to in the next section.

4.2 Two Is Company, Three Is a Crowd: Right Node Raising versus Across-the-Board Movement

The main empirical finding from chapter 3 that we want to explain is why ATB movement requires parallelism but RNR does not. In (14a–b), we repeat representative examples illustrating this contrast.

(14) a. *Tell me **who**$_i$ everyone expected $\boldsymbol{t_i}$ and $\boldsymbol{t_i}$ walked into the room.

b. Everyone expected __, and into the room walked __, **a guy in a blue suit.**

In the ungrammatical cases of ATB movement, the shared constituent occupies non-parallel positions in the two conjuncts prior to ATB extraction. For example, in (14a) *who* occupies Spec,vP in the first conjunct, defined as the path ⟨CP, C′, &P, TP, T′, vP, v′⟩, and Spec,TP in the second conjunct, defined as the path ⟨CP, C′, &P, &′, TP, T′⟩, as shown in (15).[8] When the shared *wh*-phrase is probed by C and ATB extraction takes place, the two TPs are already part of a single derivation.

(15) *Tell me

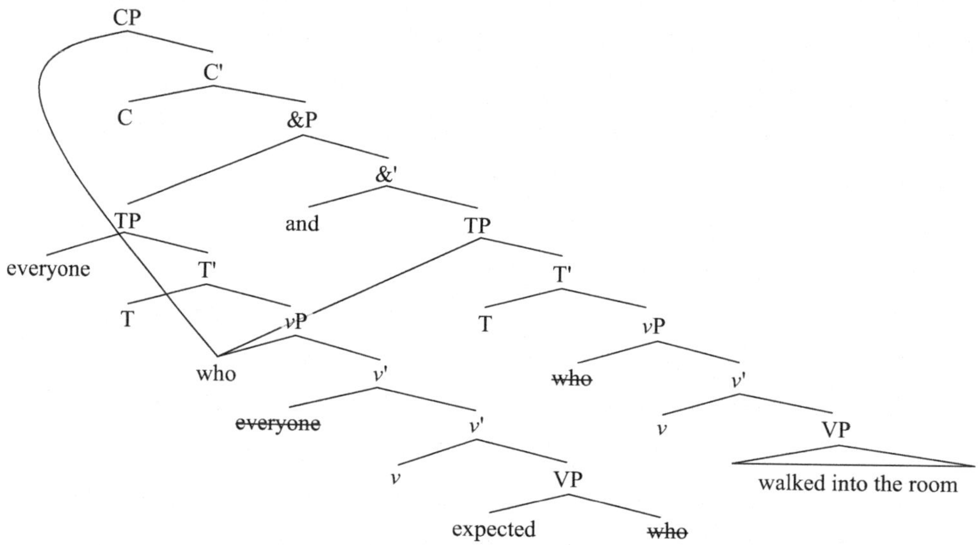

In (8), we defined a search path as the sequence of nodes from the sister of the probe to the goal. In (15), there are two paths from the sister of the probe C to the goal *who*: one in the first conjunct (⟨&P, TP, T′, vP, *who*⟩) and one in the second conjunct (⟨&P, &′, TP, *who*⟩). The two paths are shown in (16), one with solid boldfaced lines, the other with dashed boldfaced lines. Since both of the positions of the *wh*-phrase overlap with a search path, both count for the purpose of BiCoM.[9] ATB movement relates these two positions of *who* to the position of C′ (⟨CP, *who*⟩), in violation of BiCoM.

(16) *Tell me

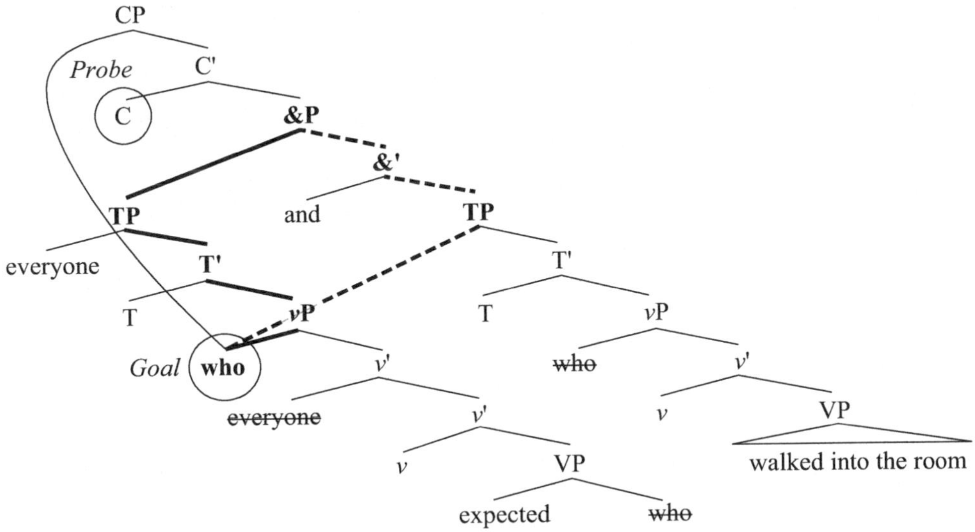

The derivation in (15)/(16) is more accurately represented by (17), where the shared constituent *who* in fact occupies four different positions that are relevant for BiCoM: the complement of V and the specifier of vP in the first conjunct, the specifier of vP and the specifier of TP in the second conjunct.[10] This is because before &P is built, the *wh*-phrase undergoes successive-cyclic movement/Internal Merge within each conjunct, which places it in multiple positions. This raises the question of whether BiCoM might be violated within individual conjuncts even before the shared constituent undergoes Internal Merge in an ATB manner. We defer our discussion of this question to section 5.4, where we examine successive-cyclic movement in light of BiCoM and show that multiple instances of Internal Merge applied to the same constituent within a single derivation (in our case, within a single conjunct) never yield a BiCoM violation. Thus, in a configuration like (17), it is only the highest position of the *wh*-phrase in each conjunct that is relevant, and it is only the final application of Internal Merge that is disallowed by BiCoM.

(17) *Tell me

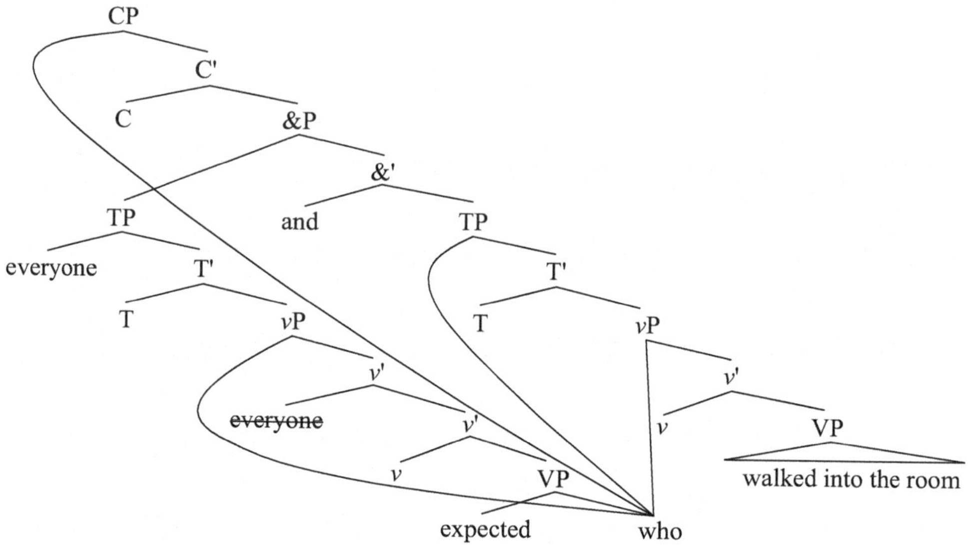

Crucially, even though in (15)–(17) the final instance of Internal Merge targets only *two objects* (the *wh*-phrase and the C′), it is still disallowed by BiCoM because it relates *three positions*: the position of *who* in Spec,vP, defined as the path ⟨CP, C′, &P, TP, T′, vP, v′⟩; the position of *who* in Spec,TP, defined as the path ⟨CP, C′, &P, &′, TP, T′⟩; and the position of C′, defined as the path ⟨CP, *who*⟩. The reason why analogous RNR examples are grammatical is that the shared element is simultaneously part of *two independent derivations* and does not undergo further instances of Merge after the two derivations are joined into one. Thus, in such examples Merge never relates more than two positions *in a single derivation*. For example, in (14b)/(18a) the shared constituent *a guy in a blue suit* is the object in the first conjunct and the subject in the second one. It occupies nonparallel positions in the two conjuncts, as shown in (18b): in the first conjunct, its position is defined by the path ⟨&P, TP, T′, vP, v′, VP, V⟩, and in the second one, by the path ⟨&P, &′, TP, T′, VP, SC, PP⟩. Nevertheless, the sentence is grammatical: its structure does not violate BiCoM since the shared constituent is merged with only one constituent in each conjunct and does not undergo any further instances of Merge after the two conjuncts become part of a single derivation.[11]

(18) a. Everyone expected __, and into the room walked __, **a guy in a blue suit.**

b.

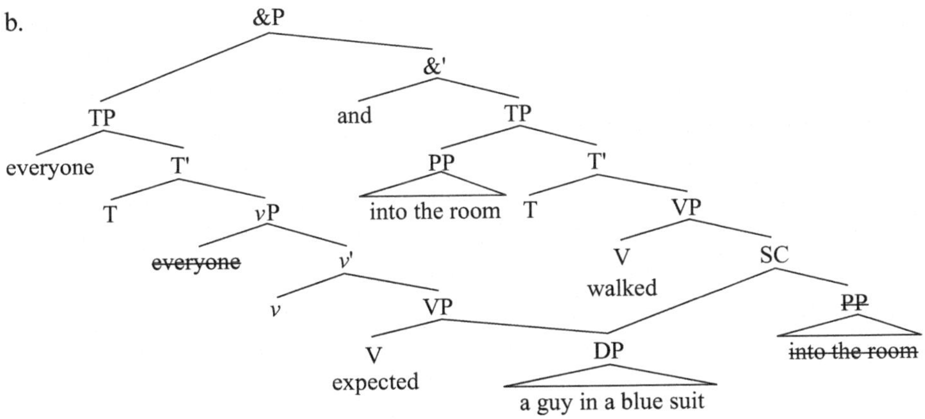

At this point, one might wonder whether the examples of RNR that we have discussed so far comply with BiCoM because they all include only two conjuncts, and whether the presence of a third conjunct, as in (19a–b), might make a difference.

(19) a. Joss wrote __, Mary was reviewing __, and Paul wanted to read __, **a paper about semiotics.**

(Sabbagh 2014: 26)

b. Josh was looking for __, Maria was waiting in __, and reporters were trying to find __, **Joss' office.**

(Sabbagh 2007: 376)

The number of conjuncts in RNR configurations is irrelevant to BiCoM. This is because violations of BiCoM are evaluated separately within each derivation. All conjuncts correspond to distinct derivations up to the point when they are conjoined with one another, so Merge always relates only two positions per derivation, as shown in (20b). Crucially, no further Merge operations apply to the shared constituent after the Conjunction Phrase is formed, uniting all conjuncts into a single derivation.[12]

(20) a. Joss wrote __, Mary was reviewing __, and Paul wanted to read __, **a paper about semiotics**.

b.

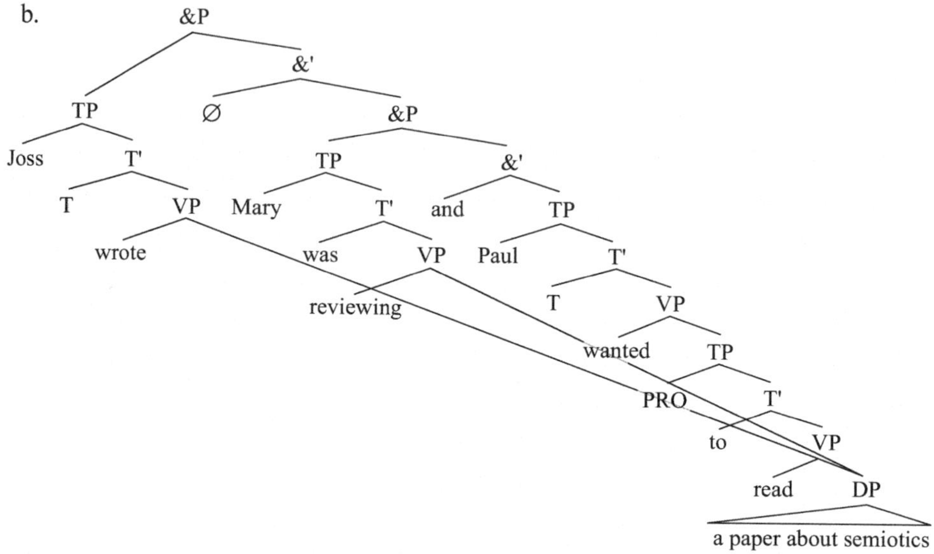

Our analysis readily carries over to Polish and Croatian, where we observe the same contrast between ATB and RNR examples. However, these languages differ from English in that they allow subjects to be extracted from postverbal positions. Nevertheless, in (21a–b) and (22a–b), repeated here from chapter 3, the RNR examples in (a) are grammatical, but analogous examples of ATB extraction in (b) are not.

(21) a. Wykładowca przepytał __, i egzamin końcowy *Polish*
lecturer quizzed and exam final
zdały __, **najmłodsze studentki na roku.**
passed youngest.F.NOM/ACC students.F.NOM/ACC on year
Int. 'The lecturer quizzed (the youngest students in this cohort) and the youngest students in this cohort passed the final exam.'

b. *?**Które studentki**$_i$ wykładowca przepytał $\boldsymbol{t_i}$
which.F.NOM/ACC students.F.NOM/ACC lecturer quizzed
i egzamin końcowy zdały $\boldsymbol{t_i}$?
and exam final passed
Int. 'Which students did the lecturer quiz and (which students) passed the final exam?'

(22) a. Organizatori su pozvali __, a jučer su dolazak *Croatian*
organizers AUX invited and yesterday AUX arrival
potvrdile __, **političarke svih europskih zemalja.**
confirmed politicians.F.NOM/ACC all.GEN European.GEN countries.GEN
Int. 'The organizers invited (female politicians from all European countries) and the female politicians from european countries yesterday confirmed their arrival.'

b. ***Koje političarke$_i$** su organizatori
which.F.NOM/ACC politicians.F.NOM/ACC AUX organizers
pozvali t_i a jučer su dolazak potvrdile t_i?
invited and yesterday AUX arrival confirmed
Int. 'Which female politicians did the organizers invite and (which female politicians) yesterday confirmed their arrival?'

Just as with the English examples above, our proposal excludes the (b) examples in (21) and (22) because they violate BiCoM: the shared *wh*-phrase is ATB-extracted from the Spec,vP position in the first conjunct and from its postverbal subject position in the second conjunct. With respect to what the postverbal subject position is, we follow Slioussar (2007, 2011), who argues that postverbal subjects in Slavic occupy Spec,TP, but the predicate moves even higher, leaving the subject in the sentence-final position. Thus, when the shared *wh*-phrase is ATB-extracted, Internal Merge relates three different positions within a single derivation: Spec,TP, Spec,vP, and the position of C′, as shown in (23). This violates BiCoM.

(23)
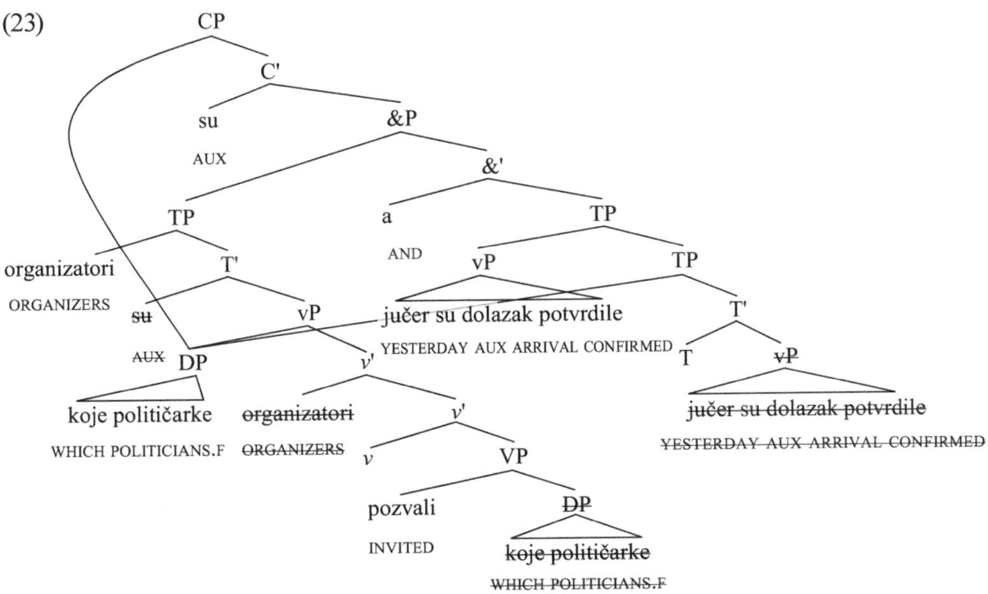

Our analysis of the ungrammaticality of ATB extraction from nonparallel positions relies on an implicit (and, we believe, uncontroversial) assumption that the position of a *wh*-object is different from the position of a *wh*-subject. We assume that in the canonical cases, prior to ATB extraction, *wh*-objects occupy Spec,vP and *wh*-subjects occupy Spec,TP. This reduces the ungrammaticality of ATB examples like (14a), repeated here, to a BiCoM violation.

(24) a. *Tell me **who**$_i$ everyone expected $\boldsymbol{t_i}$ and $\boldsymbol{t_i}$ walked into the room.

b. Everyone expected __, and into the room walked __, **a guy in a blue suit**.

However, the position of the subject in locative inversion and other types of inverted structures in Polish and Croatian is not as straightforward as the discussion above might have implied. Locative Inversion has been argued to be limited to unaccusative verbs, in which case the subject is an internal argument of the verb. If this is the case, examples like (14b)/(24b) do not show that RNR allows violations of parallelism, since the shared constituent might occupy the same position—complement of the verb—in both conjuncts. Furthermore, the Spec,TP position we assumed in (23) is not the only conceivable position for postverbal subjects in Slavic languages; postverbal subjects have also been proposed to occupy Spec,vP, in which case the ungrammaticality of the Polish and Croatian ATB examples (21b) and (22b) cannot be attributed to the lack of parallelism in the positions occupied by the *wh*-phrase. We discuss, and ultimately refute, these possibilities in the next two sections.

4.3 Subjects in Locative Inversion

In this section, we focus on the position of postverbal subjects in constructions that involve Locative Inversion and on whether the shared subject in RNR examples might occupy the same position in the locative inversion conjunct as it does in the noninverted conjunct, where it is the complement of the verb, as shown in (25b).[13]

(25) a. Into the room walked __, and everyone expected __, **a guy in a blue suit.**

b.

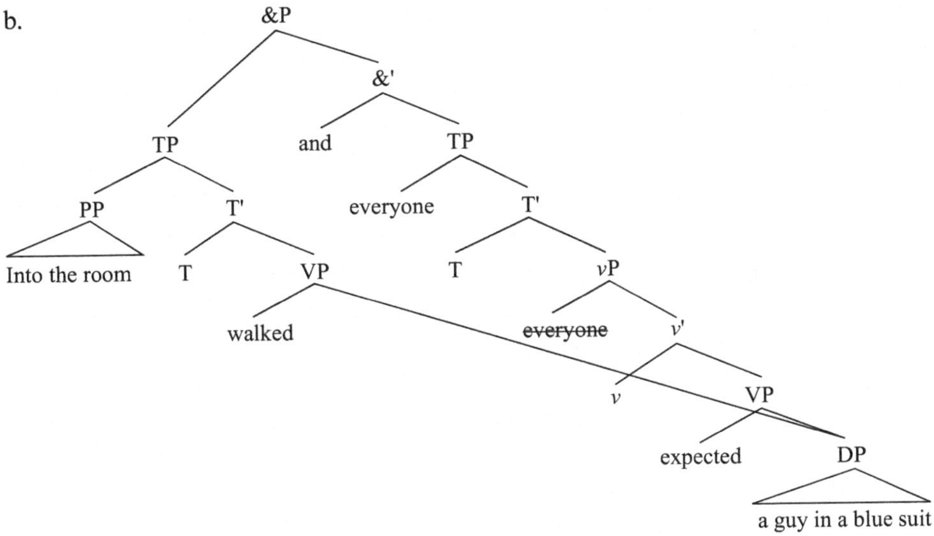

If this is the case, our RNR examples might be grammatical not because the shared constituent remains in situ, thus vacuously satisfying BiCoM, but because it occupies parallel positions in the two conjuncts, in which case rightward movement would not lead to ungrammaticality. If, on the other hand, the two positions are indeed nonparallel and RNR does not involve movement, then the absence of BiCoM violations in RNR supports our proposal that Merge is constrained by BiCoM. So let us look at the position of the subject in locative inversion in more detail.

Existing analyses of locative inversion fall into two broad families. According to some, the subject occupies the same position regardless of the type of the verb; according to others, it occupies different positions depending on the type of verb. Crucially for our purposes, both types of analysis are compatible with our proposal that the ungrammatical ATB examples violate BiCoM because they involve extraction of the shared constituent from nonparallel positions, while analogous RNR examples do not violate BiCoM because the shared constituent is not extracted.

We start with the accounts in which the subject occupies the same position regardless of the type of the verb. Some accounts of this kind place the postverbal subject inside a small clause, which itself is a complement of the verb (Hoekstra and Mulder 1990; Moro 1997; Den Dikken 2006); some place it in Spec,vP or a VP-adjoined position (Doggett 2004; Bruening 2010);[14] and some place it in Spec,TP, with the VP/vP moving "around" it to some higher position (Slioussar 2007; Wiland 2009, 2016; Bondaruk 2013).[15] According to all of these accounts, the shared constituent in our RNR examples occupies nonparallel positions in the two conjuncts. In the noninverted conjunct, it is a sister of the verb, whereas in the locative inversion conjunct, it occupies a different position: it is either the subject of a small clause or in Spec,vP or Spec,TP, depending on the analysis. If our proposal that BiCoM prevents extraction from nonparallel positions is correct, then movement from such positions should result in ungrammaticality, which is not the case. No degradation is predicted, however, if RNR does not involve movement of the shared constituent.

The other family of proposals regarding the position of the subject in locative inversion argues that the subject occupies different positions with different types of verbs. These analyses are explicitly or implicitly motivated by Levin and Rappaport Hovav's (1995) observation that although the verbs in locative inversion clauses must be intransitive, there exist unergative verbs that are allowed in this construction (see also Hoekstra and Mulder 1990), and there exist unaccusative verbs that are not allowed. Examples (26a–c) show that some verbs that are typically taken to be unergative are allowed in locative inversion, while examples (27a–c) show some unaccusative verbs that are not allowed.

(26) a. At one end, in crude bunks, SLEPT Jed and Henry . . .
[L. Bromfield, *The Farm*, 18]

b. Above them PRANCED the horses on the Parthenon frieze . . .
[P. D. James, *A Taste for Death*, 352]

c. Inside SWAM fish from an iridescent spectrum of colors . . .
[J. Olshan, *The Waterline*, 177]
(Levin and Rappaport Hovav 1995: 224–225)

(27) a. *On the top floor of the skyscraper BROKE many windows.

b. *On the streets of Chicago MELTED a lot of snow.

c. *On backyard clotheslines DRIED the weekly washing.
(Levin and Rappaport Hovav 1995: 224)

In line with these observations, several proposals regarding the subject position in locative inversion take the subject to occupy a different position with unaccusative and unergative verbs. For example, Salzmann (2013) argues that the postverbal subject is the subject of a small clause with unaccusative verbs (Hoekstra and Mulder 1990; Moro 1997; Den Dikken 2006, among others), but occupies Spec,vP with unergative verbs.[16] On the basis of data from Polish, Citko, Germain, and Witkoś (2018) take postverbal subjects in locative inversion to occupy vP/VP-internal positions: the sister of the verb with unaccusative verbs and Spec,vP with unergative verbs. Diercks (2010, 2011) also proposes two distinct types of locative inversion structures. Examining data from Lubukusu, he argues that in one type the subject remains VP-internal, and in the other it raises to Spec,TP.

Culicover and Levine (2001) also propose that there are two different types of locative inversion constructions: in one, which is limited to unaccusative verbs and which they call *light inversion*, the locative PP occupies Spec,TP and the postverbal subject remains in its original position inside the VP as a complement of the verb (Bresnan 1994; Collins 1997). In the other type, which Culicover and Levine call *heavy inversion*, the locative PP is in a topic position (higher than Spec,TP), while the subject undergoes Heavy NP Shift to a right-peripheral TP-adjoined position, having moved through Spec,TP. According to Culicover and Levine, Heavy Inversion differs from Light Inversion in that it is possible with both unaccusative and unergative verbs.[17] Light and heavy inversion also behave differently with respect to a number of independent diagnostics. For example, they differ with respect to the position of VP-level adverbs: in light inversion, the subject precedes the VP-level adverb, whereas in heavy inversion, the subject follows the adverb.

(28) a. Into the room walked **Robin** *slowly*.

b. Into the room appeared to be walking *slowly* **a very large caterpillar**.

(Culicover and Levine 2001: 288, boldface and italics ours)

All of these analyses place the postverbal subject as the sister of the verb in at least some cases of locative inversion, namely, those that involve unaccusative verbs. This position is identical to the position of the direct object in canonical, noninverted transitive structures. This means that the shared constituent in our RNR examples, which is the object in one conjunct and the subject of locative inversion in the other conjunct, occupies parallel positions in the two conjuncts when the verb is unaccusative and nonparallel positions when it is unergative. Based on this, if RNR involved movement, we would expect those RNR examples in which the locative inversion conjunct contains an unergative verb to be ungrammatical because the movement of the shared constituent would proceed from two nonparallel positions and relate them to a third position, violating BiCoM. However, this is not what we find; the status of RNR examples does not seem to covary with the type of verb used in the locative inversion conjunct, as shown in (29a–b). This again suggests that the boldfaced shared constituent undergoes no movement outside of the individual conjuncts, lending support to our analysis of the contrast between ATB extraction and RNR in terms of BiCoM.

(29) a. In the room stood __, and all the guests noticed __, **my personal assistant**.

(Unaccusative verb)

b. Into the room ran __, and all the guests noticed __, **my personal assistant**.

(Unergative verb)

In the next section, we turn to the existing analyses of postverbal subjects in Slavic, paying special attention to their syntactic position. Our analysis predicts ATB extraction to be ungrammatical only if the positions occupied by the shared constituent in the two conjuncts are not parallel. Given that prior to ATB extraction the shared *wh*-phrase in one conjunct is in Spec,vP, we need to show that in the other conjunct it does not occupy the same position. Thus, if the subject is extracted from a postverbal position, we need to show that this position is not Spec,vP.

4.4 Postverbal Subjects in Slavic

If the *wh*-subject in an ATB construction could be extracted from a postverbal Spec,vP position, as shown in (30c), the shared element would be in parallel positions in the two conjuncts.[18] This is on the assumption that the Spec,vP position of the subject "counts" as parallel in the relevant sense to the outer specifier of vP that the object comes to occupy on its way to Spec,CP. In chapter 2, we defined a position as the path from the root to the sister of the element whose position we are defining. Even though these paths are clearly different in the present case, in an intuitive sense both positions are Spec,vP positions. Therefore, it is important for us to exclude Spec,vP as the position of postverbal subjects in Slavic.

(30) a. *?**Które** **studentki**$_i$ wykładowca przepytał t_i *Polish*
which.F.NOM/ACC students.F.NOM/ACC lecturer quizzed
i egzamin końcowy zdały t_i?
and exam final passed
Int. 'Which students did the lecturer quiz and (which students) passed the final exam?'

b. ***Koje** **političarke**$_i$ su organizatori *Croatian*
which.F.NOM/ACC politicians.F.NOM/ACC AUX organizers
pozvali t_i a jučer su dolazak potvrdile t_i?
invited and yesterday AUX arrival confirmed
Int. 'Which female politicians did the organizers invite and (which female politicians) yesterday confirmed their arrival?'

c.

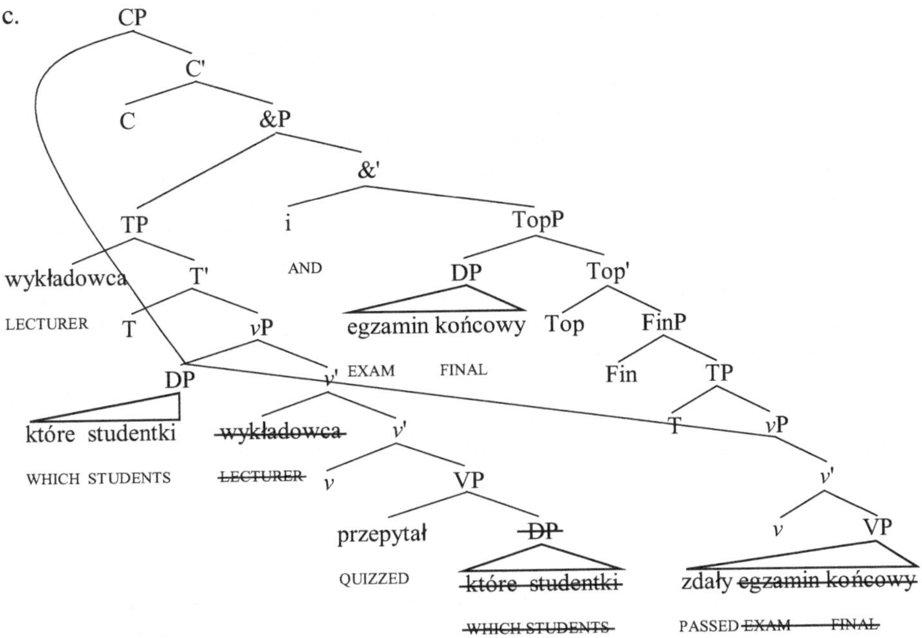

The literature offers conflicting views on the position of postverbal subjects in Slavic languages. While some authors, such as Bailyn (2004), hold that postverbal subjects remain in their base-generated Spec,vP position, there are reasons to believe that they occupy a different position.[19] Bailyn (2003, 2004) argues that postverbal subjects in Russian occupy Spec,vP because in sentences with O(bject) V(erb) S(ubject) word orders, the fronted object c-commands the postverbal nominative subject. This is evidenced by the fact that it can bind a reflexive inside the subject, as shown in (31a), and the fact that coindexing the fronted object with an R-expression contained within the subject leads to a Principle C violation, as shown in (31b).[20]

(31) a. U Petrovyx$_i$ byl [svoj$_i$ dom]. *Russian*
at the.Petrovs was [self's house].NOM
'The Petrovs had their own house.'

b. *Ego$_i$ predstavili [novye znakomye Ivana$_i$] predsedatelju.
him introduced [new friends of.Ivan] chairman.DAT
Int. 'He was introduced to the chairman by Ivan's new friends.'
(Bailyn 2003: 51–52)

Bailyn also notes that the fronted object may be coindexed with the pronoun contained in the subject phrase without incurring a Weak Crossover violation, as shown in (32). The absence of Weak Crossover effects suggests that the fronted object occupies an A-position, which Bailyn takes to be Spec,TP.

(32) [Každuju devočku]$_k$ ljubit ee$_k$ sobaka t_k. *Russian*
[every.ACC girl.ACC] loves her.NOM dog.NOM
'Every girl is loved by her dog.'
(Bailyn 2004: 27)

Note, however, that Bailyn's evidence speaks mostly to the Spec,TP position of the fronted object. His arguments are thus consistent with the subject occupying a position other than Spec,vP, as long as the object occupies a higher A-position.

There are at least two types of analyses that place the postverbal subject in a position other than Spec,vP. On one view, postverbal subjects occupy the specifier of a focus projection located in the lower TP area of the clause (Erechko 2003, Antonyuk under review). Following Belletti's (1999, 2001, 2004) analysis of postverbal subjects in Italian, Erechko (2003) proposes that postverbal subjects in Russian move from their thematic vP-internal position to a slightly higher Spec,FocP position, as shown in (33b). This movement is responsible for the fact that, unlike preverbal subjects, postverbal subjects are interpreted as focused. Since in Russian the verb does not raise to T, Erechko argues that, following the movement of the subject, the entire remnant vP moves to a higher Topic position. Finally, the object undergoes further leftward movement, yielding the correct OVS word order.

(33) a. Okno razbil Oleg. *Russian*
window.ACC broke Oleg.NOM
'Oleg broke the window.'
(adapted from Erechko 2003: 10)

b.

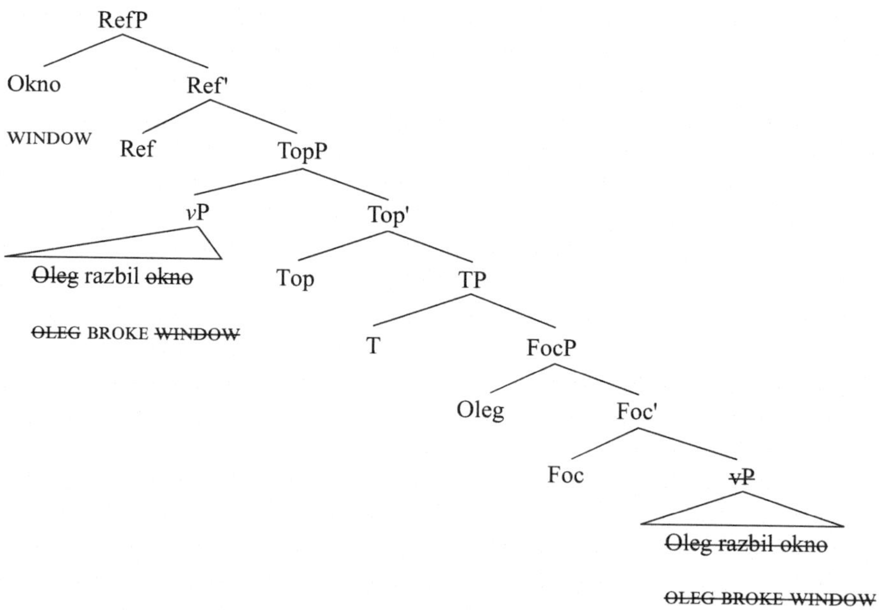

Finally, on some analyses postverbal subjects are located in, or at least pass through, Spec,TP (Sekerina 1997; Witkoś 2008b; Wiland 2009, 2016; Slioussar 2011), and the larger constituent containing the trace of the subject undergoes remnant movement around the subject in Spec,TP, which is what yields the OVS word order. Slioussar's (2007, 2011) account is a good example of such remnant movement accounts (see also Wiland 2009, 2016; Bondaruk 2013, among others).[21] Slioussar notes that in OVS sentences, no material follows postverbal subjects, which are almost exclusively sentence-final. This is unexpected if they occupy Spec,vP positions. On her analysis, the subject first moves to Spec,TP, the clausal remnant containing the trace of the subject raises around it, stranding the subject in a sentence-final position, and the object moves even higher. This is illustrated in (34).[22]

(34) a. Kašu sela Maša. *Russian*

porridge.ACC ate Masha.NOM

'The porridge was eaten by Masha.'

(Slioussar 2011: 2050)

b.

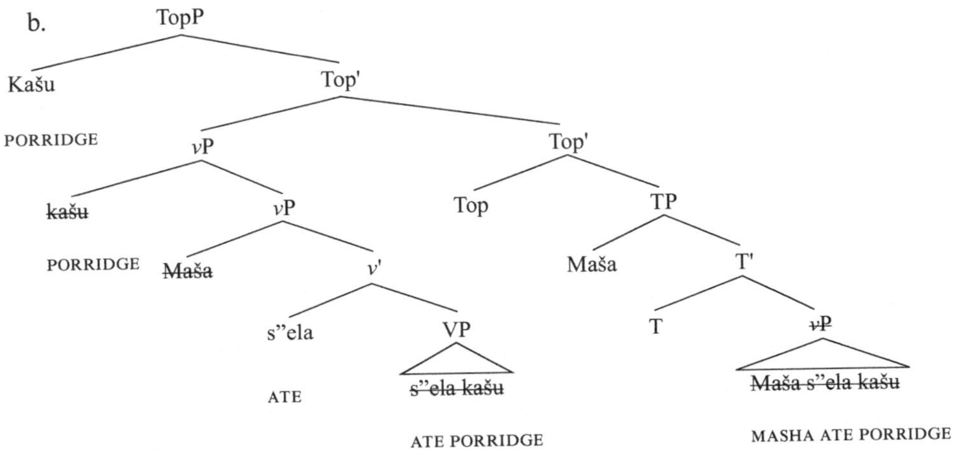

For our account of the differences between ATB extraction and RNR to hold, it is crucial that whatever position the subjects occupy prior to ATB extraction in (30a–b), repeated in (35a–b), this position *not* be Spec,vP. If it were, extraction of the shared constituent, which is the object in one conjunct and the postverbal subject in the other one, would take place from parallel positions. In that case, we would expect this movement to yield a grammatical sentence, contrary to fact. Nevertheless, some accounts of Slavic postverbal subjects place them in precisely this position. However, we have shown that these accounts are compatible with subjects occupying a different position, as long as the nonnominative preverbal constituent is placed in a higher position. We have also presented two concrete proposals that place the subject in a position different from Spec,vP, and have given reasons to believe that these accounts, which place the postverbal subject in either Spec,TP or Spec,FocP (with remnant movement around the subject), are on the right track. (35c) is one implementation of what ATB movement would look like on a remnant movement account.

(35) a. *?**Które studentki$_i$** wykładowca przepytał t_i *Polish*
which.F.NOM/ACC students.F.NOM/ACC lecturer quizzed
i egzamin końcowy zdały t_i?
and exam final passed
Int. 'Which students did the lecturer quiz and (which students) passed the final exam?'

b. ***Koje političarke$_i$** su organizatori *Croatian*
which.F.NOM/ACC politicians.F.NOM/ACC AUX organizers
pozvali t_i a jučer su dolazak potvrdile t_i?
invited and yesterday AUX arrival confirmed
Int. 'Which female politicians did the organizers invite and (which female politicians) yesterday confirmed their arrival?'

c.

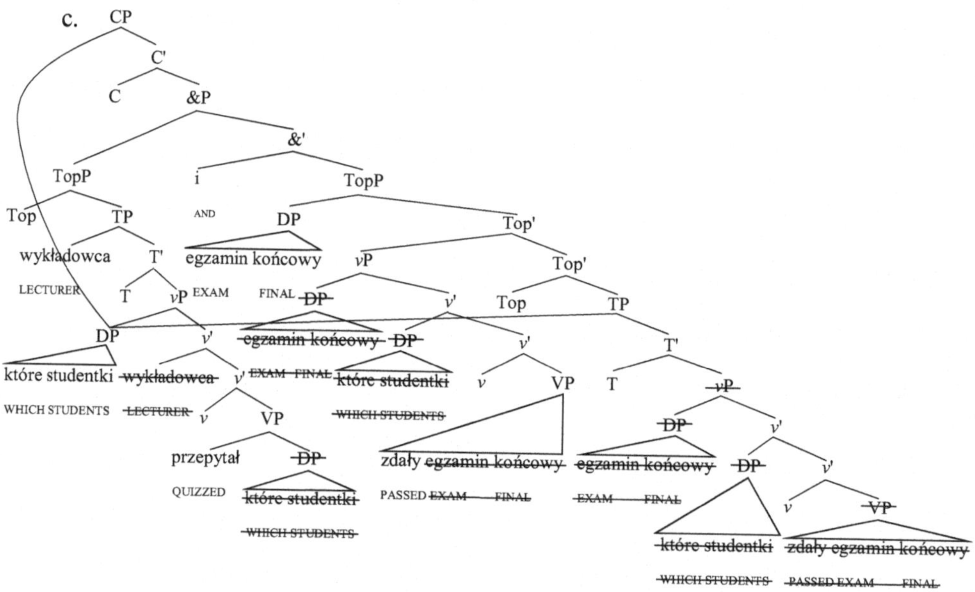

4.5 A-Movement and the Binarity Constraint on Merge

We take BiCoM to be a general constraint on Merge. We showed in section 4.1 that BiCoM applies to multidominant and non-multidominant structures alike. We also showed that for non-multidominant structures, relativizing binarity to syntactic positions yields the same results as relativizing it to syntactic objects, but for multidominant structures, it makes a difference: merging two syntactic objects does not always relate two positions. We argued that this distinction can capture the differences between RNR and ATB constructions with respect to parallelism. However, all the data we have considered so far involved only Ā-movement, which raises the question of how A-movement fares with respect to BiCoM.[23] At first glance, A-movement appears to be immune from the effects of BiCoM; in the grammatical (36a), ATB movement of the subject proceeds from non-parallel positions if the structure involves coordination just below the TP level, and if the shared DP *John* is in Spec,vP in the first conjunct and is a complement of the verb in the second conjunct.[24]

(36) a. **John**$_i$ t_i read a book and was impressed $\boldsymbol{t_i}$ by it.

b.

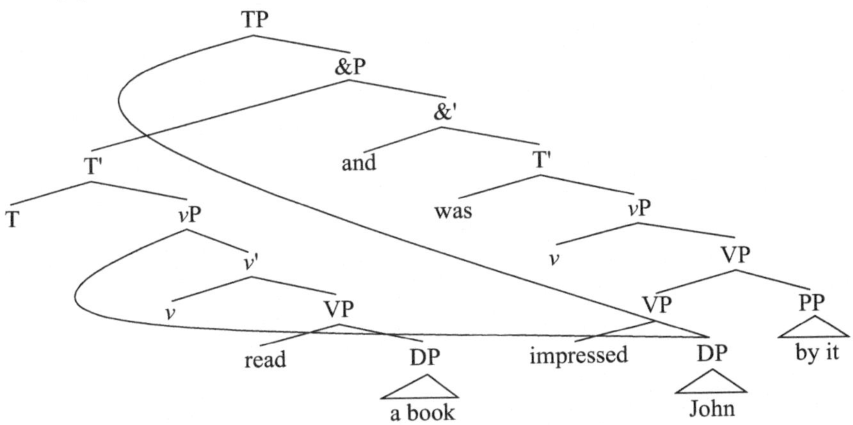

Since we do not want to exclude examples of this sort, and we also do not want to restrict BiCoM to Ā-dependencies, let us consider alternative derivations for (36a), which do not violate BiCoM. One would be for the passive movement to proceed through the edge of vP. That would allow subsequent movement to Spec,TP to proceed from the same position in the two conjuncts (i.e., Spec,vP position), as shown in (37b). This is what Kasai (2004) proposes.[25]

(37) a. **John**$_i$ [$_{vP}$ $\boldsymbol{t_i}$ read a book] and was [$_{vP}$ $\boldsymbol{t_i}$ impressed $\boldsymbol{t_i}$ by it].

b.

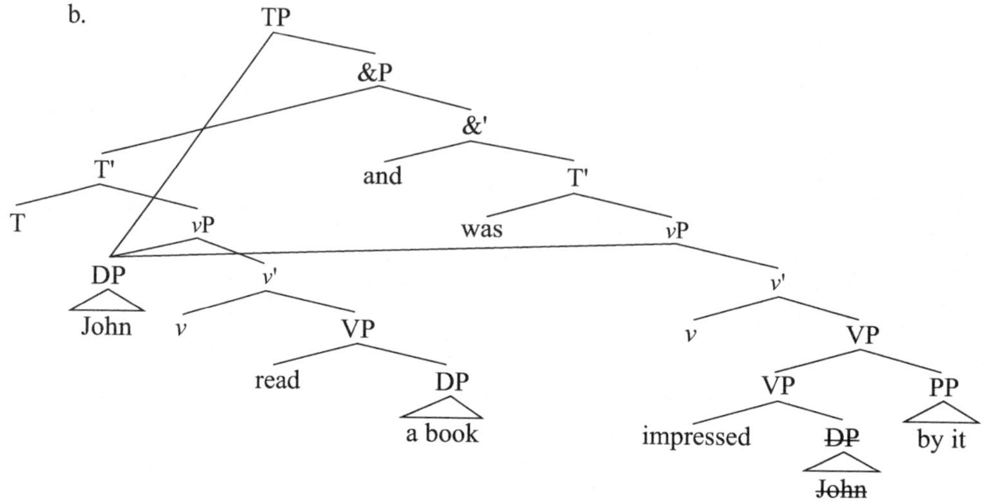

While such a derivation for passive movement looks nonstandard, this is precisely what Legate (2003) argues for, given evidence involving reconstruction, antecedent-contained deletion, parasitic gaps, and nuclear stress assignment in passive and unaccusative constructions. We present a subset of Legate's arguments. The grammaticality of (38a) on the bound variable reading of the pronoun *he* shows that the moving *wh*-phrase *at which of the parties that he invited Mary to* must be able to reconstruct to a position in which the pronoun *he* is c-commanded by *every man* but, crucially, *Mary* is not c-commanded by *her*. The edge of vP is this position. The ungrammaticality of (38b) shows that the reconstructed position cannot be the base position.[26]

(38) a. [At which of the parties that he$_i$ invited Mary$_j$ to] was every man$_i$ _✓_ introduced to her$_j$ _*_?

b. *[At which of the parties that he$_i$ invited Mary$_j$ to] was she$_j$ _*_ introduced to every man$_i$ _*_?

(Legate 2003: 507)

Similarly, the antecedent-contained deletion example in (39a) shows that the quantified DP *anyone you were* must be able to undergo Quantifier Raising to a position in which it is still c-commanded by negation, since it is a negative polarity item. Again, Spec,vP *is* this position. The fact that the universal quantifier in (39b) can scope under the existential one makes the same point.

(39) a. Mary wasn't [$_{VP1}$ introduced to [$_{DP}$ anyone you were [$_{VP2}$ *e*]]].

b. Some woman was [$_{VP1}$ given [$_{DP}$ every message you were [$_{VP2}$ *e*]]].

(Legate 2003: 509)

Another way to derive (37a) without violating BiCoM is to assume that it involves TP-coordination rather than T′-coordination, and that the shared subject does not move above the coordination level. On this analysis, the structure is BiCoM-compliant regardless of whether the subject of the passive conjunct raises to Spec,TP from its original postverbal position or moves through Spec,vP, as Legate (2003) proposes. The former option is illustrated in (40b) and the latter in (40c).

(40) a. **John**$_i$ t_i read a book and was impressed $\boldsymbol{t_i}$ by it.

b.

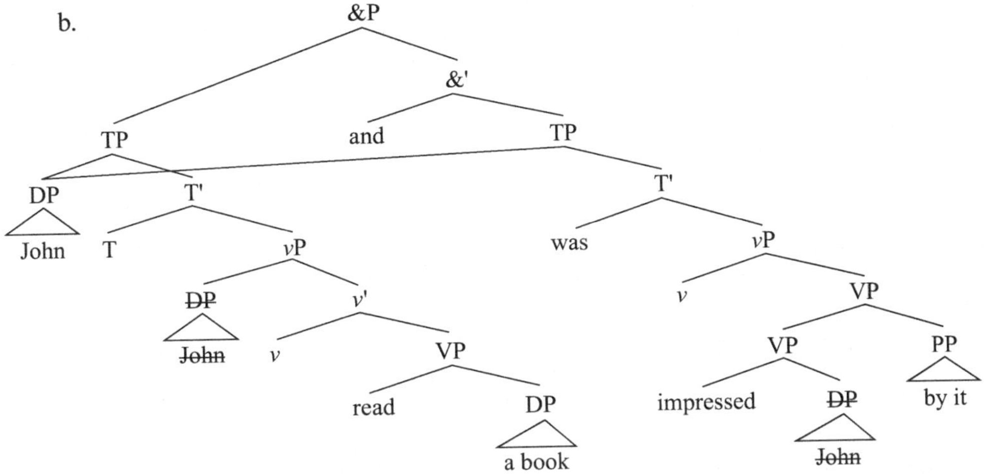

c.

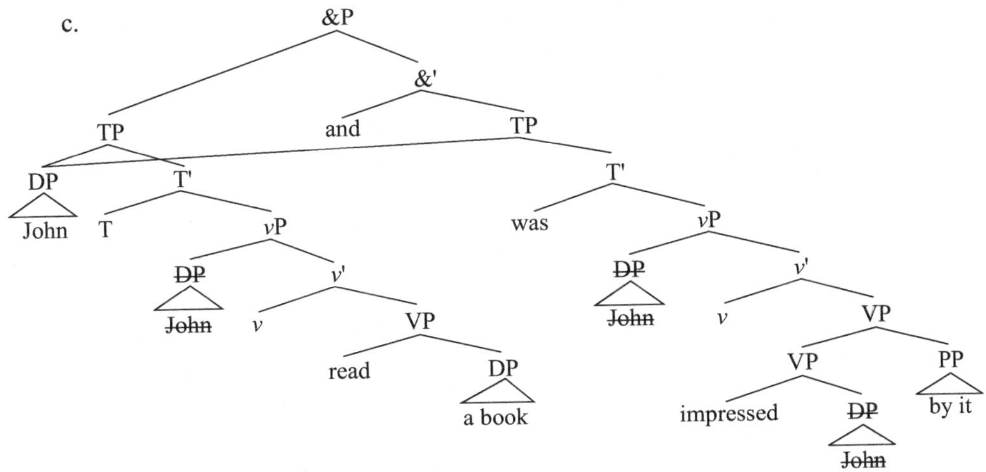

The structures in (40b) and (40c) do not violate BiCoM because the shared constituent *John* undergoes Internal Merge within each conjunct, and no further Merge applies to it after the two conjuncts have become part of a single derivation. There is, however, one question that these structures raise: how do we ensure that the shared subject is linearized in the first conjunct? On most linearization algorithms that we are aware of (Wilder 1999, 2008; Johnson 2007; Bachrach and Katzir 2009; De Vries 2009; Gračanin-Yuksek 2013), the structure containing a shared constituent can only be linearized if this constituent is placed in the final position; this is how the Right Edge Restriction in RNR is typically accounted for. While it is not inconceivable that some linearization algorithm can be developed that would allow shared constituents to occupy nonfinal positions (the possibility we leave open here), we could also resolve the linearization issue by taking the subject to move to some higher position, above the coordination level. This would not violate BiCoM because the movement would proceed from parallel positions—the Spec,TP position in each conjunct.

4.6 Conclusion

In this chapter, we have shown how BiCoM derives the contrast between ungrammatical ATB extraction from nonparallel positions and grammatical RNR in which the shared constituent occupies nonparallel positions. We argued that this contrast follows from the fact that the shared constituent in ATB constructions, unlike in RNR, undergoes Internal Merge after the two conjuncts have been united into a single derivation. Therefore, ATB extraction violates BiCoM, whereas RNR does not. The examples of RNR that we used to illustrate the relevant contrast necessarily contained clause-final subjects in one conjunct, so as not to incur violations of the Right Edge Restriction. This opened up the possibility that the postverbal position of the (shared) subject in one conjunct might be parallel to the position of the (shared) object in the other conjunct. If this were the case, both ATB and RNR examples would be predicted to be grammatical, a welcome result for RNR, but not for ATB examples. We therefore examined in detail the position of postverbal subjects in locative inversion and OVS structures in Slavic languages and showed that such subjects do not occupy positions that can be construed as parallel with the positions occupied by the objects.

However, if nothing else is said, BiCoM excludes not only the ungrammatical cases of ATB extraction—it excludes *all* cases of ATB extraction. This is because ATB extraction of an element that is shared between the two conjuncts always happens after the two conjuncts become part of a single derivation; thus, ATB movement should always violate BiCoM. However, some cases of ATB extraction—those in which the shared constituent is extracted from parallel positions—are, of course, grammatical. In the next chapter, we turn to such cases.

5 Escaping the Binarity Constraint on Merge

In this chapter, we discuss two principled exceptions to BiCoM and show how they can be incorporated into our system. One involves grammatical examples of ATB extraction, such as the one in (1a), in which the shared element occupies parallel positions in the two conjuncts prior to Internal Merge. In this case, the final instance of Merge relates three positions in a single derivation, as shown in (1b): the position of *who* in the first conjunct (defined as the path ⟨CP, C′, &P, TP, T′, vP, v′⟩), the position of *who* in the second conjunct (defined as the path ⟨CP, C′, &P, &′ TP, T′, vP, v′⟩), and the position of C′ (defined as the path ⟨CP, DP⟩). This violates BiCoM. Unlike in cases of simple Internal Merge, which we discussed in chapter 4, the number of positions related by Merge in (1b) exceeds two even if we discount the position of *who* created by the last instance of Merge.[1]

(1) a. I know a man **who**$_i$ Bill recommended $\boldsymbol{t_i}$ and Mary hired $\boldsymbol{t_i}$.

b. I know a man

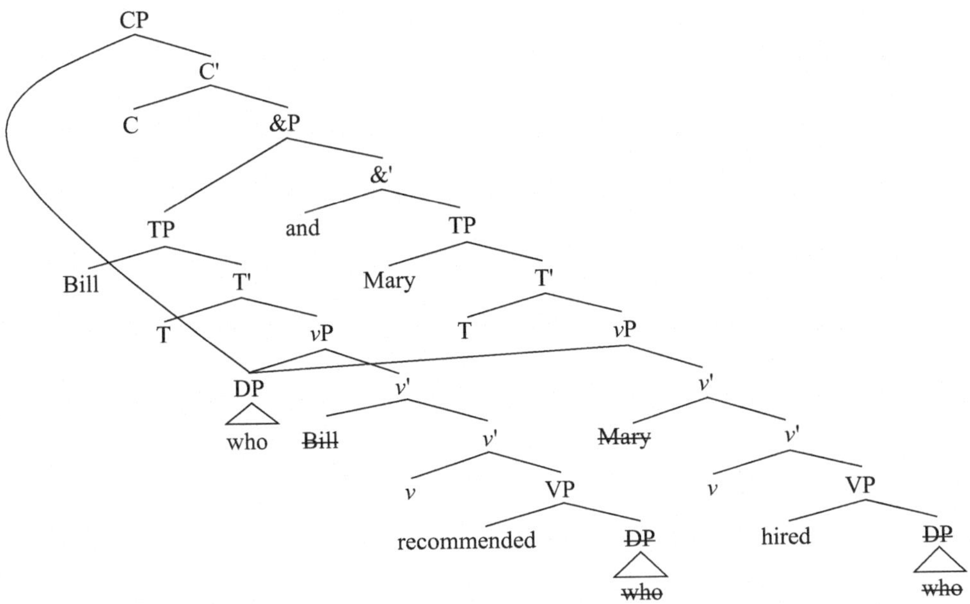

The other principled case where we would expect to find BiCoM violations, but we don't, involves successive-cyclic movement. In the run-of-the-mill long-distance *wh*-question in (2a), the *wh*-phrase comes to occupy multiple positions in a single derivation: the complement of V, the specifier of the embedded and matrix vPs, and the specifier of the embedded and matrix CPs, as shown in (2b). All Internal Merge operations apply in a single derivation, and all but the very first one relate more than two positions.

(2) a. [$_{CP}$ **What**$_i$ did John [$_{vP}$ $\boldsymbol{t_i}$ think [$_{CP}$ $\boldsymbol{t_i}$ that Mary [$_{vP}$ $\boldsymbol{t_i}$ said $\boldsymbol{t_i}$]]]]?

b.

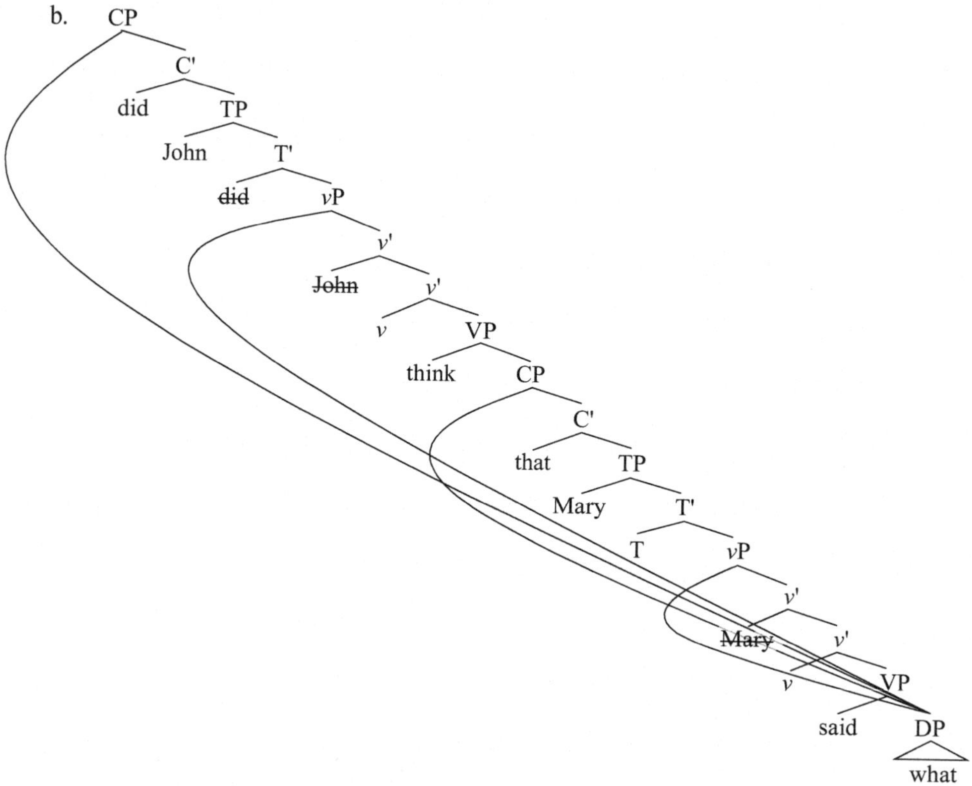

This is because each time Internal Merge takes place, the *wh*-phrase gains one position. For example, before *what* moves from the embedded Spec,vP position to the embedded Spec,CP position, it already occupies the following two positions: the embedded Spec,vP position, defined as the path ⟨CP, TP, T′, vP, v′⟩, boldfaced in (3a), and its original position, defined as the path ⟨CP, TP, T′, vP, v′, v′, VP, V⟩, boldfaced in (3b).

(3) a.

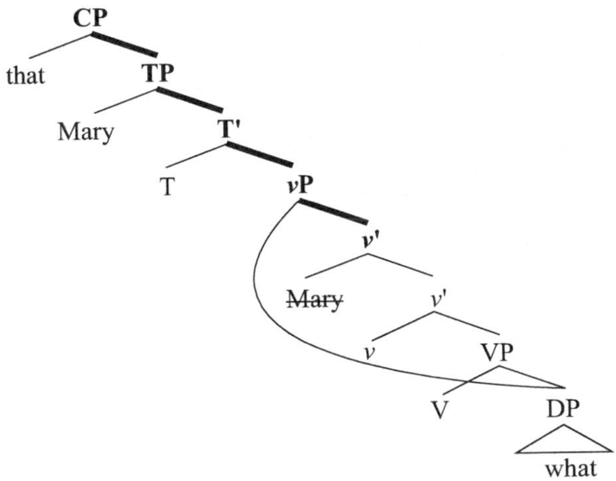

b.

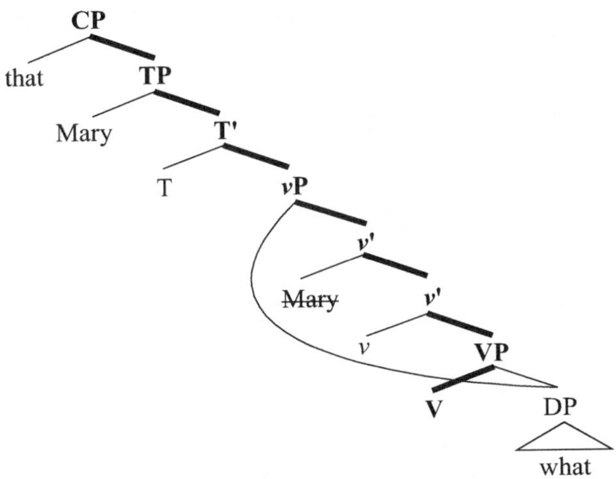

After Internal Merge applies, two additional positions are created; the new, embedded Spec,CP position of *what*, defined as ⟨CP, C′⟩, and the newly created position of C′, defined as ⟨CP, DP⟩. The changes we made to BiCoM in section 4.1 resulted in the newly created position of *what* (⟨CP, C′⟩) being excluded from the calculation. However, even if we exclude the new position of *what*, its two remaining positions, as well as the position of C′, all count. The structure in (2b) should therefore violate BiCoM.

The question we focus on in this chapter is *why* the structures in (1b) and (2b) are well-formed although prima facie they violate BiCoM. We argue that BiCoM violations may be obviated in two ways. One is for two of the three positions that Merge relates to be similar enough to count as one. We refer to this as *structural syncretism*, and show that this is how (1b) escapes BiCoM. The other way is for Merge to only "see" the latest position and "ignore" the other positions. This is what happens in (2b), where multiple positions are created through successive-cyclic movement.

5.1 Grammatical Across-the-Board Movement

Examples of well-formed ATB extraction from parallel positions are given in (4a–c). Extraction proceeds from direct object positions in (4a), from subject positions in (4b), and from indirect object positions in (4c).

(4) a. I know a man **who**$_i$ Bill recommended $\boldsymbol{t}_i$ and Mary hired $\boldsymbol{t}_i$.

b. I know a man **who**$_i$ $\boldsymbol{t}_i$ recommended Bill and $\boldsymbol{t}_i$ hired Mary.

c. I know a man **to whom**$_i$ Bill gave a book $\boldsymbol{t}_i$ and Mary sent a package $\boldsymbol{t}_i$.

In order to explain their grammaticality, we propose that in these circumstances, the grammar treats the *wh*-phrase *who/to whom*, which occupies *multiple* positions in a derivation, as if it occupied a *single* position. In (4a), for example, the final application of Internal Merge relates three positions in a single derivation: Spec,vP in the first conjunct, Spec,vP in the second conjunct, and the matrix C′. Since two of these positions are Spec,vP positions, as shown in (5), they "count" as one for the purposes of Merge.

(5) I know a man

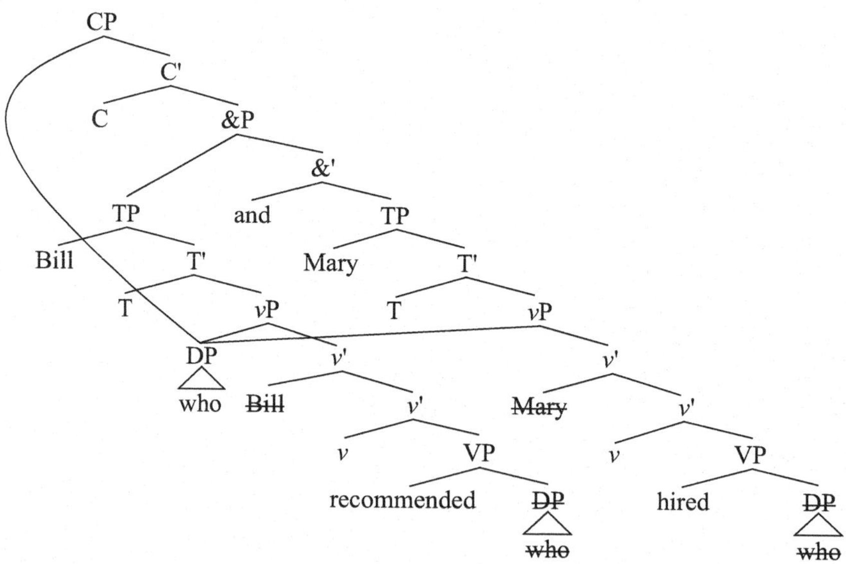

The idea that syncretism ameliorates ungrammaticality is familiar from morphosyntax; in languages with rich case morphology, such as Polish and Croatian, both RNR and ATB constructions are sensitive to the form of the shared constituent. For an RNR or

ATB construction to be grammatical, the shared constituent must be compatible with the case requirements of the predicate in each conjunct; this is known in the literature as the *case-matching requirement* (Borsley 1983; Dyła 1984; Franks 1995; Citko 2000, 2005, 2011b; Asarina 2011, 2013, among many others). This is shown in (6a–b) for ATB questions and in (7a–b) for RNR constructions. In these examples, the verbs inside the two conjuncts assign the same case to their object (accusative here), and the shared object (boldfaced) *is* accusative, thus satisfying the case requirements of both verbs.[2]

(6) *Case matching in ATB questions*

a. **Którą** **nauczycielkę**$_i$ Jan lubi t_i a Piotr lekceważy t_i? *Polish*
which.F.ACC teacher.F.ACC Jan likes$_{\text{ACC}}$ and Piotr ignores$_{\text{ACC}}$
'Which teacher does Jan like and Piotr ignore?'

b. **Koju** **učiteljicu**$_i$ Jan mrzi t_i a Vid obožava t_i? *Croatian*
which.F.ACC teacher.F.ACC Jan hates$_{\text{ACC}}$ and Vid adores$_{\text{ACC}}$
'Which teacher does Jan hate and Vid adore?'

(7) *Case matching in RNR*

a. Jan lubi __, a Piotr krytykuje __, **nauczycielkę historii.** *Polish*
Jan likes$_{\text{ACC}}$ and Piotr criticizes$_{\text{ACC}}$ teacher.F.ACC history.GEN
'Jan likes and Piotr criticizes the history teacher.'

b. Jan voli __, a Vid prezire __, **učiteljicu iz povijesti.** *Croatian*
Jan loves$_{\text{ACC}}$ and Vid despises$_{\text{ACC}}$ teacher.F.ACC from history
'Jan loves and Vid despises the history teacher.'

If the case requirements imposed on the shared object in the two conjuncts are distinct, the result becomes ungrammatical. This is shown in (8a–b) for ATB questions and in (9a–b) for RNR constructions. In these examples, the verb in one conjunct requires accusative case, whereas the verb in the other conjunct requires dative case; the outcome is bad regardless of which case the shared constituent bears.[3]

(8) *Case mismatches in ATB questions*

a. ***Którą** **nauczycielkę**$_i$ / **Której** **nauczycielce**$_i$ *Polish*
which.F.ACC teacher.F.ACC which.F.DAT teacher.F.DAT
Jan ufa t_i a Piotr uwielbia t_i?
Jan trusts$_{\text{DAT}}$ and Piotr adores$_{\text{ACC}}$
'Which teacher does Jan trust and Piotr adore?'

b. ***Koju učiteljicu**$_i$ / **Kojoj učiteljici**$_i$ Jan *Croatian*
which.F.ACC teacher.F.ACC which.F.DAT teacher F.DAT Jan
vjeruje t_i a Vid obožava t_i?
trusts$_{DAT}$ and Vid adores$_{ACC}$
'Which teacher does Jan trust and Vid adore?'

(9) *Case mismatches in RNR*

a. Jan lubi __, a Piotr ufa __, ***nauczycielkę** *Polish*
Jan likes$_{ACC}$ and Piotr trusts$_{DAT}$ teacher.F.ACC
historii / ?nauczycielce historii.
history.GEN / teacher.F.DAT history.GEN
'Jan likes and Piotr trusts the history teacher.'

b. Jan voli __, a Vid ne vjeruje __, ***učiteljicu iz** *Croatian*
Jan loves$_{ACC}$ and Vid NEG trusts$_{DAT}$ teacher.F.ACC from
povijesti / ??učiteljici iz povijesti.
history / teacher.F.DAT from history
'Jan loves and Vid doesn't trust the history teacher.'

Crucially, syncretic forms ameliorate case conflicts in both ATB and RNR constructions. If the verbs in the two conjuncts of an ATB construction assign different cases, but the *form* of the shared constituent can satisfy the case requirements of both verbs, the outcome is grammatical, as in (10a–b). The same is true of RNR, as shown in (11a–b).

(10) *Case syncretism in ATB questions*

a. **Kogo**$_i$ Jan lubi t_i a Maria się boi t_i? *Polish*
who.ACC/GEN Jan likes$_{ACC}$ and Maria REFL fears$_{GEN}$
'Who does Jan like and Maria fear?'

b. **Koga**$_i$ Jan voli t_i a Petra se boji t_i? *Croatian*
who.ACC/GEN Jan likes$_{ACC}$ and Petra REFL fears$_{GEN}$
'Who does Jan like and Petra fear?'

(11) *Case syncretism in RNR*

a. Jan lubi __, a Maria się boi __, **dużego klauna.** *Polish*
Jan likes$_{ACC}$ and Maria REFL fears$_{GEN}$ big.ACC/GEN clown.ACC/GEN
'Jan likes and Maria fears a/the big clown.'

b. Jan voli __, a Petra se boji __, **velikog klauna.** *Croatian*
Jan loves$_{ACC}$ and Petra REFL fears$_{GEN}$ big.ACC/GEN clown.ACC/GEN
'Jan loves and Petra fears a/the big clown.'

5.2 Structurally Syncretic Positions

We propose that syncretism, broadly understood as identity in form, can be translated into syntactic terms. Two *distinct* syntactic positions can be regarded as syncretic (i.e., *nondistinct*) if they can be given sufficiently similar configurational descriptions. Such nondistinct positions can then count as *a single position* for the purposes of BiCoM. In chapter 2, we defined a position of a syntactic object as a path from the root of the tree to the sister of the syntactic object whose position we are defining. We repeat the relevant definition in (12).

(12) A position of SO_n in SO_1 is a path from SO_1 to SO_m, SO_1 the set^W formed by Merge, SO_m a sister of SO_n, where a path is a sequence of syntactic objects $\langle SO_1, SO_2, \ldots, SO_m \rangle$, and for all i, $0 < i < m$, $SO_{i+1} \in SO_i$.

We further propose that for two objects α and β to occupy syncretic positions, they must share immediate syntactic environments. Since positions are defined in terms of paths, we propose that the relevant paths (i.e., the path from the root to the sister of α and the path from the root to the sister of β) must share the last two members: the mother and the sister of α and β. We provide the definition of syncretic positions in (13).

(13) *Syncretic positions*

A position of SO_n in SO_1 is syncretic with a position of SO_m in $SO_{1'}$ if and only if:

- the path from SO_1 to $SO_{n'}$, SO_1 the set^W formed by Merge, $SO_{n'}$ a sister of SO_n, is a sequence of syntactic objects $\langle SO_1, SO_2, \ldots, SO_{n'} \rangle$ where for all $0 < i < n'$, $SO_{i+1} \in SO_i$ and
- the path from $SO_{1'}$ to $SO_{m'}$, $SO_{1'}$ the set^W formed by Merge, $SO_{m'}$ a sister of SO_m, is a sequence of syntactic objects $\langle SO_{1'}, SO_{2'}, \ldots, SO_{m'} \rangle$ where for all $0 < i < m'$, $SO_{i+1} \in SO_i$ and
- the last two members of the path from SO_1 to $SO_{n'}$ and the last two members of the path from $SO_{1'}$ to $SO_{m'}$ are the same.[4]

Our definition of syncretic positions captures the intuition that, for example, a Spec,vP position is syncretic with a distinct Spec,vP position irrespective of whether the two are within the same derivation (in distinct clauses with one clause containing the other) or within separate derivations (in two distinct conjuncts or two distinct sentences). It also holds irrespective of whether the syncretic positions are occupied by the same element, as in the grammatical cases of ATB extraction we discuss here, or by two different elements: for example, a Spec,vP position occupied by a DP is syncretic with a Spec,vP position occupied by a CP. According to the definition in (13), the shared constituent *who* in (14a), repeated from (1a), occupies syncretic positions in the two conjuncts prior to ATB extraction. Its position in the first conjunct is defined as the path ⟨CP, C′, &P, TP, T′, **vP, v′**⟩, and its position in the second conjunct is defined as ⟨CP, C′, &P, &′, TP, T′, **vP, v′**⟩. The last two members in these two paths are identical, which is what makes the two positions syncretic.

(14) a. I know a man **who**$_i$ Bill recommended $\boldsymbol{t_i}$ and Mary hired $\boldsymbol{t_i}$.

b. I know a man

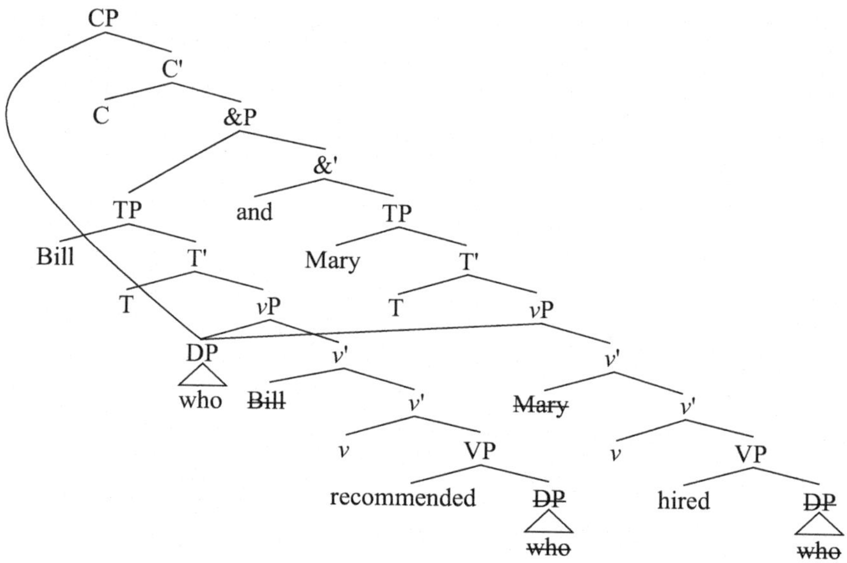

Since *who* occupies syncretic positions in the two conjuncts (Spec,vP positions), the Internal Merge that places *who* in the specifier of the matrix CP can treat them as one.[5] This Merge thus relates only two positions, so BiCoM is not violated.

Structural syncretism obviates BiCoM violations in all cases of ATB extraction from parallel positions. In (15a–b), we illustrate grammatical ATB extraction of the subject. This is allowed by BiCoM because the shared *wh*-phrase, *which students*, occupies syncretic Spec,TP positions in both conjuncts before it is internally merged with the matrix C′. These positions are syncretic because the last two members of the paths defining them are the same: ⟨TP, T′⟩.

(15) a. **Which students**$_i$ ***t***$_i$ passed the exam and ***t***$_i$ earned the scholarship?

b.

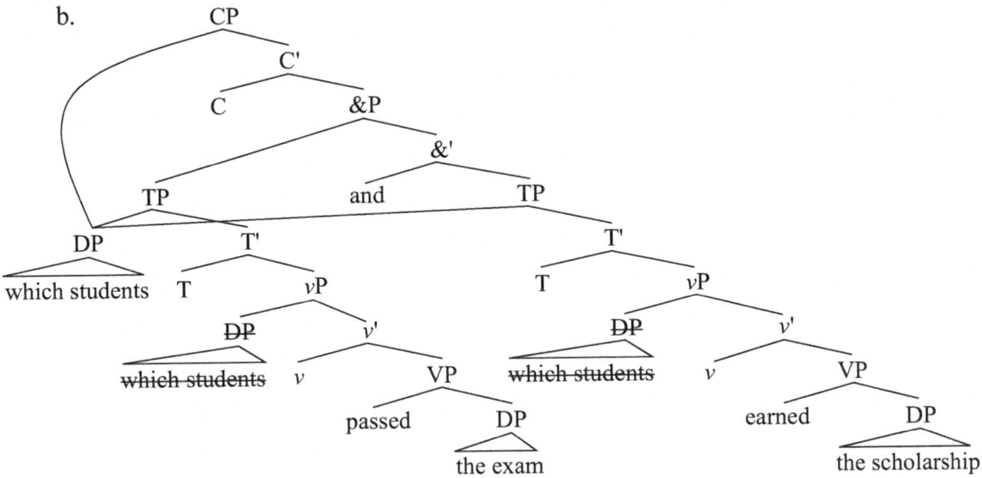

5.3 The Syncretism Effect

In the previous section, we attributed the amelioration of BiCoM violations in ATB extraction from parallel positions to structural syncretism (by analogy to morphological syncretism) and proposed that Merge can relate three (or more) positions without violating BiCoM only if two (or more) of these positions are syncretic. We defined syncretic positions as positions whose sisters and mothers are the same. The question we focus on in this section is *why* syncretism should matter: what is it about syncretism, morphological and syntactic alike, that allows it to remedy morphological and syntactic violations?[6] Since morphological syncretism has received considerable attention in the relevant literature, we start with an overview of representative approaches to that topic, with an eye toward determining how, if at all, their insights might help us explain the effects of structural syncretism that we are investigating here.

To put the discussion in concrete terms, consider the case paradigms of *wh*-pronouns in Polish and Croatian, given in (16a) and (16b), with the syncretic forms boldfaced. In both Polish and Croatian, the animate *wh*-pronoun *kto/tko* 'who' exhibits syncretism in the genitive and accusative forms (in Polish *kogo*, in Croatian *koga* for both cases), and the inanimate *wh*-pronoun *co/što* 'what' exhibits syncretism in the nominative and accusative forms (*co/što* for both cases). Furthermore, both *kto* and *co* in Polish have syncretic forms in the instrumental and locative cases (*kim* and *czym*, respectively) while in Croatian, *tko* and *što* are both syncretic in the dative and locative (*komu* and *čemu*, respectively).

(16) a. Nominative kto 'who' **co** 'what' *Polish*

a. Nominative	kto 'who'	**co** 'what'	*Polish*
Genitive	**kogo**	czego	
Dative	komu	czemu	
Accusative	**kogo**	**co**	
Locative	**kim**	**czym**	
Instrumental	**kim**	**czym**	
b. Nominative	tko 'who'	**što** 'what'	*Croatian*
Genitive	**koga**	čega	
Dative	**komu**	**čemu**	
Accusative	**koga**	**što**	
Locative	**komu**	**čemu**	
Instrumental	kim	čim	

Within the framework of Distributed Morphology, which we adopt here, there are two main ways that we are aware of to account for syncretism effects.[7] One relies on the underspecification of Vocabulary items in the lexicon and the other on impoverishment rules. In what follows, we present both types of approaches, starting with underspecification. We then show that an impoverishment-based approach, coupled with basic assumptions of set theory, offers the best way to capture the effects of structural syncretism that we are interested in here.

On the underspecification view, individual cases are broken down into more primitive (sets of) features, and individual forms may lack some of these features—that is, may be underspecified with respect to these features. We illustrate this view with Jakobson's classic feature system, which "decomposes" cases into three more primitive features: [+/−quantified], [+/−directional], and [+/−marginal] (Jakobson 1958), as shown in (17).[8]

(17)

Nominative	=	[−marg, −quant, −dir]
Accusative	=	[−marg, −quant, +dir]
Genitive	=	[−marg, +quant, −dir]
Instrumental	=	[+marg, −quant, −dir]
Dative	=	[+marg, −quant, +dir]
Locative	=	[+marg, +quant, −dir]

(Franks 1995: 42, citing Jakobson 1958)

The feature system in (17) can capture the nominative/accusative syncretism if these two cases are simply underspecified with respect to the [directional] feature (i.e., lack this feature), as shown in (18).[9]

(18) *co*, *što* [−marg, −quant] Nominative/Accusative

Crucially, on the underspecification view, syncretism is not a result of the lexicon containing two lexical items with two different feature specifications that happen to be pronounced in the same way, as shown in (19a–b).[10] Instead, there is only a single form specified for some features but underspecified for others, as shown in (18), which makes this form compatible with two or more different environments.

(19) a. co_1, $što_1$ [−marg, −quant, −dir] Nominative

b. co_2, $što_2$ [−marg, −quant, +dir] Accusative

The syntactic syncretism discussed in section 5.2 concerns two positions that are the same in the relevant sense, which is what allows Merge to treat them as one for the purposes of BiCoM. This is closer to the view of morphological syncretism in (19), where the lexicon contains two distinct forms, than to the underspecification view in (18). It is not clear, however, how the approach in (19) would explain *why* syncretism should have the power that it has to ameliorate grammaticality violations. Consider the free relative clause examples in (20a–b). In both, the matrix and relative clauses impose different case requirements on the (boldfaced) *wh*-pronoun; the matrix verb requires its complement (the free relative clause, whose case is determined by the case of the *wh*-pronoun that introduces it) to be accusative, but the *wh*-pronoun is assigned nominative case inside the relative clause.[11] The fact that the inanimate *wh*-pronoun *co* 'what' in Polish has a syncretic nominative/accusative form but its animate counterpart *kto* 'who' does not is what explains the contrast in grammaticality between (20a) and (20b).

(20) a. *Polish*

Kupimy	**[co(kolwiek)**	jest	na	wyprzedaży].
we.buy$_{ACC}$	what(ever).NOM/ACC	is$_{NOM}$	on	sale

'We will buy whatever is on sale.'

b.

*Zaprosimy	**[kogo(kolwiek)/kto(kolwiek)**	jest	na	liście	gości].
we.invite$_{ACC}$	who(ever).ACC/who(ever).NOM	is$_{NOM}$	on	list	guests

'We will invite whoever is on the guest list.'

Only the underspecification view allows the representation in (20a). If, instead, the lexicon contains two distinct forms, the result is predicted to be ungrammatical no matter which of the two forms is selected. If the nominative form is selected, as in (21a), the case requirements of the matrix verb will not be satisfied. If the accusative form is selected instead, as in (21b), the case requirements of the relative clause predicate will not be satisfied.

(21) a. Kupimy [**co(kolwiek)** jest na wyprzedaży]. *Polish*
we.buy$_{ACC}$ what(ever).NOM is$_{NOM}$ on sale
'We will buy whatever is on sale.'

b. Kupimy [**co(kolwiek)** jest na wyprzedaży].
we.buy$_{ACC}$ what(ever).ACC is$_{NOM}$ on sale
'We will buy whatever is on sale.'

The only way to satisfy the case requirements of both the matrix and the relative clause would be to include both the accusative and nominative *wh*-pronouns in the structure and delete one of them, as shown in (22).

(22) Kupimy **co(kolwiek)** [~~**co(kolwiek)**~~ jest na wyprzedaży]. *Polish*
we.buy$_{ACC}$ what(ever).ACC what(ever).NOM is$_{NOM}$ on sale
'We will buy whatever is on sale.'

We will come back to the accounts that rely on deletion when we discuss impoverishment, which will serve as the basis for our analogy between the effects of morphological and syntactic syncretism. First, however, let us present in some detail Asarina's (2011, 2013) account, which also relies on underspecification. It is directly relevant here, as it discusses the effects of morphological case syncretism on the grammaticality of RNR constructions.

Focusing on the Russian nominal system and the syncretisms exhibited by different declension classes, Asarina (2011, 2013) distinguishes among the following three types of syncretism: neutrality, morphological ambiguity, and phonological ambiguity, illustrated in (23a–c).

(23) a. Neutrality: NOM-ACC (neuter, class Ib)
Example: *bljudc-e* 'saucer-NOM/ACC'

b. Morphological ambiguity: PART-DAT (masculine, class Ia; lexically specified subset)
Example: *chaj-u* 'tea-PART/DAT'

c. Phonological ambiguity: ACC-PREP (neuter with unstressed ending, class Ib)
Example: *pól-i* 'field-ACC/PREP'
(Asarina 2011: 182)

Neutrality arises when a single form is underspecified with respect to a certain feature (or set of features). Ambiguity, in Asarina's terms, arises when "two sets of features are *accidentally* represented in the same way" (Asarina 2011: 174). Asarina's experimental results demonstrate that only neutrality resolves case mismatches. This is shown by the contrast between (24a), which involves the neutral/underspecified form (*bljudc-e* 'saucer-NOM/ACC'), and (24b), which involves the ambiguous form (*chaj-u* 'tea-PART/DAT').

(24) a. On ne ostavil, tak kak emu nadoelo *Russian*
he not $kept_{ACC}$ as him $sick.of_{NOM}$
bljudc-e s **krasnoj kaëmkoj**.
saucer-**ACC/NOM** with red border
'He didn't keep, as he was sick of, the saucer with a red border.'
(Asarina 2011: 182)

b. *On otlil, no poradovalsja, **chaju**.
he $poured_{PART}$ but was $glad_{DAT}$ tea.**PART/DAT**
'He poured off, but was glad of, the tea.'
(Asarina 2011: 195)

Similarly to what we have done, Asarina adopts a multidominance analysis of RNR, which allows the shared constituent to bear two sets of features, as shown in (25), which represents the shared constituent in (24a).

(25)

CLASS	Ib
NUMBER	singular
CASE	nonoblique: **ACC**

CLASS	Ib
NUMBER	singular
CASE	nonoblique: **NOM**

(Asarina 2011: 194)

The result is grammatical if the two feature structures can be spelled out by a *single* Vocabulary Insertion rule, in accordance with the principle Asarina proposes, given in (26).

(26) *Spell-out of multiple feature structures*
All feature structures on a single item must be spelled out by a single insertion rule.
(Asarina 2011: 191)

For the syncretism at hand (NOM/ACC), Asarina proposes the Vocabulary Insertion rule in (27), where NOM/ACC are realizations of nonoblique case.

(27) Nonoblique, singular, class Ib → -o
(Asarina 2011: 194)

Examples involving nonsyncretic cases, such as the one in (28), are ungrammatical because they would have to involve two distinct Vocabulary Insertion rules.

(28) *On ne sosedu podlil, a naoborot poradovalsja, *Russian*
he not neighbor.DAT poured$_{PART}$ but opposite was.glad$_{DAT}$
moloku s saxarom i likërom.
milk.DAT with sugar and liqueur
'He didn't pour some for his neighbor, but rather was glad of, milk with sugar and liqueur.'
(Asarina 2011: 191)

In this example, the shared nominal has the two feature structures given in (29), which means that there are two Vocabulary Insertion rules, given in (30a–b). Since neither one is more specific than the other and they are not ordered with respect to each other, Vocabulary Insertion cannot apply.

(29)

CLASS	ib		CLASS	Ib
NUMBER	singular		NUMBER	singular
CASE	GEN–**PART**		CASE	**DAT**

(Asarina 2011: 192)

(30) a. GEN, singular, class Ib → -a
b. DAT, singular, class Ib → -u
(Asarina 2011: 192)

As discussed by Harley (2008) and Kramer (2016), among others, while underspecification can account for the types of syncretism that apply to particular forms, it is less well-equipped to handle so-called metasyncretism, which refers to the kind of syncretism that holds across paradigms and is not tied to particular Vocabulary items (Williams 1994).[12] In Distributed Morphology, the morphological operation that is used to capture metasyncretism is called *impoverishment*: it "removes a feature from a syntactic feature bundle" (Kramer 2016: 102; see also Halle 1997; Harley 2008; Calabrese 2011, among others, for relevant discussion). One example of metasyncretism that Harley discusses (from Bobaljik 2002) is the lack of gender distinctions in the following plural forms in Russian:

(31) a. *Third person nominative pronouns*

Gender	Singular	Plural
Masculine	*on-Ø*	
Feminine	*on-a*	*on-i*
Neuter	*on-o*	

b. *Third person dative pronouns*

Gender	Singular	Plural
Masculine	*emu*	
Feminine	*ej*	*im*
Neuter	*emu*	

c. *Nominative adjective suffixes*

Gender	Singular	Plural
Masculine	*-yi*	
Feminine	*-aja*	*-ye*
Neuter	*-oe*	

(Harley 2008: 255–256)

This can be captured by the impoverishment rule given in (32), which simply deletes gender features in the plural.[13]

(32) [+plural, +{masculine, feminine, neuter}] → [+plural]
(Harley 2008: 258)

Even though she ultimately does not adopt it, Asarina (2011) discusses an impoverishment-based account of the syncretism effects in RNR constructions, and our account of syntactic syncretism builds on her insights. She ends up arguing against this account on the grounds that not all cases of syncretism can be reduced to impoverishment/feature deletion.[14] However, impoverishment does seem to work for RNR examples like (24a), in which the noun *bljudce* 'saucer' has two feature structures, given in (33a). The impoverishment rule deletes NOM and ACC case features, yielding (33b). Now the two are the same, which means that (33b) is equivalent to (33c).

(33) a.

CLASS	Ib
NUMBER	singular
CASE	non-oblique: **ACC**

CLASS	Ib
NUMBER	singular
CASE	non-oblique: **NOM**

b.

CLASS	Ib
NUMBER	singular
CASE	non-oblique

CLASS	Ib
NUMBER	singular
CASE	non-oblique

c.

CLASS	Ib
NUMBER	singular
CASE	non-oblique

(Asarina 2011: 197)

For present purposes, it is not crucial which kinds of syncretism can be handled by underspecification and which ones require impoverishment. We take both to be necessary and, in the rest of this section, we suggest a way to analogize syntactic syncretism to morphological syncretism viewed as the result of impoverishment.

We take the input to Merge to be lexical items taken from the lexicon or the sets previously constructed by Merge, and the output of Merge to be a set. BiCoM constrains the number of positions that the members of this set may occupy.

In its simplest form, abstracting away from the provisions we made for Internal Merge, BiCoM states that the number of positions that Merge relates cannot exceed two. Suppose that we state BiCoM in set-theoretical terms so that the set of positions that Merge relates cannot have more than two members. If two positions in this set are identical, then the set in (34a) is equivalent to the set in (34b), which reduces the number of positions in the set from three to two.[15]

(34) a. $S = \{P_1, P_1, P_2\}$

b. $S = \{P_1, P_2\}$

We illustrate with a concrete example in (35), repeated from (14).

(35) a. I know a man **who**$_i$ Bill recommended $\boldsymbol{t_i}$ and Mary hired $\boldsymbol{t_i}$.

b. I know a man

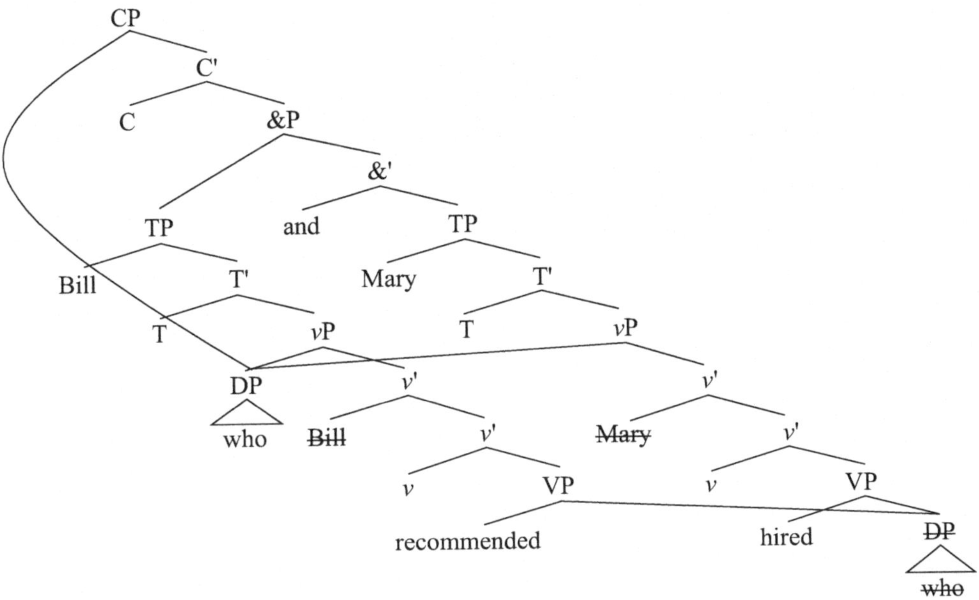

The *wh*-pronoun *who* occupies the following two positions (defined in terms of paths), which are not identical:

(36) a. P_1 = ⟨CP, C′, &P, TP, T′, **vP, v′**⟩ (the position of *who* in the first conjunct)

b. P_2 = ⟨CP, C′, &P, &′, TP, T′, **vP, v′**⟩ (the position of *who* in the second conjunct)

When Internal Merge applies, these two positions are related to a third one, which is the position of C′.

(37) P_3 = ⟨CP, DP⟩

We assumed that for the purposes of BiCoM, syncretic positions are evaluated on the basis of their immediate context (i.e., the last two members of the path). This could be accomplished by means of an impoverishment/deletion rule that would delete all but the last two members of the two paths in (36a–b). This makes two of the three subpaths identical (these are boldfaced in (38a)). This in turn makes the set in (38a) equivalent to the set in (38b), which means that the set of positions that Merge relates does not exceed two.

(38) a. S_1 = {⟨**vP, v′**⟩, ⟨**vP, v′**⟩, ⟨CP, DP⟩}

b. S_2 = {⟨vP, v′⟩, ⟨CP, DP⟩}

This impoverishment-based account allows us to capture the effects of syntactic syncretism in a way that parallels existing accounts of morphological syncretism. It provides an answer to the question that we started this section with: why should BiCoM violations be ameliorated by the parallelism of positions that the *wh*-phrase occupies in the two conjuncts? We derived this effect by proposing that the paths defining the relevant positions of the shared *wh*-phrase in the two conjuncts get impoverished to all but the last two members. This makes the paths that define the two syncretic positions identical. If BiCoM is seen as a constraint that limits to two the number of elements that a set of positions created by Merge may contain, then a set that contains three elements, two of which are identical, satisfies this constraint; this in turn explains why ATB extraction from parallel positions is grammatical.

In the next section, we turn to the other construction in which BiCoM violations are obviated: successive-cyclic movement.

5.4 Successive-Cyclic Movement

In our view, movement does not involve a copying operation: in successive-cyclic movement configurations, Internal Merge creates multidominant representations in which a single constituent is remerged in multiple positions. The first application of Internal Merge relates only two positions within a derivation, which is not problematic for BiCoM. However, given that merging a constituent into a new position does not remove it from its previous position(s), the second instance of Internal Merge that applies to the same constituent necessarily relates three positions in a single derivation and should therefore be disallowed by BiCoM whenever these positions are not syncretic. The same is true of every subsequent application of Internal Merge. The long-distance *wh*-question in (39) is an example of this scenario.

(39) $[_{CP}$ **What**$_i$ did Mary $[_{vP}$ $\boldsymbol{t_i}$ say $[_{CP}$ $\boldsymbol{t_i}$ that Peter $[_{vP}$ $\boldsymbol{t_i}$ borrowed $\boldsymbol{t_i}]]]]$?

Already in the embedded clause, the *wh*-phrase in (39) undergoes Internal Merge twice (in addition to External Merge), as shown in (40a–b).

(40) a.

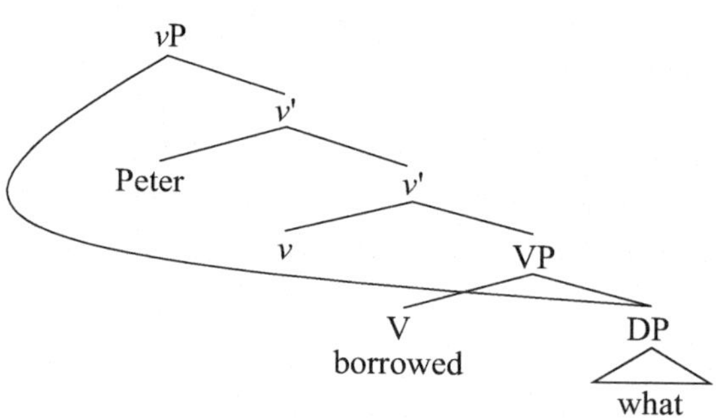

b.

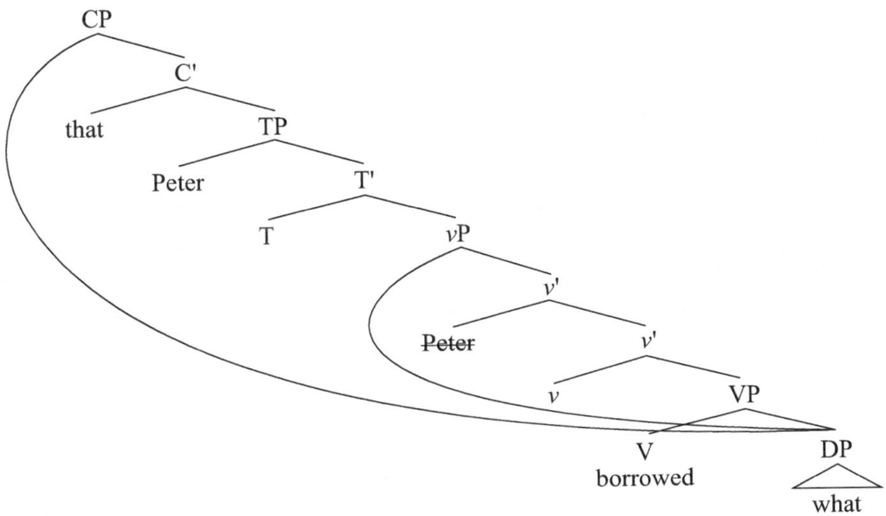

By the time the derivation has reached the stage in (40a), Internal Merge has related two positions in a single derivation: the original position of the *wh*-phrase (the complement of the verb, defined by the path ⟨vP, v′, v′, VP, V⟩) and the position of v′ (defined by the path ⟨vP, DP⟩). The newly created position of the *wh*-phrase (Spec,vP, defined as the path ⟨vP, v′⟩) does not count for BiCoM because it does not overlap with the search path from the probe v to the goal *what*, which is the sequence ⟨VP, DP⟩.[16] Thus, (40a) satisfies BiCoM.

However, the next step, illustrated in (40b), violates BiCoM. Now the *wh*-phrase occupies *three* positions: Spec,CP, Spec,vP, and its original (complement-of-the-verb) position. The newly created Spec,CP position, defined by the path ⟨CP, C′⟩ does not count for the purposes of BiCoM because it does not overlap with the search path from the probe C to the goal in Spec,vP; this search path is the sequence ⟨TP, T′, vP, DP⟩. The remaining two positions of the *wh*-phrase, however, do overlap with this search path. The position of *what* in Spec,vP is defined as the path ⟨CP, C′, TP, T′, vP, v′⟩, and the original position of *what* is defined as the path ⟨CP, C′, TP, T′, vP, v′, v′, VP, V⟩. Both paths include the nodes TP, T′, and vP, which are also part of the search path. When Merge relates these two positions of *what*, which are not syncretic, to a third position, the position of C′, BiCoM is violated. The situation only gets worse with every subsequent application of Internal Merge, as is obvious from (41), which gives the entire structure.

(41)

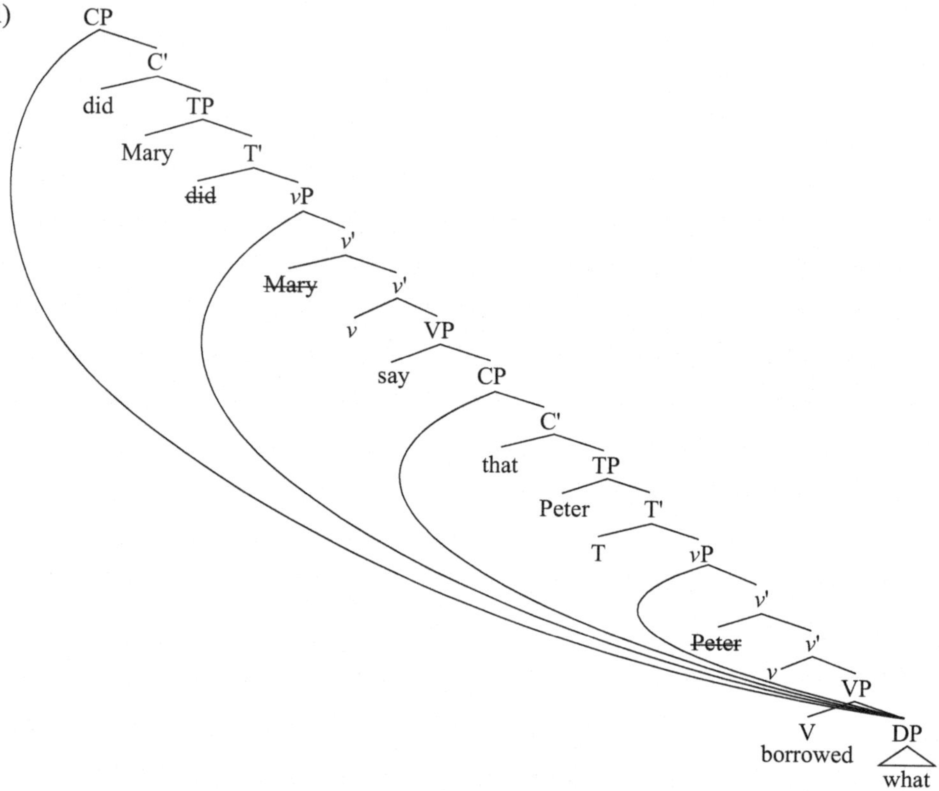

On our view, the reason why BiCoM is not violated in (40b) and (41) is that only the closest position occupied by the multiply-dominated constituent is visible to any higher probe. Simply put, the computational system is constrained by locality. Suppose that in evaluating BiCoM violations, the system "counts" only the positions in which the constituent that undergoes Internal Merge (the goal) was *accessed* by the probe that triggered this Internal Merge. Since the highest position that the goal occupies prior to Merge is necessarily closer to the probe than its other positions, the probe accesses the goal *only* in this position. Thus, the probe always reaches the goal via the *shortest* search path. We assume that, for the purpose of assessing possible locality violations, the lengths of two search paths can only be compared to one another if one path is contained in the other, as stated in (42).

(42) A search path SP is shorter than a search path SP′ if and only if SP is contained in SP′.[17]

According to (42), the search path to the highest position of the shared goal in successive-cyclic movement is necessarily shorter than the search paths to all the other positions of the goal because the sequence of syntactic objects making up this search path is contained in the sequence of syntactic objects making up the search paths to all the other positions of the shared goal. Thus, in (43), which is a more detailed representation of (41), the shortest search path, marked in boldface and given in (44a), is shorter than the other search paths, given in (44b–d), because it is contained in all of them.

(43)

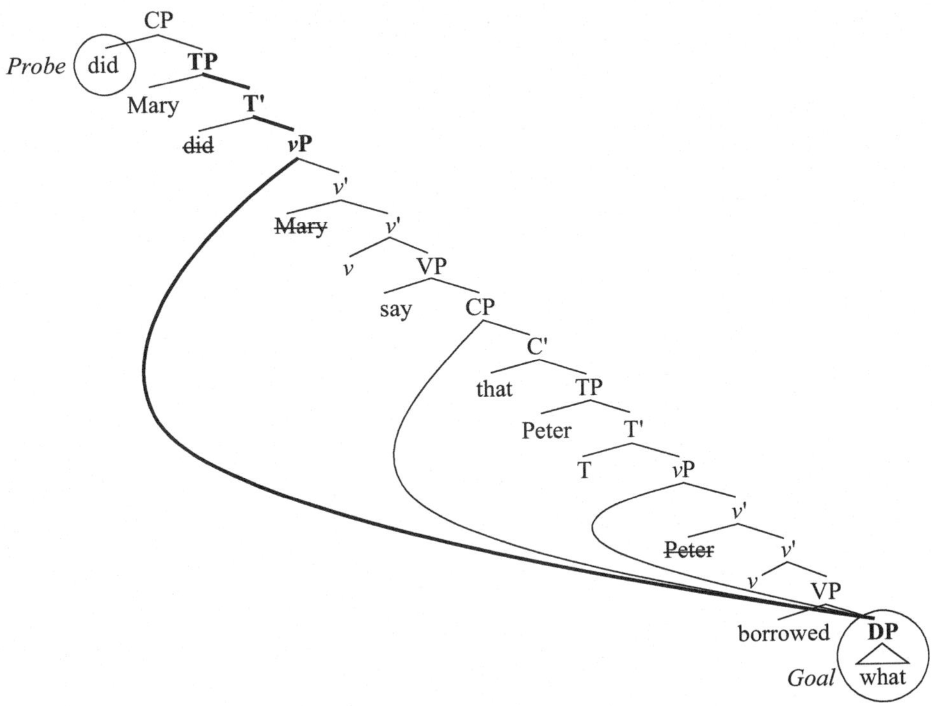

(44) a. ⟨TP, T', *v*P, DP⟩

b. ⟨TP, T', *v*P, *v*', *v*', VP, CP, DP⟩

c. ⟨TP, T', *v*P, *v*', *v*', VP, CP, C', TP, T', *v*P, DP⟩

d. ⟨TP, T', *v*P, *v*', *v*', VP, CP, C', TP, T', *v*P, *v*', *v*', VP, DP⟩

The search ends as soon as it reaches the position of the goal that is closest to the probe. Since all positions of the shared constituent except the highest one remain invisible for the purposes of BiCoM, and only the highest position occupied by the multiply-dominated constituent is related to the root, the number of positions related by Internal Merge in successive-cyclic configurations *never* exceeds two; therefore, BiCoM is not violated.[18]

Having explained why successive-cyclic movement does not violate BiCoM, we turn to locality in the context of ATB extraction. In the ATB configurations that we examined in chapters 3 and 4, the goal probed by C (i.e., the shared *wh*-phrase) also occupies two (or more) positions prior to being ATB-extracted. This violates BiCoM unless the goal moves from syncretic positions. The question now is what makes ATB configurations different from successive-cyclic movement configurations with respect to BiCoM. We attribute this difference to the fact that in ATB configurations, neither of the two positions of the shared *wh*-phrase is closer to the probe than its other position is.[19] More specifically, when the C head, introduced into the structure above the &P level, probes the &P in search of a goal, the search path from the probe to the highest position of the shared goal in one conjunct *neither* contains *nor* is contained within the search path from the probe to the highest position of the shared goal in the other conjunct. In (45), we illustrate the two shortest search paths: in the first conjunct the shortest search path is the sequence of nodes ⟨&P, TP, T′, vP, DP⟩, boldfaced in (45), while in the second conjunct the shortest path is ⟨&P, &′, TP, DP⟩, boldfaced and dashed in (45). According to (42), if neither of the two search paths is contained within the other, as is the case here, neither is shorter nor longer than the other. Thus, in ATB configurations the shared constituent is reached in the highest position that it occupies in *each* conjunct because there are multiple shortest paths from the probe to the goal.[20] Consequently, the search "detects" both positions of the shared constituent and Merge relates both of these positions to a third one within a single derivation, which violates BiCoM whenever the two positions are not syncretic.[21]

(45) *Tell me

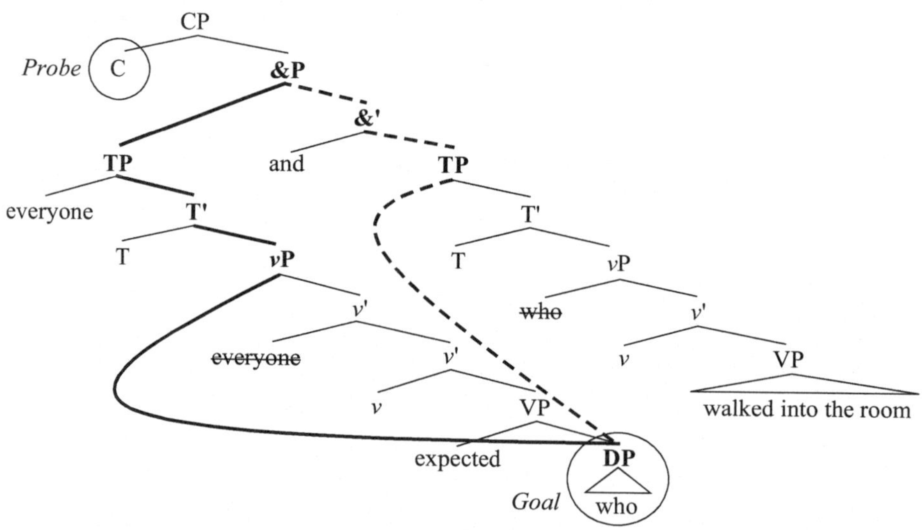

Locality thus leads to obviations of BiCoM violations in cases in which one position of the shared element c-commands the other(s), that is, in successive-cyclic movement. This is also why in ATB configurations, any conjunct-internal movements that the shared constituent undergoes before the two conjuncts become part of a single derivation "do not count" for the purposes of BiCoM, as we also noted in section 4.2. For example, in the ungrammatical (46a) the shared constituent is parallel-merged as the sister of the verb in both conjuncts (one containing a transitive verb and the other an unaccusative verb). These two positions are syncretic. However, the shared *wh*-phrase subsequently moves to Spec,vP in the first conjunct and Spec,TP in the second conjunct. Once the matrix interrogative C initiates the search for the closest *wh*-goal, it accesses *these* two positions, which are no longer syncretic. Given that the subsequent Internal Merge relates two non-syncretic positions to a third one within a single derivation, the sentence is ungrammatical, even though the lower positions of the shared constituent are syncretic. This is because locality prevents the system from considering lower positions of a multiply-dominated element when evaluating BiCoM violations.

(46) a. *the letter **which**$_i$ John wrote $\boldsymbol{t_i}$ and $\boldsymbol{t_i}$ was mailed by Bill
(Franks 1995: 90)

b. *the letter

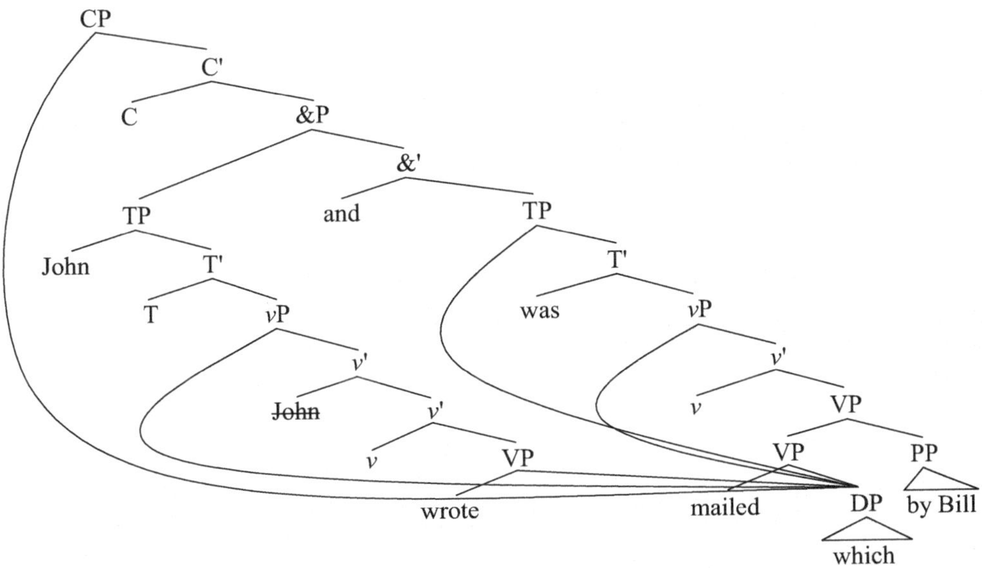

Given what we just said about lower positions being inaccessible, the grammaticality of similar examples in Catalan, reported by Valmala (2013: 240), is somewhat surprising. In his examples, repeated here from note 10 in chapter 3, the extracted *wh*-phrase is also the object of a transitive verb in one conjunct and the subject of an unaccusative verb in the other conjunct.

(47) a. **Quines mostres d'ADN$_i$** dius que vas portar t_i dilluns i t_i no van ser analitzades fins dijous? *Catalan*
which samples of+DNA say.2SG that AUX bring Monday and not AUX be analyzed until Thursday
'Which DNA samples do you say you brought on Monday and were not analyzed until Thursday?'

b. **Quines mostres d'ADN$_i$** dius que et va enviar t_i el jutge el dimarts i t_i van desaparèixer el dijous?
which samples of+DNA say.2SG that you AUX send the judge the Tuesday and AUX disappear the Thursday
'Which DNA samples do you say that you sent to the judge on Tuesday and disappeared on Thursday?'[22]
(Valmala 2013: 240)

Valmala's explanation for the grammaticality of (47a–b) relies on the assumption that in Catalan (and Spanish) subjects do not have to raise to Spec,TP, but can remain in situ. This allows ATB extraction in (47a–b) to proceed from parallel positions since the shared *wh*-phrase is the complement of the verb in both conjuncts before it undergoes ATB movement. If this analysis is on the right track, (47a–b) do not violate BiCoM because ATB extraction proceeds from syncretic positions. For Valmala's analysis to derive the grammaticality of (47a–b), it is necessary for both the *wh*-subject of an unaccusative verb and the *wh*-object of a transitive verb to remain in their original positions. However, if we assume that *wh*-movement proceeds through phase edges, as we have throughout this monograph, this becomes difficult to maintain. In particular, we would expect that the shared *wh*-phrase *quines mostres d'ADN* 'which samples of DNA' moves successive-cyclically at least in the first conjunct, which contains a transitive verb. This movement places the *wh*-phrase in Spec,vP in the first conjunct prior to ATB extraction. This position is not syncretic with the position of the complement of the verb, occupied on Valmala's analysis by the *wh*-subject in the second conjunct, as shown schematically in (48). Thus, we would expect (47a–b) to violate BiCoM.

(48) **WH$_i$** [$_{vP}$ . . . say [$_{CP}$ that
[$_{\&P}$ [$_{TP}$ . . . [$_{vP}$ t_i . . . [$_{VP}$ . . . send t_i . . .]]] and
[$_{TP}$ . . . [$_{VP}$ . . . disappear t_i . . .]]]]]

One way of accounting for the grammaticality of these examples without abandoning the assumption that *wh*-movement proceeds successive-cyclically is to follow Legate

(2003), who argues that a passive/unaccusative v is a phase head, in which case *wh*-movement out of a passive must proceed through Spec,vP in order to escape Spell-Out.[23] If Valmala is correct in assuming that subjects in Catalan do not necessarily raise to Spec,TP (presumably because T does not have an EPP feature), the *wh*-phrase in the second conjunct would remain in Spec,vP until it is ATB-extracted. Thus, (47a–b) escape BiCoM because the *wh*-phrase is ATB-extracted from syncretic Spec,vP positions, which count as one for the purpose of BiCoM violations. The English example in (46a) is still expected to be ungrammatical because T in English does have an EPP feature, so the *wh*-subject of the passive second conjunct must stop off in Spec,TP before being ATB-extracted, and this position is not syncretic with Spec,vP, which is the position that the *wh*-phrase occupies in the first conjunct.

Although this analysis accounts for the contrast between English examples like (46a) and comparable Catalan examples like (47a–b), it cannot explain the fact that even in English, some ATB constructions in which the *wh*-phrase is the subject of an unaccusative or a passive verb in one conjunct are grammatical even though ATB extraction proceeds from nonparallel positions. We give some examples of this kind in (49a–c), repeated from chapter 3.

(49) a. We went to see a movie **which**$_i$ the critics praised $\boldsymbol{t_i}$ but $\boldsymbol{t_i}$ was too violent for my taste.

(Anderson 1983: 3)

b. Here is a book **which**$_i$ I haven't read $\boldsymbol{t_i}$ but $\boldsymbol{t_i}$ was recommended by several professors.

(Anderson 1983: 3)

c. These are the medicines **OP**$_i$ that the government won't fund $\boldsymbol{t_i}$ but $\boldsymbol{t_i}$ are desperately needed.

(Jason Merchant, pers. comm.)

The shared *wh*-phrase in all of these examples is the object of a transitive verb in one conjunct and the subject of an unaccusative or passive verb in the other conjunct. Given that prior to ATB extraction the *wh*-phrase occupies nonsyncretic positions in the two conjuncts, we would expect all of them to violate BiCoM and be ungrammatical, but they are not. In what follows, we show that such examples have somewhat different properties from regular, run-of-the-mill examples of ATB extraction, which leads us to believe that they might involve a different structure, with the conjuncts being potentially larger. First, to the extent that the examples where the shared subject is extracted from a passive construction in the second conjunct are acceptable at all, they are only acceptable if the passive auxiliary is present, as shown in (50a–b). This is different from examples of ATB extraction such as (50c), in which extraction proceeds from parallel positions, where the presence or absence of the passive auxiliary does not make a difference.

(50) a. Tell me **which children**$_i$ Lady Di was visiting $\boldsymbol{t_i}$ and $\boldsymbol{t_i}$ *(were) given presents.

b. Tell me **which child**$_i$ Lady Di was visiting $\boldsymbol{t_i}$ and $\boldsymbol{t_i}$ *(was) given presents.

c. **Which wife of Henry VIII**$_i$ $\boldsymbol{t_i}$ was arrested on Monday and $\boldsymbol{t_i}$ (was) beheaded on Tuesday?

Furthermore, analogous examples in Croatian allow case mismatches across the two conjuncts, as shown in (51a). Such case mismatches otherwise result in sharp ungrammaticality, as shown in (51b) (where the subscript on the verb indicates the case required/assigned by the verb).

(51) a. *Croatian*

Kojeg	**mafijaša**$_i$	policija	traži $\boldsymbol{t_i}$
which.ACC	Mafia.boss.ACC	police	seeks$_{\text{ACC}}$

a	$\boldsymbol{t_i}$	izručen	je	FBIu?
and		turned.over$_{\text{NOM}}$	AUX	to.FBI

'Which Mafia boss are the police looking for and was turned over to the FBI?'

b.

***Kojeg**	**mafijaša**$_i$	policija	traži $\boldsymbol{t_i}$	a	FBI	vjeruje	$\boldsymbol{t_i}$?
which.ACC	Mafia.boss.ACC	police	seeks$_{\text{ACC}}$	and	FBI	trusts$_{\text{DAT}}$	

Int. 'Which Mafia boss are the police looking for and the FBI trusts?'

This also suggests to us that such examples might involve a different structure and, more generally, that their grammatical status is not necessarily incompatible with BiCoM and our view of successive-cyclic movement.

5.5 Possible Alternatives

A different but related way of explaining why successive-cyclic movement is insensitive to BiCoM is to say that what would be a BiCoM-violating Merge operation applies after all but the highest position of the multiply-dominated constituent have been spelled out. This possibility is illustrated in (52b) for the derivation of the long-distance question in (52a). In this case, by the time the matrix C initiates its search for the multiply-dominated *wh*-goal, all positions of the goal but the highest Spec,vP position have been spelled out.

(52) a. $[_{CP}$ **What**$_i$ did Mary $[_{vP}$ $\boldsymbol{t_i}$ say $[_{CP}$ $\boldsymbol{t_i}$ that Peter $[_{vP}$ $\boldsymbol{t_i}$ borrowed $\boldsymbol{t_i}]]]]$?

b.

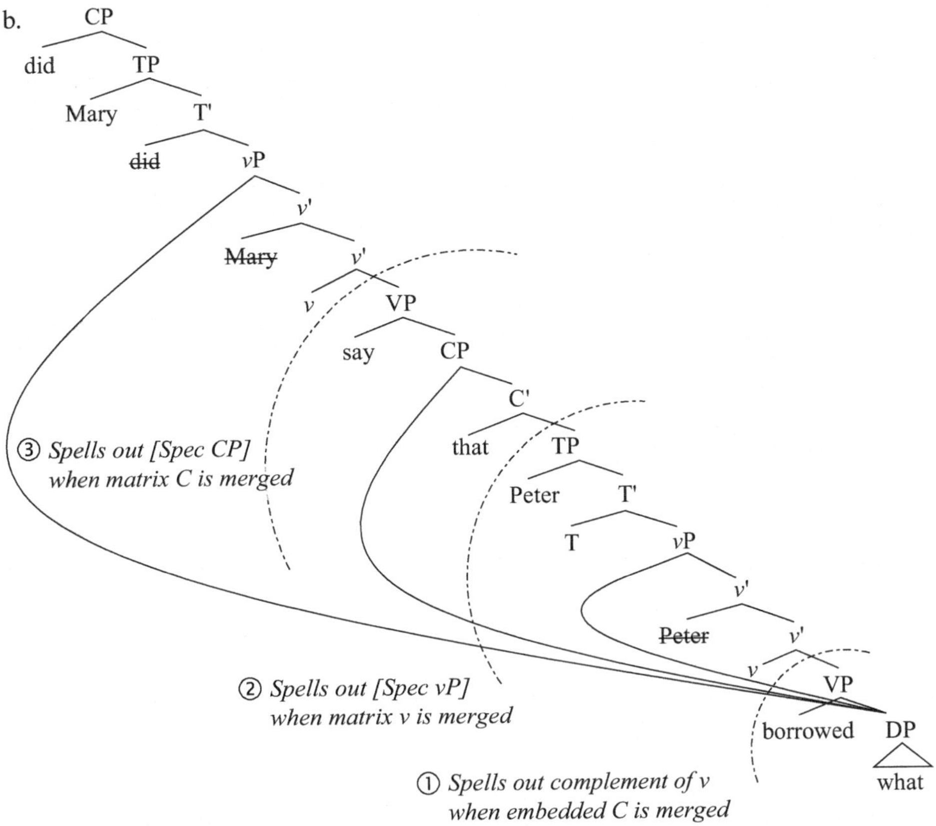

At first sight, it might seem counterintuitive to conceive of a position of a syntactic object as being spelled out, but of the syntactic object itself as still being available for further operations. Recall, however, that we define the position of a syntactic object as a path from the root of the tree to the sister of the object itself. Since Spell-Out removes parts of the structure, it will "obliterate" paths and consequently remove positions of a syntactic object. However, the object itself might still be available by virtue of occupying another position, which has not yet been spelled out; that is, there might exist an alternative path from the root of the tree to a different sister of the syntactic item, which remains intact.[24] In this way, a multiply dominated constituent that has undergone successive-cyclic movement may escape Spell-Out (as proposed by Bachrach and Katzir [2009] for independent reasons) and at the same time obviate a BiCoM violation (by remaining accessible to subsequent Merge operations in only one of its multiple positions). In an ATB context, on the other hand, the Spell-Out operation would remove lower positions of the shared constituent within individual conjuncts, but it would never preserve the highest position in one conjunct without preserving the highest position in the other conjunct(s) as well. Consequently, appealing to Spell-Out would not ameliorate BiCoM violations in ATB extraction.

We believe that the view of Spell-Out outlined above is correct in that it explains how a multiply-dominated element can in principle be exempt from Spell-Out while an element occupying a single position cannot. However, it is probably not the correct way to answer the question of why successive-cyclic movement does not incur BiCoM violations, because it relies on the assumption that the only targets for successive-cyclic movement are phase edges. This is certainly the case in (52), where movement proceeds only through Spec,vP and Spec,CP positions, but the proposal that appeals to Spell-Out will not generalize to cases like (53), where successive-cyclic movement targets Spec,TP positions as well. Since TPs are not (typically) considered to be phases, and raising predicates embed TPs, not CPs, there will be no "intermediate" Spell-Out operations that would "remove" the embedded Spec,TP from the structure before the next instance of Internal Merge applies. Thus, in (53a), at the point in the derivation when the *wh*-phrase is probed by T of the clause underlined in (53a), neither Spec,vP nor Spec,TP of the lower clause has been spelled out. Subsequent Internal Merge should therefore violate BiCoM, as illustrated in (53b), but it does not.

(53) a. $[_{CP}$ **Who**$_i$ $[_{TP}$ $\boldsymbol{t_i}$ seems $[_{TP}$ $\boldsymbol{t_i}$ <u>to be likely</u> $[_{TP}$ $\boldsymbol{t_i}$ to $[_{vP}$ $\boldsymbol{t_i}$ leave]]]]]?

b.

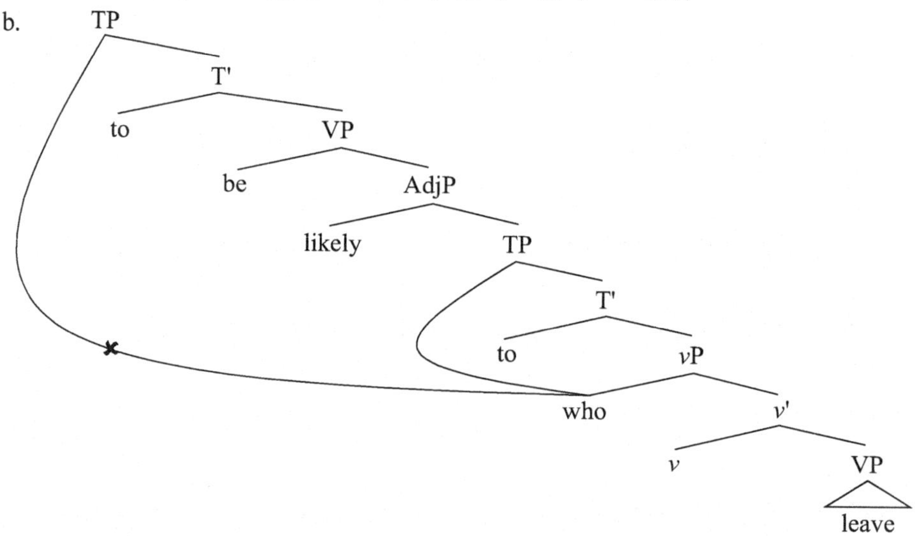

There is another logical possibility that would allow successive-cyclic configurations to be exempt from BiCoM. This would involve treating all the positions involved in successive-cyclic movement as syncretic. It is not clear to us, though, what the relevant notion of syncretism would be. Even allowing phase edges (Spec,CP and Spec,vP) to count as structurally syncretic would not be sufficient. To derive the grammaticality of (53a), for example, we would need syncretism to hold of Spec,vP, Spec,CP, *and* Spec,TP. However, it is hard to see what property would make these three positions syncretic.[25]

5.6 Structural Syncretism and Improper Movement

Our definition of syncretic positions does not require them to be in separate derivations (e.g., separate conjuncts in a coordinate structure) and allows one of the syncretic positions to c-command another one within a single derivation. This opens up an intriguing possibility that BiCoM can derive the ban on improper movement, which Müller and Sternefeld (1993) capture in terms of the Principle of Unambiguous Binding.[26]

In most general terms, improper movement refers to the type of movement that proceeds from a position of a certain type to a position of a different type, and is followed by movement to a position of the first type. This ban accounts for the contrast between the permissible derivations schematized in (54a–b) and the impermissible one in (54c).[27] The derivation in (54a) is allowed because the *wh*-phrase undergoes a sequence of movements to Spec,TP before undergoing a single movement to Spec,CP; the one in (54b) is allowed because, once the *wh*-element moves to Spec,CP, it undergoes subsequent movements to positions of the same type. In (54c), however, the *wh*-phrase starts out in Spec,TP and moves to another Spec,TP after passing through Spec,CP, which is disallowed.[28]

(54) a. $[_{CP}$ **WH**$_i$ $[_{TP}$ t_i $[_{TP}$ t_i $[_{TP}$ $t_i]]]]$? Who seems to be likely to have arrived late?

b. $[_{CP}$ **WH**$_i$ $[_{CP}$ t_i $[_{CP}$ t_i $[_{TP}$ $t_i]]]]$? Who did Bill think Mary said arrived late?

c. *$[_{CP}$ **WH**$_i$ $[_{TP}$ t_i $[_{CP}$ t_i $[_{TP}$ $t_i]]]]$? *Who seems that arrived late?

Given our proposal regarding the alleviating effects of structural syncretism, it is worth examining whether (54a) and (54b) might be allowed because some of the positions related by Internal Merge are syncretic. However, the contrast between the grammatical (54a–b) and the ungrammatical (54c) cannot be attributed to structural syncretism.[29] While our proposal makes correct predictions for the grammatical (54a) and the ungrammatical (54c), it also incorrectly predicts (54b) to be ungrammatical. In (54a), the final Internal Merge, which ends up creating the matrix Spec,CP, applies to the root (C′) and the *wh*-phrase, which at that point in the derivation occupies three syncretic Spec,TP positions, as shown schematically in (55a). Thus, for the purposes of BiCoM, Merge relates only two different positions here (the position of C′ and Spec,TP), so the structure is allowed. However, in (54b) and (54c), at the same point in the derivation, shown in (55b–c), before being merged with the root, the *wh*-phrase occupies three positions, only two of which are syncretic: two Spec,CP positions in (54b) and two Spec,TP positions in (54c). Since the final instance of Merge in both examples relates three different positions (those of C′, Spec,CP, and Spec,TP), we predict both of them to be excluded due to a BiCoM violation. However, only one of them—namely, (54c)—is ungrammatical.

(55) a.

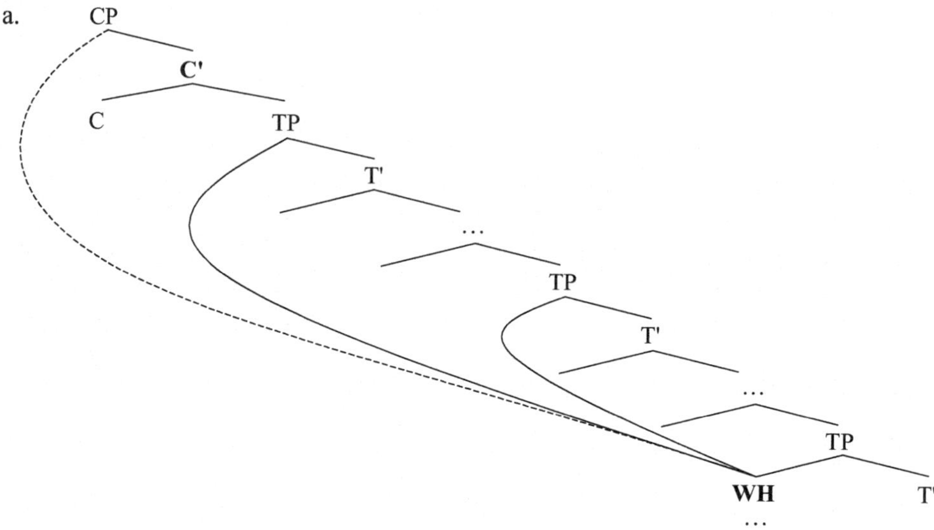

b.

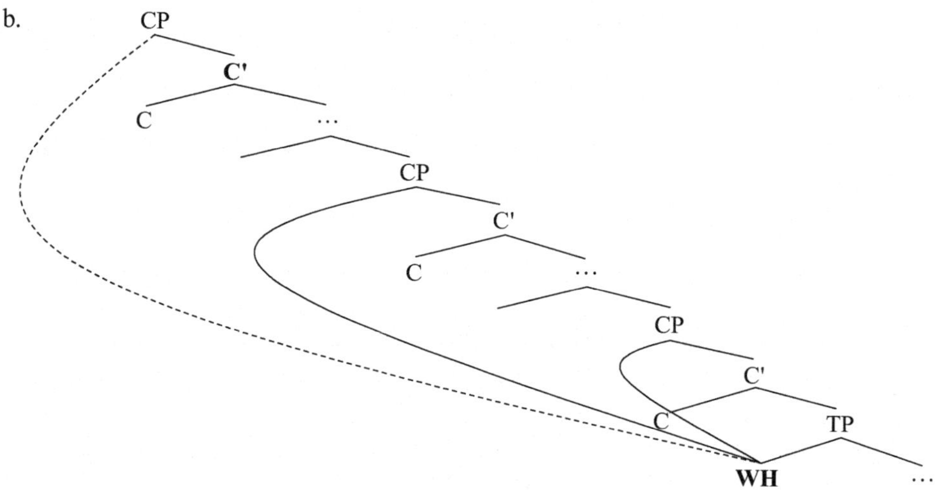

c.

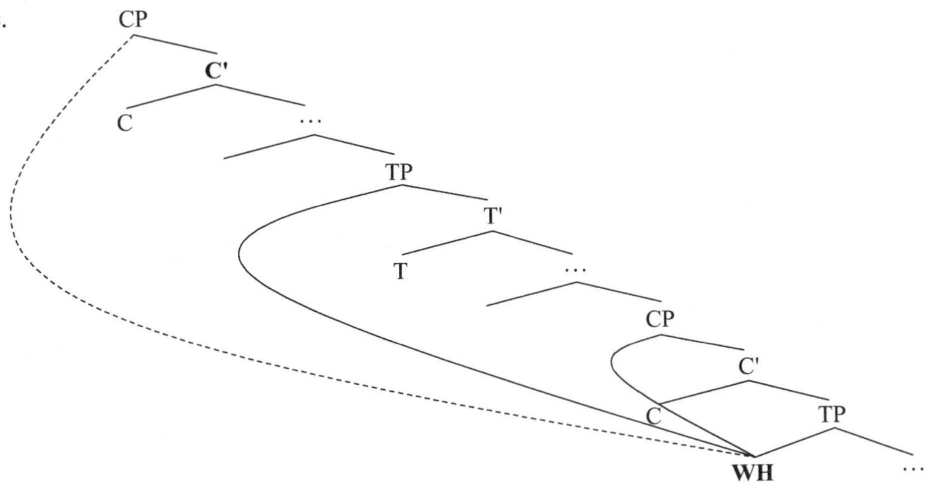

Given that BiCoM cannot derive the contrast in (54a–c), we do not think that it can capture the ban on improper movement.

5.7 Conclusion

We started this chapter by discussing grammatical cases of ATB extraction—cases where the shared constituent undergoes ATB extraction from parallel positions. We proposed that they are exempt from BiCoM because parallel positions are *structurally syncretic*. By analogy to morphological syncretism and, in particular, to impoverishment-based accounts of morphological syncretism, we argued that structural syncretism affects the evaluation of BiCoM violations by allowing two (or more) syncretic positions to count as one. We then proceeded to examine another principled exception to BiCoM, involving successive-cyclic movement, and we argued that such configurations are allowed by BiCoM because the computational system is constrained by locality: all positions of a multiply-dominated element except the highest are "invisible" to further Merge operations and are therefore disregarded by BiCoM. We also explored the possibility that BiCoM might derive the ban on improper movement, concluding that it cannot—at least not without some extra, potentially unwarranted assumptions.

6 Consequences of Structural Syncretism

In this chapter, we take a closer look at more complex ATB configurations and examine the consequences of structural syncretism for such configurations. We first look at the effects of embedding one or both conjuncts and show that it sometimes improves examples of ATB extraction that were ungrammatical with no embedding, sometimes degrades examples that were grammatical with no embedding, and sometimes has no effect at all. We show how the effects of embedding can be derived from our proposal that structural syncretism alleviates BiCoM violations. We next show that the same proposal, in conjunction with the Vacuous Movement Hypothesis, can capture the otherwise mysterious contrast between cases of nonparallel ATB extraction in which the subject is extracted from the first versus the second conjunct. We then examine ATB extraction in raising-to-object configurations, and we conclude with a discussion of the so-called adverb effect: the ameliorating effect that adding an adverbial has on the grammaticality of ATB extraction from nonparallel positions.

6.1 Embedding in Across-the-Board Configurations

Besides explaining the grammaticality of ATB extraction from parallel positions, the proposal that structural syncretism obviates BiCoM violations can explain how embedding inside one or both conjuncts affects the grammaticality of ATB configurations. The proposal predicts that embedding should improve an ungrammatical ATB structure *only if* it creates a configuration in which, prior to ATB extraction, the highest position of the shared constituent in one conjunct is syncretic with the highest position of the shared constituent in the other conjunct, as shown schematically in (1a–b). In (1a), the shared *wh*-phrase occupies nonsyncretic positions in the two conjuncts: its mothers and sisters are different: ⟨Z, W⟩ versus ⟨X, Y⟩. In (1b), by contrast, the shared *wh*-phrase is embedded deeper in one conjunct, which allows it to move to a position that is syncretic with the position it occupies in the other conjunct (its mother and sister are ⟨X, Y⟩ in both conjuncts).

(1) a.

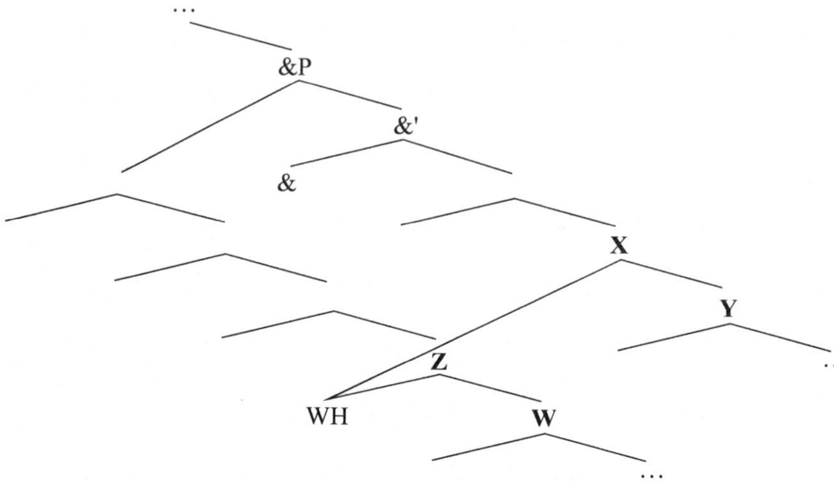

b.

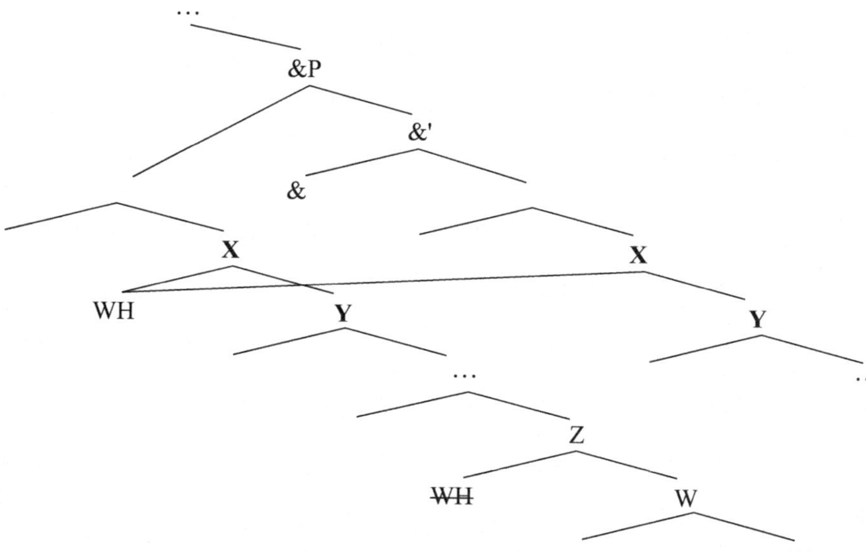

Conversely, embedding should degrade a grammatical ATB example if the added structure destroys the configuration in which, prior to ATB extraction, the shared constituent occupied syncretic positions and movement of the *wh*-phrase inside one conjunct results in its occupying nonsyncretic positions, as shown in (2a–b).

(2) a.

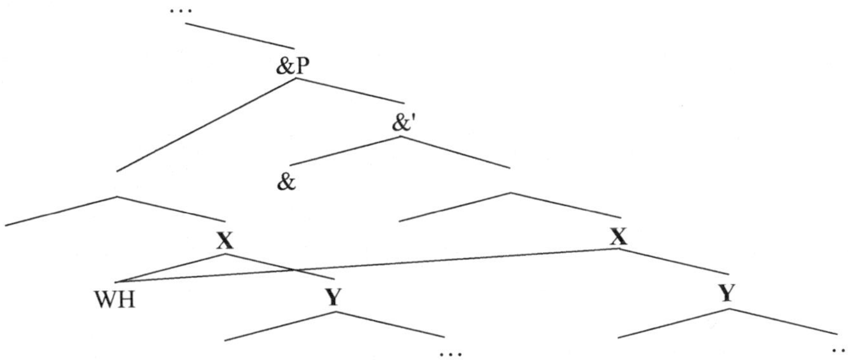

b.

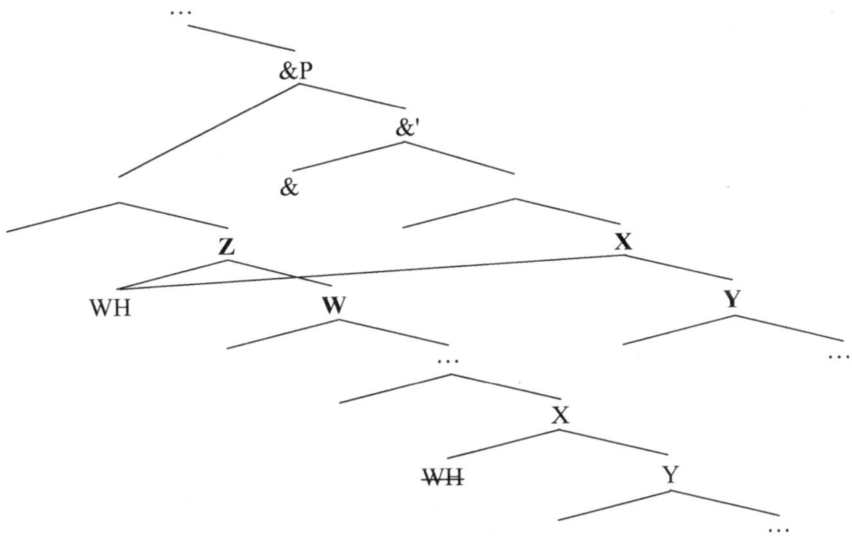

One way the configurations in (1b) and (2b) arise is by embedding the shared constituent deeper in one conjunct than in the other. The result is a Conjunction Phrase in which one conjunct is monoclausal and the other is biclausal, and the biclausal conjunct, regardless of whether it is the first or the second conjunct, contains an embedded gap. We refer to this configuration, schematized in (3a–b), as *asymmetric embedding*.

(3) a. [**WH**$_i$ [$_{\&P}$ [$_{TP}$ . . . $\boldsymbol{t_i}$ . . .] and [$_{TP}$ . . . [$_{\mathbf{CP}}$ . . . $\boldsymbol{t_i}$ . . .]]]] *Asymmetric embedding*

b. [**WH**$_i$ [$_{\&P}$ [$_{TP}$ . . . [$_{\mathbf{CP}}$ . . . $\boldsymbol{t_i}$ . . .]] and [$_{TP}$ . . . $\boldsymbol{t_i}$ . . .]]]

If both conjuncts are embedded, the result is a Conjunction Phrase in which both conjuncts are biclausal and contain embedded gaps. We refer to this configuration, illustrated in (4), as *symmetric embedding.*

(4) [**WH**$_i$ [$_{\&P}$ [$_{TP}$ . . . [$_{CP}$ . . . t_i . . .]] and [$_{TP}$ . . . [$_{CP}$ . . . t_i . . .]]]] *Symmetric embedding*

In what follows, we explore these embedding options in more detail. We begin our discussion with symmetric embedding (section 6.1.1). Next, we discuss cases where asymmetric embedding has no effect on grammaticality. These include examples in which ungrammatical coordination of monoclausal conjuncts does not improve with asymmetric embedding, as well as examples in which grammatical coordination of monoclausal conjuncts remains grammatical with asymmetric embedding (section 6.1.2). We then take up more interesting cases of asymmetric embedding, in which embedding does have an effect on grammaticality: cases in which coordination of monoclausal conjuncts yields a BiCoM violation, which disappears with asymmetric embedding (section 6.1.3), and cases in which BiCoM violations arise only with asymmetric embedding (section 6.1.4).

6.1.1 Symmetric Embedding

Extra embedding in both conjuncts from which a shared *wh*-phrase is ATB-extracted always yields a grammatical result, whether or not an analogous sentence with monoclausal conjuncts violates BiCoM. This is because in all such examples, the shared *wh*-phrase moves successive-cyclically to Spec,vP of the higher clause in each conjunct and, as a result of this movement, is ATB-extracted from syncretic positions. Thus, BiCoM violations are obviated. For example, in (5a), the shared *wh*-phrase is ATB-extracted from nonsyncretic positions, yielding a BiCoM violation. However, in (5b), where both conjuncts are embedded, the *wh*-phrase first moves to the higher Spec,vP in each conjunct, which allows ATB extraction to proceed from syncretic positions, as shown in (6).

(5) a. *This is the man **who**$_i$ [$_{TP}$ John hired t_i] and [$_{TP}$ t_i impressed Mary].

b. This is the man **who**$_i$ [$_{TP}$ Bill t_i thinks [$_{TP}$ John hired t_i]] and [$_{TP}$ Sue t_i thinks [$_{TP}$ t_i impressed Mary]].

(6) This is the man

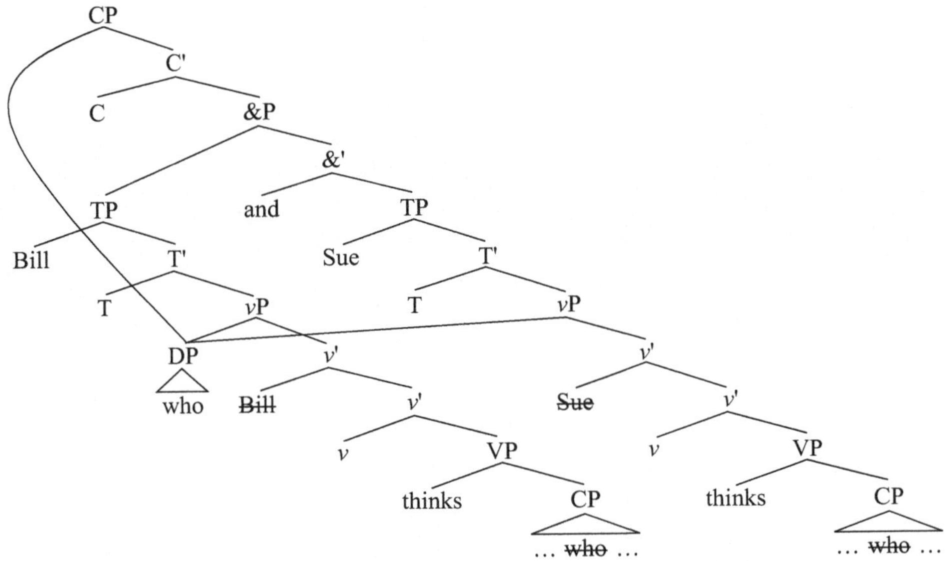

Not surprisingly, adding an extra clause in each conjunct in examples that were BiCoM-compliant to begin with, as in (7a) and (8a), does not affect the grammaticality of these examples, as noted by Goodall (1987). Subject and object extractions from parallel positions in (7a) and (8a) remain grammatical when they are more deeply embedded because the shared *wh*-phrase is ATB-extracted from syncretic positions, as shown in (7b) and (8b), respectively.[1]

(7) a. This is the kind of movie **which**$_i$ [$_{\text{TP}}$ $\boldsymbol{t}_i$ pleases Americans] and [$_{\text{TP}}$ $\boldsymbol{t}_i$ frightens Canadians].

b. This is the kind of movie **which**$_i$ [$_{\text{TP}}$ Tom $\boldsymbol{t}_i$ thinks [$_{\text{TP}}$ $\boldsymbol{t}_i$ pleases Americans]] and [$_{\text{TP}}$ Bill $\boldsymbol{t}_i$ thinks [$_{\text{TP}}$ $\boldsymbol{t}_i$ frightens Canadians]].

(Goodall 1987: 76)

(8) a. This is the kind of movie **which**$_i$ [$_{\text{TP}}$ Americans like $\boldsymbol{t}_i$] and [$_{\text{TP}}$ Canadians hate $\boldsymbol{t}_i$].

b. This is the kind of movie **which**$_i$ [$_{\text{TP}}$ Tom $\boldsymbol{t}_i$ thinks [$_{\text{TP}}$ Americans like $\boldsymbol{t}_i$]] and [$_{\text{TP}}$ Bill $\boldsymbol{t}_i$ thinks [$_{\text{TP}}$ Canadians hate $\boldsymbol{t}_i$]].

(Goodall 1987: 76)

6.1.2 Asymmetric Embedding with No Effects

In this section, we discuss ATB extraction where asymmetric embedding has no effect on BiCoM violations. We consider two scenarios: ungrammatical ATB extraction that remains ungrammatical with asymmetric embedding, and grammatical ATB extraction that remains grammatical with asymmetric embedding.

The first scenario is illustrated in (9a–b). The ungrammatical (9a), involving extraction from nonparallel (i.e., nonsyncretic) positions (the object position in the first conjunct and the subject position in the second one), remains ungrammatical when the object gap is embedded, as shown in (9b).[2]

(9) a. *Tell me **who**$_i$ [$_{TP}$ Chris invited $\boldsymbol{t_i}$] and [$_{TP}$ $\boldsymbol{t_i}$ brought Sam].

b. *Tell me **who**$_i$ [$_{TP}$ Pat $\boldsymbol{t_i}$ believes [$_{TP}$ Chris invited $\boldsymbol{t_i}$]] and [$_{TP}$ $\boldsymbol{t_i}$ brought Sam].

This is because the shared constituent in (9b) is ATB-extracted from the *same* positions in the two conjuncts as in (9a): in the first (biclausal) conjunct, it is extracted from the matrix Spec,vP position, and in the second (monoclausal) conjunct, from Spec,TP, just as it was in (9a). Since Spec,vP is not syncretic with Spec,TP, ATB extraction violates BiCoM because it relates more than two positions in a single derivation, as shown in (10).

(10) *Tell me

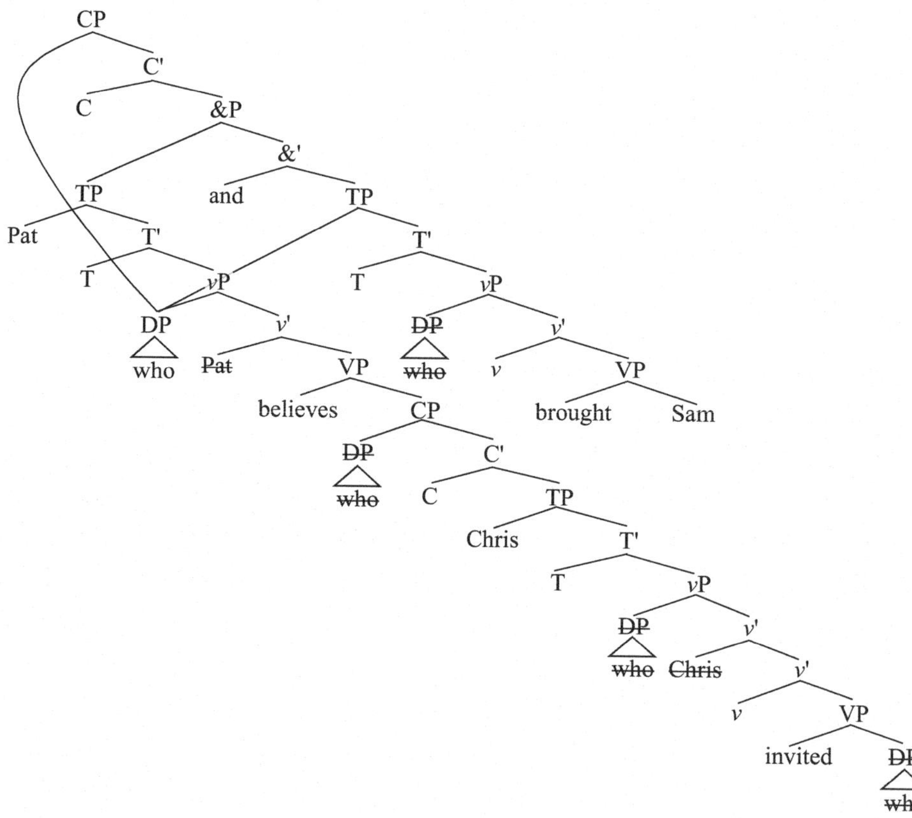

It is also possible for asymmetric embedding to preserve the grammatical status of the nonembedded variant.[3] This is what happens when the shared *wh*-constituent occupies a direct object position in both conjuncts and is embedded in one conjunct but not the other, as shown in (11a–b).

(11) a. Tell me **who**$_i$ [$_{TP}$ Chris recommended $\boldsymbol{t_i}$] and [$_{TP}$ Sam hired $\boldsymbol{t_i}$].

b. Tell me **who**$_i$ [$_{TP}$ Chris recommended $\boldsymbol{t_i}$] and [$_{TP}$ Ian $\boldsymbol{t_i}$ thought [$_{TP}$ Sam hired $\boldsymbol{t_i}$]].

Our proposal predicts the lack of contrast in (11a–b). The addition of structure to the second conjunct in (11b) causes the shared *wh*-phrase to move through the Spec,CP of the embedded clause (*Sam hired*) and into the Spec,vP of the higher clause (*Ian thought*). When ATB extraction applies, it proceeds from syncretic positions (Spec,vP positions in both conjuncts), obviating the BiCoM violation, as shown in (12).

(12) Tell me

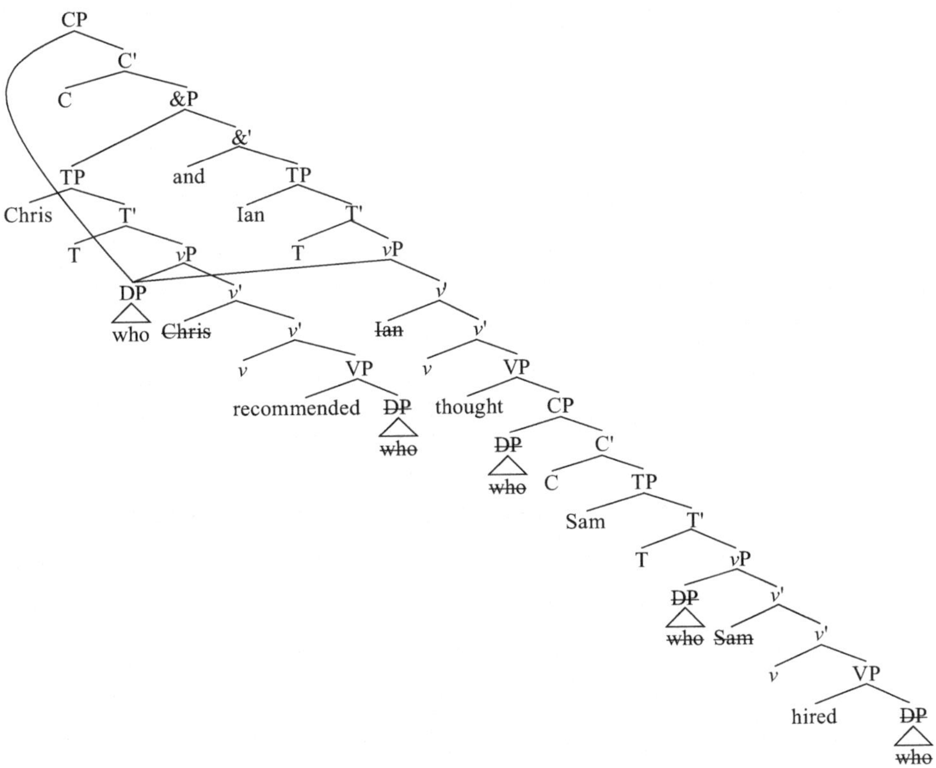

6.1.3 Asymmetric Embedding with Ameliorating Effects

In this section, we turn to the observation, due to Williams (1978), that the ungrammatical cases of ATB extraction in which the *wh*-phrase is the object in one conjunct and the subject in the other one improve if the subject extraction site is embedded, as shown in (13a–b).

(13) a. *Tell me **who**$_i$ [$_{TP}$ Bill saw $\boldsymbol{t_i}$] and [$_{TP}$ $\boldsymbol{t_i}$ likes Mary].

b. Tell me **who**$_i$ [$_{TP}$ Bill saw $\boldsymbol{t_i}$] and [$_{TP}$ John $\boldsymbol{t_i}$ believes [$_{TP}$ $\boldsymbol{t_i}$ likes Mary]].

The improvement is also predicted by our proposal. In (13b), unlike in (13a), the shared *wh*-phrase occupies syncretic positions in both conjuncts (Spec,vP) prior to being ATB-extracted, due to conjunct-internal successive-cyclic movement. Thus, at the point in the derivation when the shared *wh*-phrase is attracted by the matrix C, illustrated in (14), it occupies Spec,vP positions in both conjuncts and therefore no BiCoM violations ensue.

(14) Tell me

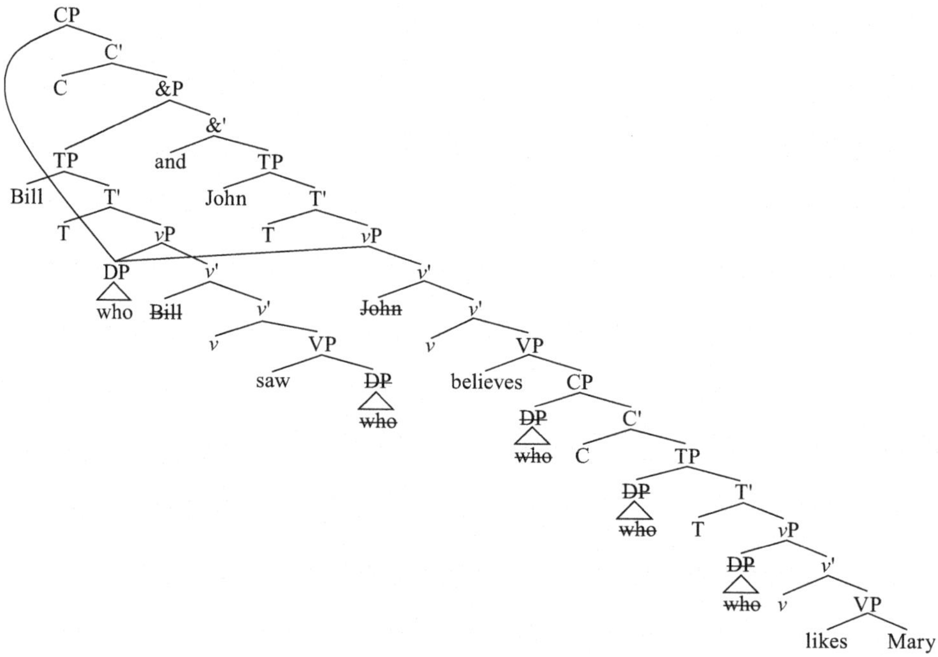

6.1.4 Asymmetric Embedding with Detrimental Effects

Finally, embedding one of the gaps in an ATB configuration may have a detrimental effect on the grammaticality of the sentence. This is what happens when the shared *wh*-phrase is the subject in both conjuncts and is embedded in one conjunct but not the other, as shown in (15b).[4] At a certain point in the derivation, the shared *wh*-phrase occupies Spec,TP positions in both conjuncts. However, in the biclausal (second) conjunct it undergoes successive-cyclic movement to the Spec,vP position of the higher clause. Consequently, it occupies nonsyncretic positions when the two conjuncts are conjoined, and ATB extraction applies. As expected, movement to the matrix Spec,CP, illustrated in (15c), becomes impossible because it violates BiCoM.

(15) a. This is the guy **who**$_i$ [$_{TP}$ $\boldsymbol{t_i}$ embezzled the money] and [$_{TP}$ $\boldsymbol{t_i}$ should be indicted $\boldsymbol{t_i}$].

b. %This is the guy **who**$_i$ [$_{TP}$ $\boldsymbol{t_i}$ embezzled the money] and [$_{TP}$ the prosecutor $\boldsymbol{t_i}$ thinks [$_{TP}$ $\boldsymbol{t_i}$ should be indicted $\boldsymbol{t_i}$]].

c. *This is the guy

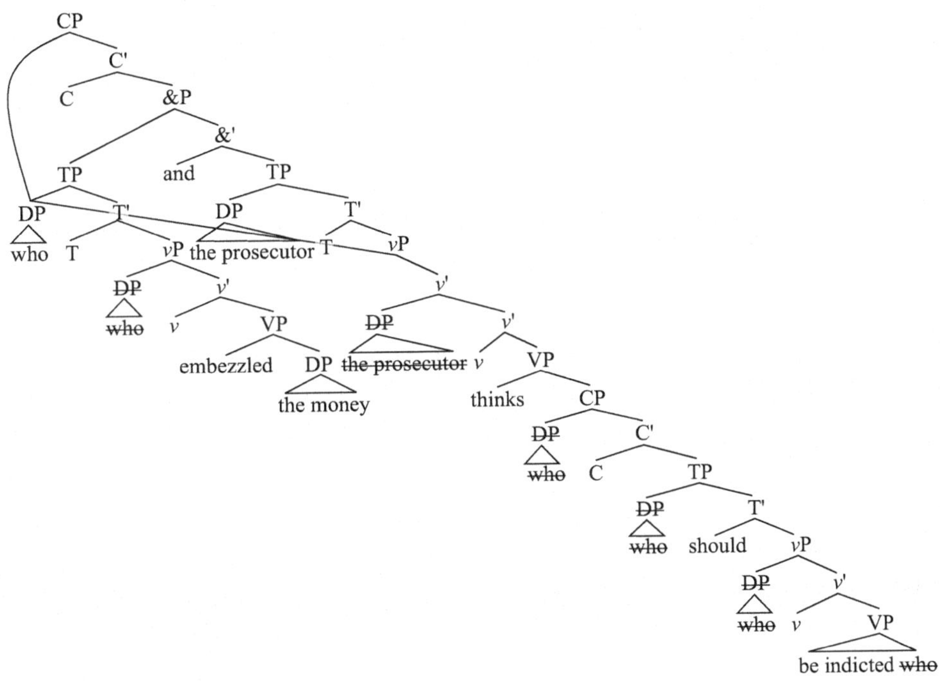

As mentioned in note 4, some speakers find (15b) grammatical. This is unexpected under our analysis, given that the structure violates BiCoM.

6.2 The Vacuous Movement Hypothesis

We ended the previous section with a puzzle concerning the status of examples like (15b), where extraction proceeds from nonparallel positions and the result is grammatical, contra the predictions made by BiCoM. Structural syncretism will not help in this case since no two of the three relevant positions (i.e., the positions of C′, Spec,TP, and Spec,vP) are syncretic. To account for the judgments of the speakers who accept (15b), we adopt the so-called *Vacuous Movement Hypothesis* (following George 1980; Chomsky 1986; Kasai 2004; Agbayani 2006, among others). On this hypothesis, the matrix *wh*-subject does not undergo movement to Spec,CP, but remains in Spec,TP, as shown in (16b).[5]

(16) a. [$_{CP}$ C [$_{TP}$ Who works hard]]?

b.

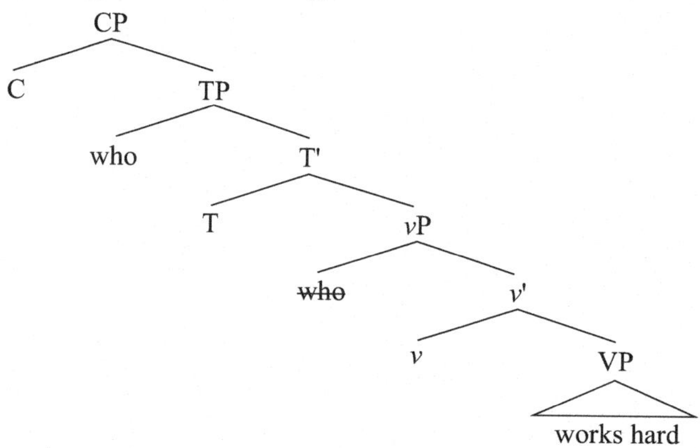

Applied to the case under discussion, this hypothesis states that the shared *wh*-subject remains in Spec,TP in the first, monoclausal conjunct, as shown in (17). This configuration does not violate BiCoM because even though the shared *wh*-phrase occupies nonsyncretic positions (Spec,TP in the monoclausal conjunct and Spec,vP in the biclausal one), it does not undergo Merge after the two conjuncts become part of a single derivation. Therefore, Merge never relates more than two positions in the same derivation. The configuration in (17) is thus similar to RNR configurations, in which, as we demonstrated in chapter 4, the shared constituent may freely occupy nonparallel positions: in neither configuration does the shared constituent undergo Internal Merge after the conjuncts have merged with *and*.[6]

(17) This is the guy

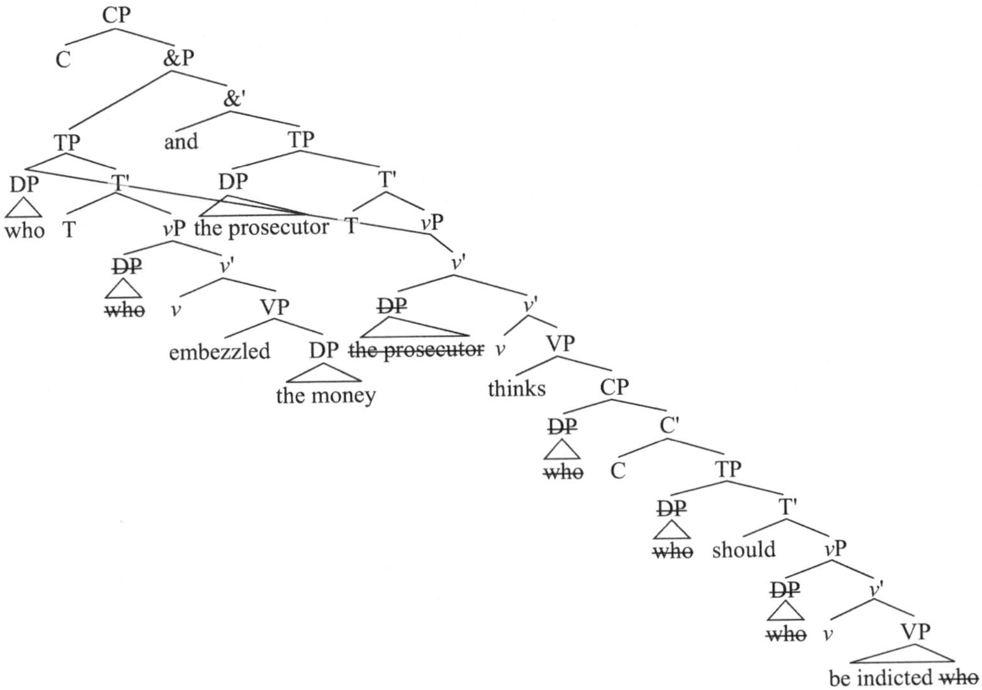

If, however, the first conjunct is embedded instead, as in (18), vacuous movement can no longer save the structure since the embedded *wh*-subject cannot remain in Spec,TP, but must move successive-cyclically to Spec,vP of the higher clause. From there, as shown in (18), the *wh*-phrase moves to Spec,CP, which violates BiCoM. Therefore, we would expect (18) to be ungrammatical, but this is not what we find.

(18) This is the guy **who**$_i$ the prosecutor $\boldsymbol{t_i}$ thought $\boldsymbol{t_i}$ embezzled the money and $\boldsymbol{t_i}$ should be indicted $\boldsymbol{t_i}$.

We propose that (18) is grammatical because it is structurally ambiguous, and only one of its two possible structures, namely (19b), violates BiCoM. It does so because the shared *wh*-subject, asymmetrically embedded only in the first conjunct, is ATB-extracted from Spec,vP in that conjunct and from Spec,TP in the second, monoclausal conjunct. Thus, in this case subsequent Merge relates three distinct positions.

(19) a. This is the guy **who**$_i$ [$_{TP}$ the prosecutor $\boldsymbol{t_i}$ thought $\boldsymbol{t_i}$ embezzled the money] and [$_{TP}$ $\boldsymbol{t_i}$ should be indicted $\boldsymbol{t_i}$].

b. This is the guy

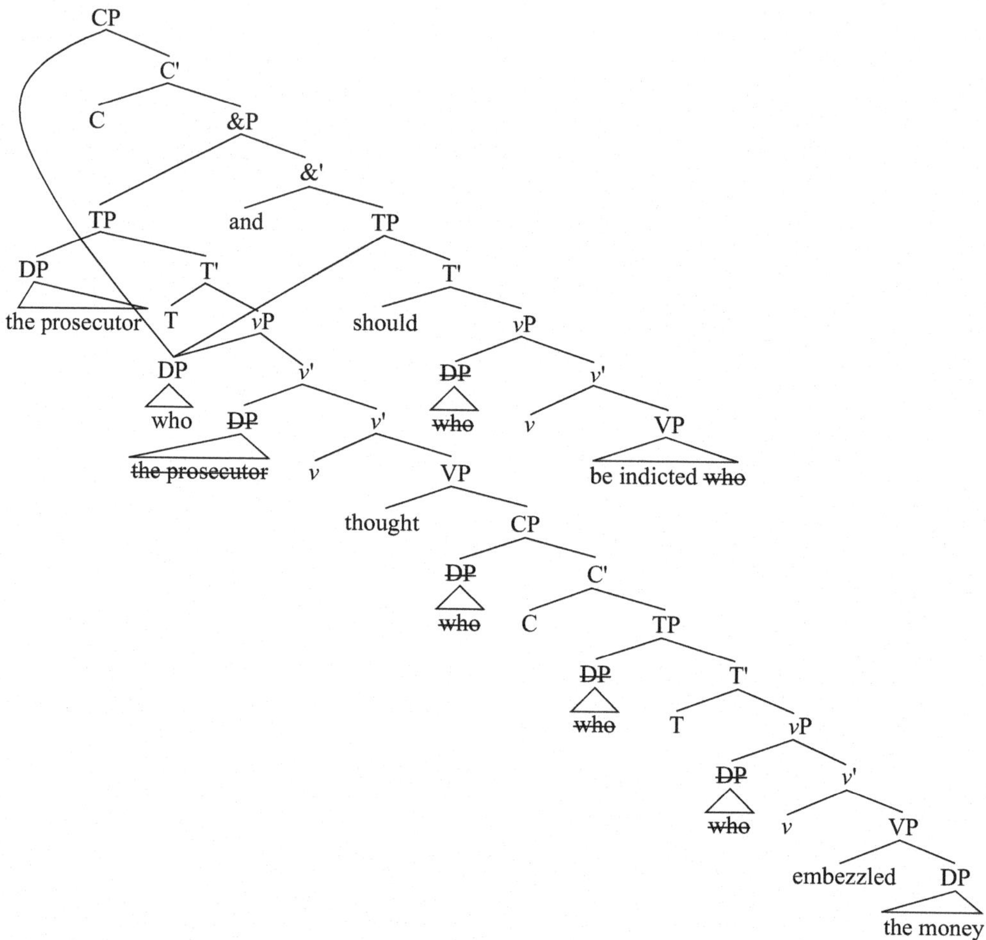

However, this example has an alternative structure, given in (20b), in which two monoclausal conjuncts are embedded under *This is the guy who the prosecutor thought.* In this structure, the *wh*-phrase is ATB-extracted from syncretic Spec,TP positions. This derivation does not violate BiCoM, which explains the grammaticality of the sentence.

(20) a. This is the guy **who**$_i$ the prosecutor thought [$_{TP}$ $\boldsymbol{t_i}$ embezzled the money] and [$_{TP}$ $\boldsymbol{t_i}$ should be indicted $\boldsymbol{t_i}$].

b. This is the guy

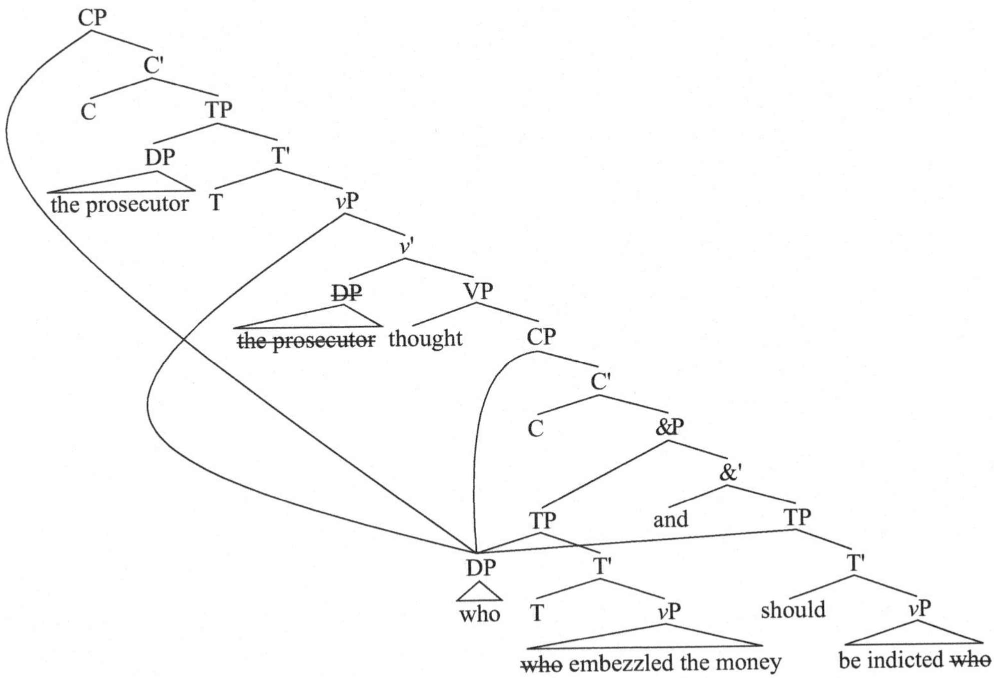

Support for the availability of the structure in (20b) comes from the ungrammaticality of (21), where the matrix subject pronoun *he* in the first conjunct is coindexed with the R-expression *the prosecutor* in the second conjunct.

(21) *This is the guy who **he**$_i$ thought embezzled the money and offered **the prosecutor**$_i$ a bribe.

This example also has two possible structures, given in (22a–b). The one with asymmetric embedding, given in (22a), does not involve a Principle C violation because the pronoun *he* in the first conjunct does not c-command the R-expression *the prosecutor* in the second conjunct, with which it is coindexed. However, it violates BiCoM because ATB extraction of the subject *wh*-phrase proceeds from nonsyncretic positions, just like in (19b). The structure in (22b), in which the two monoclausal conjuncts are both embedded, does not violate BiCoM since the *wh*-phrase is ATB-extracted from syncretic positions (Spec,TP positions in both conjuncts). However, the coindexation between *he* and *the prosecutor* causes a Principle C violation because in this case, the pronoun in the matrix clause does c-command the R-expression inside the Conjunction Phrase. Thus, (21) is ungrammatical on either analysis.

(22) a. *This is the guy **who**$_j$ [$_{TP}$ **he**$_i$ ***t***$_j$ thought [$_{TP}$ ***t***$_j$ embezzled the money]] and [$_{TP}$ ***t***$_j$ offered **the prosecutor**$_i$ a bribe].

b. *This is the guy **who**$_j$ **he**$_i$ thought [$_{TP}$ ***t***$_j$ embezzled the money] and [$_{TP}$ ***t***$_j$ offered **the prosecutor**$_i$ a bribe].

The proposal that the matrix *wh*-subject may remain in situ predicts that ATB examples in which the shared *wh*-phrase occupies nonparallel positions and is the subject in the first conjunct should be better than those in which it is the subject in the second conjunct, regardless of the level of embedding. This is what the contrast in (23) shows.

(23) a. ?Tell me **who**$_i$ [$_{TP}$ ***t***$_i$ walked into the room] and [$_{TP}$ everyone's eyes turned to ***t***$_i$].

b. *Tell me [$_{TP}$ **who**$_i$ everyone's eyes followed ***t***$_i$] and [$_{TP}$ ***t***$_i$ left the room].

Judgments along these lines are also reported by Goodall (1987: 74), who notes that "sentences in which the extraction sites are linearly adjacent are worse than sentences in which they are nonadjacent." Goodall's examples, together with his judgments, are given in (24).

(24) a. *This is the man **who**$_i$ [$_{TP}$ John saw ***t***$_i$] and [$_{TP}$ ***t***$_i$ kissed Mary].

b. *?This is the man **who**$_i$ [$_{TP}$ ***t***$_i$ kissed Mary] and [$_{TP}$ John saw ***t***$_i$].

(Goodall 1987: 74)

This contrast follows from the proposal that BiCoM violations are obviated if a *wh*-subject remains in Spec,TP. If the *wh*-subject in the first conjunct remains in Spec,TP, the structure does not violate BiCoM: following Parallel Merge, the shared constituent undergoes movement only conjunct-internally. Thus, Merge never relates more than two positions per derivation, as shown in (25).

(25)

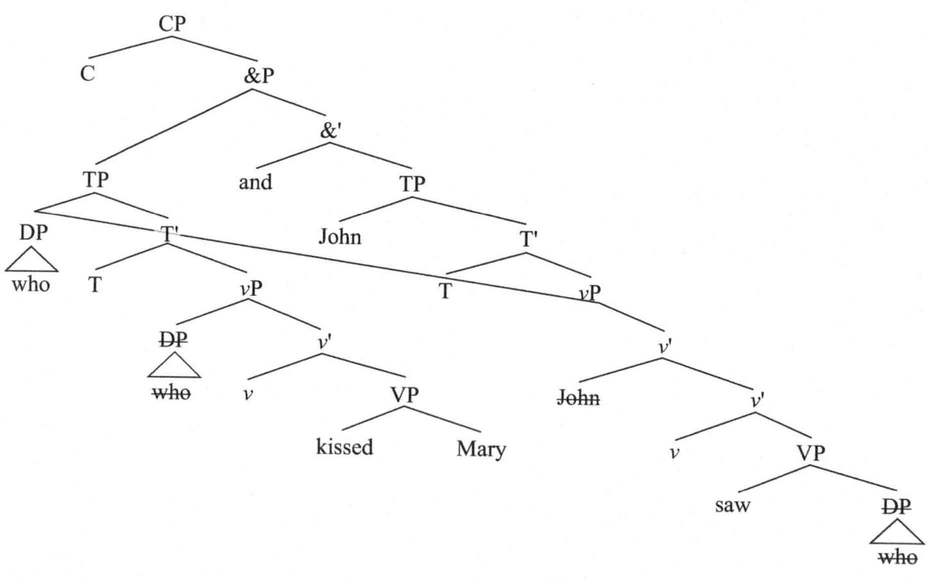

However, if the shared *wh*-phrase is the subject in the second conjunct, it necessarily undergoes ATB extraction, which proceeds from nonsyncretic positions, as shown in (26). This violates BiCoM since Merge relates three positions relevant for the constraint.

(26)

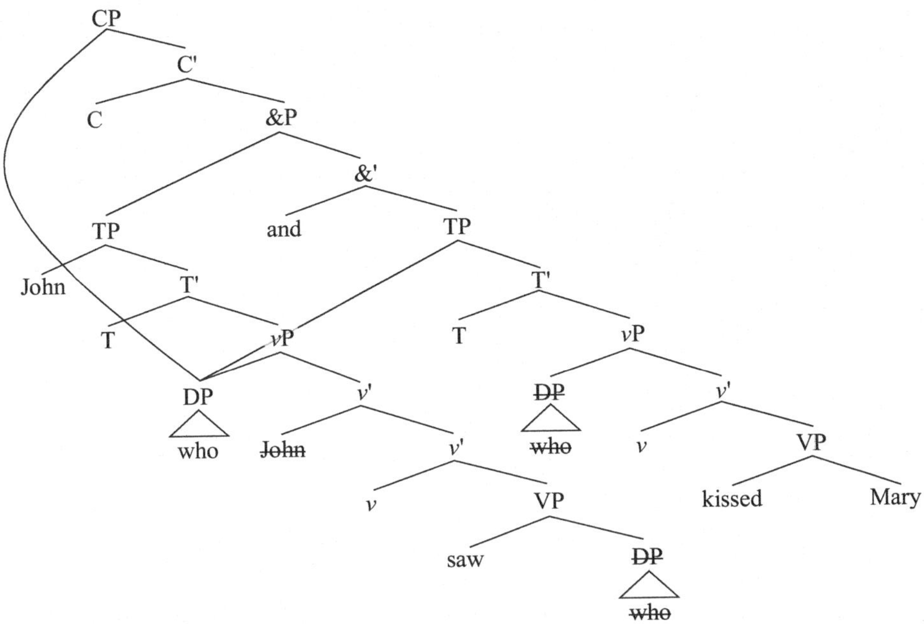

The Vacuous Movement Hypothesis can also explain examples (27a–c), due to Anderson (1983), which involve grammatical ATB extraction from nonparallel positions: the subject position in the first conjunct and the object position in the second conjunct. They involve the same configuration as (17): a violation of BiCoM if the shared element moves to Spec,CP, and no violation if it is allowed to remain in its conjunct-internal Spec,TP position(s).

(27) a. Jackson is the candidate **who**$_i$ $\boldsymbol{t_i}$ supported Reagan and the Democrats refused to endorse $\boldsymbol{t_i}$.

b. Caruso was a tenor **who**$_i$ $\boldsymbol{t_i}$ sang like an angel and audiences adored $\boldsymbol{t_i}$.

c. We are trying to fire the chairman **who**$_i$ $\boldsymbol{t_i}$ is terribly inflexible and Committee members strongly dislike $\boldsymbol{t_i}$.

(Anderson 1983: 4)

In the next section, we turn to ATB examples that involve raising to object, originally discussed by Woolford (1987), which also seem unexpected from the perspective of BiCoM. In these examples, what looks like extraction from nonparallel subject and object positions is grammatical, but extraction from parallel subject positions is not. The analysis we present builds on Woolford's original insight that the relevant contrasts become quite expected once raising to object is taken into account.

6.3 Raising to Object

Woolford (1987) discusses the contrast between (28a) and (28b), where the first conjunct involves raising to object. In the ungrammatical (28a), the shared *wh*-phrase originates as the subject in both conjuncts, whereas in the grammatical (28b), it originates as the subject in the first conjunct and the object in the second one.

(28) a. *Tell me **who**$_i$ everyone allows $\boldsymbol{t_i}$ to win and $\boldsymbol{t_i}$ is a jerk.

b. Tell me **who**$_i$ everyone allows $\boldsymbol{t_i}$ to win and Margaret loathes $\boldsymbol{t_i}$.

(Woolford 1987: 166)

The ungrammatical example (28a) cannot be represented as in (29a), with two TP conjuncts embedded under *Tell me who everyone allows*. Such an analysis is impossible because the matrix predicate *allow* cannot embed the tensed complement clause *is a jerk* in the second conjunct, as shown in (29b).

(29) a. *Tell me **who**$_i$ everyone allows [$_{TP}$ $\boldsymbol{t_i}$ to win] and [$_{TP}$ $\boldsymbol{t_i}$ is a jerk].

b. *Tell me **who**$_i$ everyone allows [$_{TP}$ $\boldsymbol{t_i}$ is a jerk].

If the structure in (29a) were allowed, example (28a) would not violate BiCoM since ATB extraction of the shared *wh*-subject would proceed from syncretic Spec,TP positions in both conjuncts. However, given that (28a) can only have the structure in (30), the sentence is ruled out by BiCoM.

(30) *Tell me **who**$_i$ [[$_{TP}$ everyone allows $\boldsymbol{t_i}$ to win] and [$_{TP}$ $\boldsymbol{t_i}$ is a jerk]].

The reason why it violates BiCoM is that the subject of the infinitival clause undergoes raising into the matrix clause, as argued by Postal (1974), Lasnik and Saito (1992), Runner (1998), and Chomsky (2015), among others. Existing accounts of raising to object differ with respect to the exact position in which the embedded subject ends up, with some possibilities being Spec,VP, Spec,vP, or Spec,AgrOP. Crucially, all concur that the raised object does not remain in the Spec,TP position of the lower clause. For concreteness' sake, we adopt the analysis presented by Chomsky (2015), according to which the raised subject lands in Spec,VP of the higher clause.[7] Under this analysis, the *wh*-subject in the first, biclausal conjunct in (28a) first lands in Spec,VP of the higher clause, from where it undergoes movement to Spec,vP. This is the position it occupies when it is ATB-extracted to the matrix Spec,CP, as shown in (31). In the second, monoclausal conjunct, on the other hand, it occupies Spec,TP. Since these two positions are not syncretic (one is Spec,vP and the other is Spec,TP), BiCoM is violated when these two positions are related to a third one by Internal Merge.

(31) *Tell me

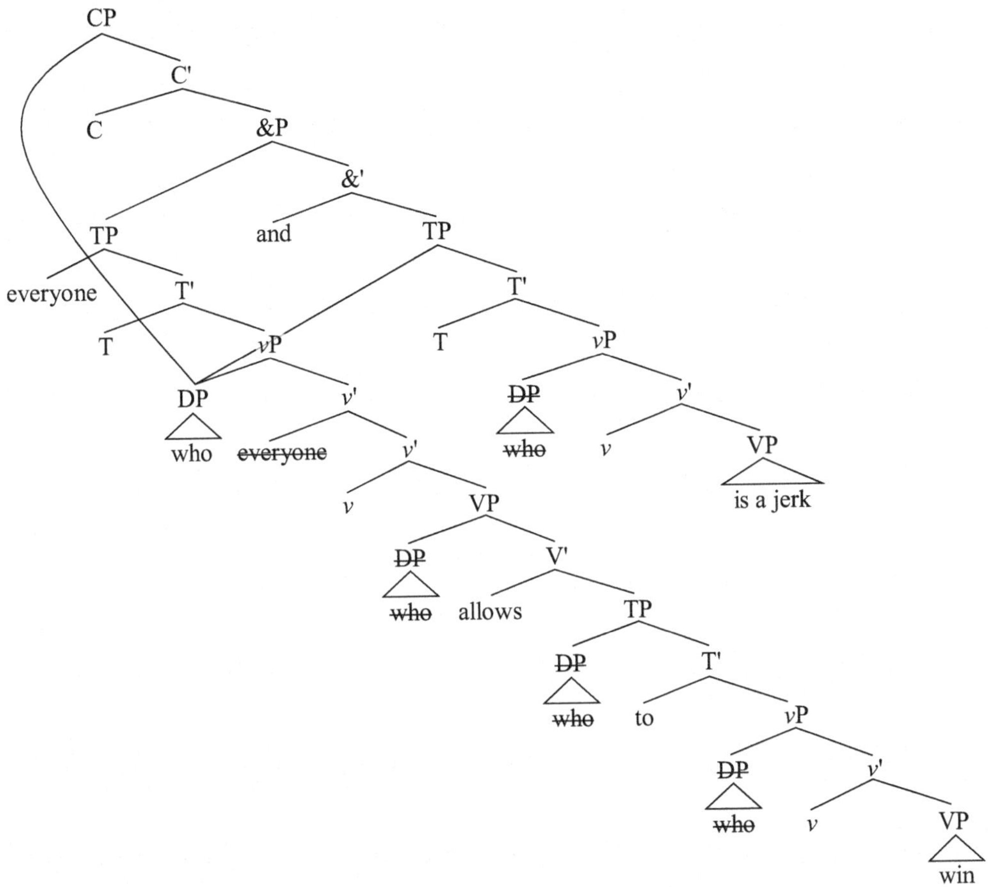

By contrast, in the grammatical (28b), the second (monoclausal) conjunct involves the object *wh*-phrase, so before the two conjuncts are united into a single derivation, the *wh*-phrase in this conjunct undergoes successive-cyclic movement to Spec,vP. Since the derivation of the first conjunct proceeds exactly the same way as the one in (28a), the *wh*-phrase in (28b) is ATB-extracted from syncretic Spec,vP positions in both conjuncts, obviating a BiCoM violation, as shown in (32).

(32) Tell me

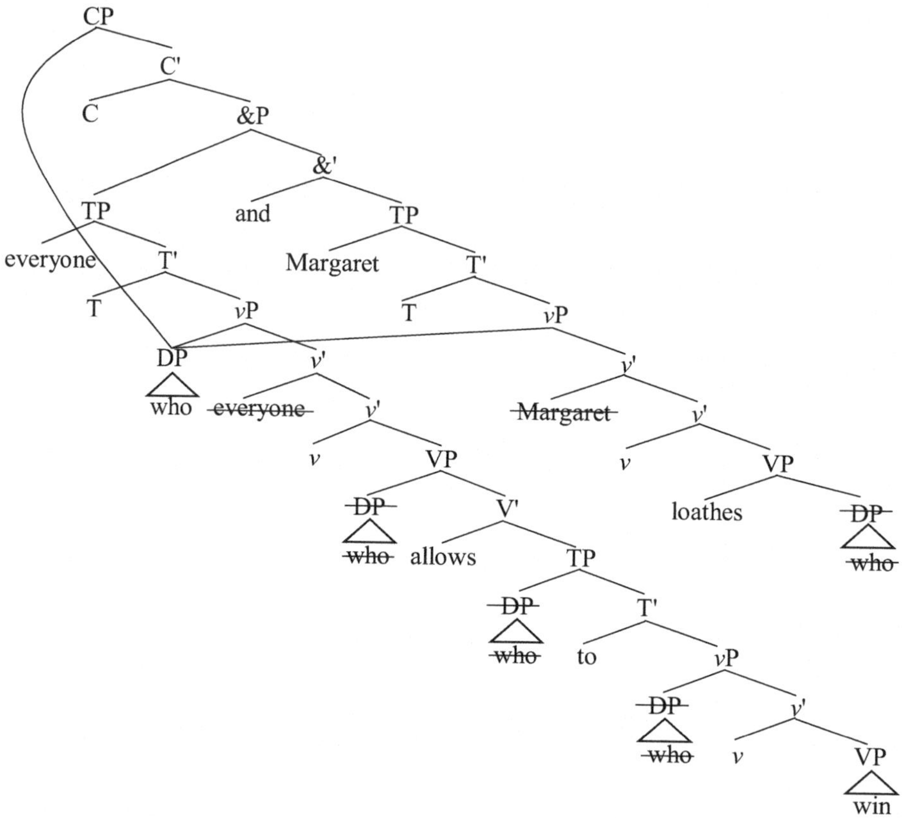

The contrast in (28a–b) shows once more that the parallelism constraint on ATB movement is not about subjecthood or objecthood, the point made already by Williams (1978). If it were, we would expect (28a) to be grammatical given that the shared *wh*-phrase is a thematic subject in both TP conjuncts, so there is a sense in which the two are parallel. The fact that (28a) is nevertheless ungrammatical and (28b) is grammatical lends additional support to our proposal that the ungrammaticality of (28a)—and other examples of illegitimate ATB extraction we have presented—is related to the question of whether the positions occupied by the shared element immediately prior to extraction are syncretic or not, and consequently, whether or not the extraction violates BiCoM.

6.4 The Adverb Effect

Our account can also explain the fact, discussed by Bruening (2010), that examples of ATB extraction from nonparallel positions improve if an adverbial is added on top of the conjunct containing the subject gap.[8] This is illustrated by the contrast in (33a–b) and (34a–b).

(33) a. *She is someone **OP**$_i$ that cooking amuses t_i and t_i hates jogging.

b. She is someone **OP**$_i$ that cooking amuses t_i and, according to her personal trainer, t_i hates jogging.[9]

(Bruening 2010: 55)

(34) a. ***Who**$_i$ did you say t_i that the law firm hired t_i and t_i acts as its manager?

b. **Who**$_i$ did you say t_i that the law firm hired t_i and, for all intents and purposes, t_i acts as its manager?

Bruening proposes the constraint in (35) to account for this contrast.

(35) *The Parallelism Constraint*

In across-the-board extraction, if one gap is the highest constituent within its conjunct, all other gaps must be as well.

(Bruening 2010: 55)

We propose that the contrast in (33) and (34) can also be reduced to BiCoM. In (33a) and (34a), the shared *wh*-phrase or the null operator is ATB-extracted from nonsyncretic positions, which leads to a BiCoM violation because Merge relates three different positions in the same derivation: Spec,vP in the first conjunct, Spec,TP in the second conjunct, and the position of C′. We argue that in (33b) and (34b), BiCoM is not violated because ATB extraction of the *wh*-phrase or the null operator proceeds from syncretic positions in the two conjuncts. These positions are Spec,CP positions, as shown in (36a–b).[10]

(36) a. She is someone [$_{CP}$ **OP**$_i$ [$_{CP}$ t_i that [$_{TP}$ cooking amuses t_i]] and, [$_{CP}$ t_i according to her personal trainer, [$_{TP}$ t_i hates jogging]]].

b. **Who**$_i$ did you say [[$_{CP}$ t_i that [$_{TP}$ the law firm hired t_i]] and, [$_{CP}$ t_i for all intents and purposes, [$_{TP}$ t_i acts as its manager]]]?

To motivate our analysis of the contrast in (33) and (34), we need to provide support for the claim that the conjuncts in (33b) and (34b) are CPs and also for the claim that the conjuncts in (33a) and (34a) are TPs and *cannot* be CPs: if the conjuncts were CPs in both (a) and (b) examples, we would lose the explanation for the contrast because the shared constituent would be extracted from syncretic positions in both. In the remainder of the chapter, we argue for these two claims in turn. We first provide support for the CP status of the conjuncts in (33b) and (34b) by invoking a particular family of analyses of the analogous ameliorating effect of adverbials in examples that involve the *that*-trace effect. Next, by considering examples in which one or both conjuncts are introduced by an overt complementizer *that*, we provide the details of the structure in (33b) and (34b), arguing that it involves a recursive CP layer. In doing so, we draw heavily on Bjorkman's (2013) discussion of the so-called *asymmetric* uses of the coordinator *and*. Following Bjorkman's arguments, we also defend the claim that the conjuncts in (33a) and (34a) are necessarily TPs and cannot be CPs introduced by null complementizers.

We begin our discussion of the CP status of the conjuncts in (33b) and (34b) by noting that the adverb effect observed in BiCoM-violating nonparallel ATB extraction is reminiscent of the effect that the addition of an adverbial has in structures involving the *that*-trace violation, as shown in (37a–b) (Bresnan 1977; Culicover 1993a, b; Kandybowicz 2006, among others).[11]

(37) a. ***Who**$_i$ did you say **that** $\boldsymbol{t_i}$ acts as the law firm's manager?

b. **Who**$_i$ did you say **that**, for all intents and purposes, $\boldsymbol{t_i}$ acts as the law firm's manager?

However, we are not dealing with the *same* phenomenon: the ungrammatical example of nonparallel ATB extraction in (38a) does not display the *that*-trace effect, but is nevertheless improved by the addition of the adverbial in (38b). Thus, our analysis has to explain both Bruening's original contrast in (33a–b), where an overt complementizer precedes the two conjuncts, and the contrast in (38a–b), where an overt complementizer is absent.

(38) a. ***Who**$_i$ did you say the law firm hired $\boldsymbol{t_i}$ and $\boldsymbol{t_i}$ acts as its manager?

b. **Who**$_i$ did you say the law firm hired $\boldsymbol{t_i}$ and, for all intents and purposes, $\boldsymbol{t_i}$ acts as its manager?

Many analyses of the ameliorating effect of an adverbial on the *that*-trace effect, illustrated by the contrast in (37), involve expanding the structure in order to accommodate the adverbial. For example, Browning (1996) proposes that the adverbial occupies Spec,CP, the overt complementizer moves to a higher C position, and the extracted subject moves to the specifier of this higher CP. The expanded structure that hosts the adverbial no longer contains a *that*-trace violation because the trace of the subject *wh*-phrase is properly governed.[12] The steps in the derivation are sketched in (39a–d).[13]

(39) a. **Who**$_i$ did you say **that**, for all intents and purposes, $\boldsymbol{t_i}$ acts as the law firm's manager?

b. [$_{CP}$ for all intents and purposes [$_{C'}$ **that** [$_{TP}$ **who** acts as the law firm's manager]]]

c. [$_{CP}$ **that**$_j$ [$_{CP}$ for all intents and purposes [$_{C'}$ $\boldsymbol{t_j}$ [$_{TP}$ **who** acts as the law firm's manager]]]]

d. [$_{CP}$ **who**$_i$ [$_{C'}$ **that**$_j$ [$_{CP}$ for all intents and purposes [$_{C'}$ $\boldsymbol{t_j}$ [$_{TP}$ $\boldsymbol{t_i}$ acts as the law firm's manager]]]]]

The adverbial that ameliorates the *that*-trace effect occupies a position that is higher than TP, somewhere in the C-system of the clause.[14] If this is correct, it is reasonable to assume that the second conjunct in (38b), in which the adverbial improves nonparallel ATB extraction, also involves a structure bigger than TP, in order to accommodate the adverbial. According to the Law of the Coordination of Likes, proposed by Williams (1981), only constituents of the same syntactic category can be conjoined. Thus, if the second conjunct in (38b) is a CP, the first conjunct must also be a CP. What matters for our system is that the extra structure provides extra—potentially syncretic—positions for the movement of the shared *wh*-phrase. With both conjuncts the size of a CP, the shared *who* now moves through the Spec,CP position in both conjuncts before it is ATB-extracted out of them. Since the two Spec,CP positions are syncretic, the Internal Merge that extracts *who* from both conjuncts no longer violates BiCoM. Consequently, the sentence improves.[15]

One difference between the adverb effect in ATB configurations and the adverb effect in *that*-trace configurations concerns the position of the complementizer *that*. As shown in (40a–b), in *that*-trace configurations the complementizer immediately precedes the adverbial, but in the relevant ATB configurations it does not; instead, in (40b) the complementizer and the adverbial are separated by the first conjunct, which does not contain the adverbial. Thus, while in (40a) the complementizer and the adverbial most probably belong to the same CP, this is not the case in (40b).

(40) a. **Who**$_i$ did you say **<u>that</u>**, <u>for all intents and purposes</u>, ***t***$_i$ acts as the law firm's manager?

b. **Who**$_i$ did you say ***t***$_i$ **<u>that</u>** the law firm hired ***t***$_i$ and, <u>for all intents and purposes</u>, ***t***$_i$ acts as its manager?

Since in (40b) the complementizer does not introduce the second conjunct (i.e., the conjunct containing the adverbial), it must be the case that this conjunct is headed by a null complementizer. Such an analysis in turn requires that a CP headed by a null C be able to host an adverbial in the left periphery. It has been claimed in the literature (e.g., Rizzi 1997) that this is not possible, as shown in (41).

(41) She thought *(that) never in her life would she accept this solution.

(Rizzi and Shlonsky 2007: 151, adapted from Grimshaw 1997)

However, Sobin (2002) reports that his consultants found such examples to be quite acceptable, as shown in (42a–b).

(42) a. Who did you say just last week saw Elvis?

b. Who do they think next year might visit the Pope?

(Sobin 2002: 544)

Given the grammaticality of (42a–b), it is not implausible to propose, as we did, that even in the absence of an overt complementizer in the second conjunct in (40b), that conjunct is a CP. Thus, the shared constituent can end up occupying syncretic positions in the two conjuncts prior to ATB extraction.

Another issue raised by (40b) concerns the exact position of *that*. There are at least two possibilities to consider. One is for the complementizer *that* to embed the entire coordination phrase, with CP conjuncts headed by null complementizers ($C_{\varnothing}$), as shown schematically in (43a). Another option is for the complementizer *that* to introduce the first CP conjunct, which is conjoined with a CP introduced by a null complementizer, as shown in (43b).

(43) a. $[_{CP}$ **that** $[_{\&P}$ $[_{CP}$ $C_{\varnothing}$ . . .] and $[_{CP}$ $C_{\varnothing}$ . . .]]]

b. $[_{\&P}$ $[_{CP}$ **that** . . .] and $[_{CP}$ $C_{\varnothing}$ . . .]]

We believe that the analysis in (43a) is correct. There are several reasons for this conclusion, which we discuss in turn. First, if the second conjunct is a subject relative clause, as in (36a), an overt complementizer or a relative pronoun is required, as shown in (44a–b) (Kayne 1981; Lasnik and Saito 1984; Rizzi 1990; Grimshaw 1997; Postal 2004, among others). This requirement is met by the structure in (43a), where the second conjunct CP *is* embedded under an overt *that*, but not by the structure in (43b).

(44) a. It was those towns (that) he studied.

b. It was those towns *(that) were studied.

(Postal 2004: 21)

Next, there are reasons to believe that coordination of a CP introduced by a null complementizer and one introduced by an overt complementizer is disallowed. One reason comes from Bjorkman's (2013) discussion of the so-called *asymmetric* uses of the coordinator *and*. Bjorkman argues that examples like (45a), in which a single instance of *that* introduces the embedded coordination, are best analyzed as involving TP conjuncts embedded under a single CP layer, as in (46a). By contrast, examples like (45b), where each conjunct is introduced by *that*, involve coordination of CPs, as in (46b). Bjorkman's argument for the difference in the size of the conjuncts is based on the interpretive possibilities of examples like (45a–b): she shows that while (45b) is most naturally interpreted as reporting two events that are independent from one another (symmetric interpretation), (45a) receives an interpretation in which the first conjunct temporally or causally precedes the other (asymmetric interpretation).

(45) a. The newspaper reported **that** a new government was elected and there was a riot.

b. The newspaper reported **that** a new government was elected and **that** there was a riot.

(Bjorkman 2013: 396)

(46) a. report [$_{CP}$ that [$_{TP}$ . . .] and [$_{TP}$ . . .]]
b. report [$_{CP}$ that . . .] and [$_{CP}$ that . . .]
(Bjorkman 2013: 396)

Bjorkman's discussion implicitly (but see her footnote 5) argues against the analysis in (47), in which the two conjuncts are CPs, the first conjunct being introduced by an overt complementizer and the second conjunct by a null one. It is precisely this possibility that we also argue against.

(47) *report [$_{CP}$ that [$_{TP}$ . . .]] and [$_{CP}$ $C_{\varnothing}$ [$_{TP}$ . . .]]

The observation that (48a), in which only the second conjunct contains an overt complementizer, is ungrammatical provides an additional argument against (47). If it were possible to coordinate a CP headed by *that* with a CP headed by a null complementizer, (48a) should be grammatical. Since it is not, we conclude that what excludes it is a violation of the Law of the Coordination of Likes: (48a) necessarily involves coordination of a CP with a TP, as shown in (48b).[16]

(48) a. ***Who**$_i$ did Mary say John recommended $\boldsymbol{t_i}$ and that Bill criticized $\boldsymbol{t_i}$?
b. ***Who**$_i$ did Mary say [$_{TP}$ John recommended $\boldsymbol{t_i}$] and [$_{CP}$ that Bill criticized $\boldsymbol{t_i}$]?

We thus conclude that a CP introduced by an overt complementizer cannot be coordinated with a CP introduced by a null complementizer. With this in mind, let us return to the question of what position the overt complementizer occupies in examples of ATB extraction in which the addition of an adverbial alleviates BiCoM violations. We started out by suggesting the following possibilities, repeated here from (43).

(49) a. [$_{CP}$ that [$_{\&P}$ [$_{CP}$ $C_{\varnothing}$ . . .] and [$_{CP}$ $C_{\varnothing}$ . . .]]]
b. [$_{\&P}$ [$_{CP}$ that . . .] and [$_{CP}$ $C_{\varnothing}$ . . .]]

In light of the conclusion that a CP with an overt complementizer cannot be coordinated with a CP introduced by a null complementizer, it seems to us that examples of ATB extraction that display the adverb effect—examples like (34b), repeated here as (50)—are best analyzed as an instance of CP-recursion in which the C hosting an overt complementizer embeds the coordination of CPs headed by null complementizers, as in (49a).[17]

(50) Who did you say that the law firm hired and, for all intents and purposes, acts as its manager?

Thus, the final representation of (50) is as shown in (51).

(51)

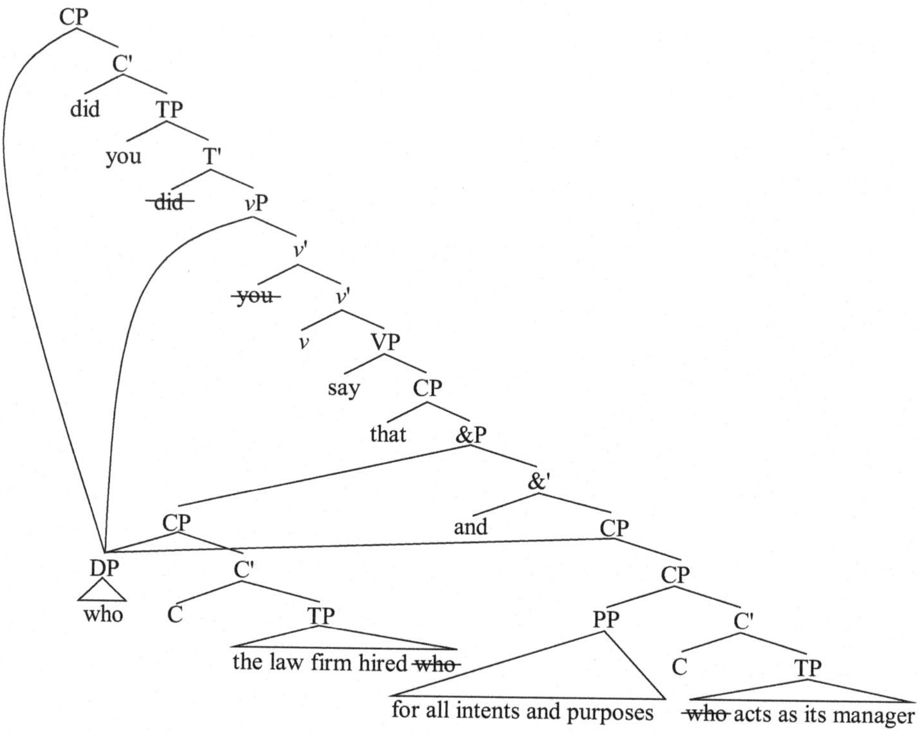

This analysis also captures the grammaticality of examples like (52a), in which the conjoined CPs are *not* introduced by an overt complementizer. The corresponding structure is given in (52b).[18]

(52) a. **Who**$_i$ did you say

[$_{CP}$ $\boldsymbol{t_i}$ [$_{C'}$ $C_\varnothing$ [$_{TP}$ the law firm hired $\boldsymbol{t_i}$]] and

[$_{CP}$ $\boldsymbol{t_i}$ [$_{C'}$ for all intents and purposes [$_{C'}$ $C_\varnothing$ $\boldsymbol{t_i}$ acts as its manager]]]]?

b.

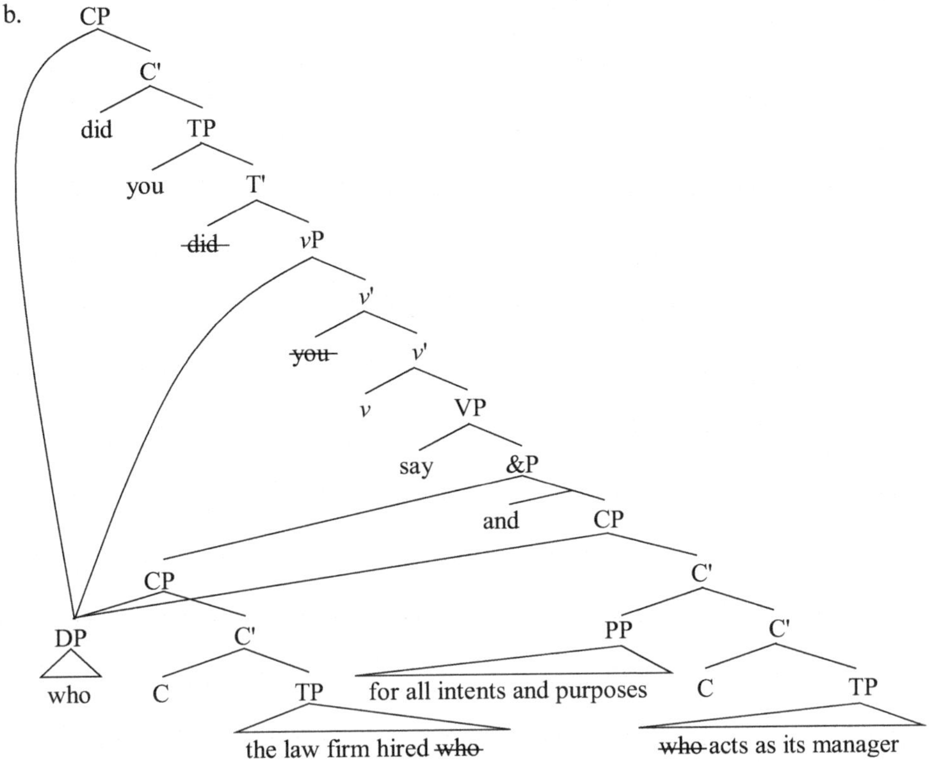

Note also that if it were possible to coordinate a CP introduced by *that* with a CP introduced by a null complementizer, examples of ungrammatical ATB extraction without an adverbial could be given the representations in (53a–b), in which both conjuncts are CPs. This in turn would mean that the shared constituent (a null operator in (53a) and *who* in (53b)) could undergo successive-cyclic movement to Spec,CP in each conjunct before being ATB-extracted. Since ATB extraction would proceed from syncretic positions, this step should obviate the BiCoM violation. Thus, we would expect such examples to be grammatical, but they are not.

(53) a. *She is someone $\mathbf{OP}_i$ [$_{CP}$ $\boldsymbol{t}_i$ that cooking amuses $\boldsymbol{t}_i$] and [$_{CP}$ $\boldsymbol{t}_i$ $C_{\varnothing}$ $\boldsymbol{t}_i$ hates jogging].

b. *$\mathbf{Who}_i$ did you say [$_{CP}$ $\boldsymbol{t}_i$ that the law firm hired $\boldsymbol{t}_i$] and [$_{CP}$ $\boldsymbol{t}_i$ $C_{\varnothing}$ $\boldsymbol{t}_i$ acts as its manager]?

If such examples necessarily involve TP coordination embedded under a *single* overt complementizer, they also necessarily violate BiCoM, since prior to ATB extraction, the shared constituent occupies nonsyncretic positions in the two conjuncts: Spec,vP in the first one and Spec,TP in the second one, as shown in (54).

(54) She is someone

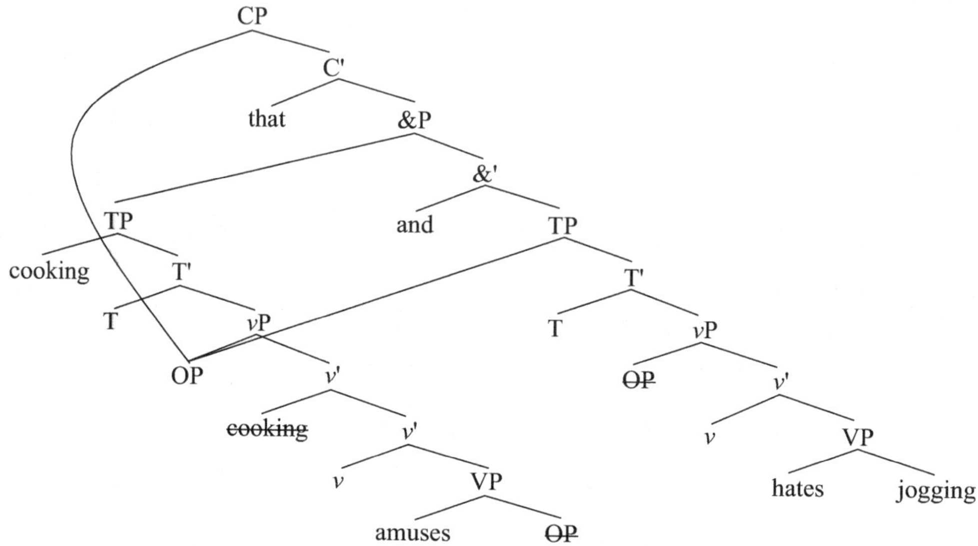

Finally, we need to address the question of *why* examples like (55a), which contains neither an overt *that* nor an adverbial, cannot be rescued by "big," CP-sized coordination, as shown in (55b).

(55) a. ***Who**$_i$ did you say the law firm hired $\boldsymbol{t_i}$ and $\boldsymbol{t_i}$ acts as its manager?

b. ***Who**$_i$ did you say

[$_{CP}$ $\boldsymbol{t_i}$ $C_\varnothing$ [$_{TP}$ the law firm hired $\boldsymbol{t_i}$]] and

[$_{CP}$ $\boldsymbol{t_i}$ $C_\varnothing$ [$_{TP}$ $\boldsymbol{t_i}$ acts as its manager]]?

On a TP-coordination analysis, (55a) violates BiCoM because ATB extraction of the shared constituent *who* proceeds from nonsyncretic positions. However, if it involves coordination of CPs, as in (55b), *who* would be ATB-extracted from syncretic Spec,CP positions, and this would result in a BiCoM-compliant structure.

If our analysis of the adverb effect is on the right track, the ungrammaticality of (55a) suggests that the grammar, perhaps by some principle of economy, prefers small conjunctions whenever possible and allows for expanded structure only when some overt material—such as an adverbial or an overt complementizer—requires it (see also Bjorkman 2013: 401n9). This is reminiscent of the Minimal Structure Constraint (Law 1991; Grimshaw 1994; Speas 1994; Bošković 1996; Bhatt and Takahashi 2011), which gives preference to small rather than big constituents. For example, Grimshaw (1994) argues for a principle she calls *Minimal Projection*, given in (56).

(56) *Minimal Projection*

Projections are legitimate only when they are motivated.

(Grimshaw 1994: 76)

Similarly, Bošković (1996) proposes the Minimal Structure Principle in (57).

(57) *The Minimal Structure Principle*

Provided that lexical requirements of relevant elements are satisfied, if two representations have the same lexical structure and serve the same function, then the representation that has fewer projections is to be chosen as the syntactic representation serving that function.

(Bošković 1996: 290)

The absence of overt complementizers and adverbials in both conjuncts makes the sentence in (55a) compatible with both a CP- and a TP-coordination analysis. However, both Minimal Projection and the Minimal Structure Principle force the smaller, TP-sized coordination. On the other hand, the selectional requirements of the embedding verb *say*, which takes a CP complement, are incompatible with TP-coordination. Arguably, the most economical way to reconcile these two considerations, the lack of motivation for the presence of a CP layer in the coordination structure and the requirement that *say* embed a CP, is to posit TP-coordination under a single, null C. However, in such a configuration, illustrated in (58), ATB extraction of the shared *wh*-phrase necessarily violates BiCoM and results in ungrammaticality.

(58) ***Who**$_i$ did you say [$_{CP}$ $\boldsymbol{t_i}$ $C_{\varnothing}$ [$_{TP}$ the law firm hired $\boldsymbol{t_i}$] and [$_{TP}$ $\boldsymbol{t_i}$ acts as its manager]]?

Support for TP-coordination under a single C comes from the interpretation of grammatical examples in which ATB extraction proceeds from syncretic positions, as in (59a). Such sentences have only the asymmetric interpretation, on a par with sentences where the Conjunction Phrase is embedded under an overt complementizer, as in (59b). Both (59a) and (59b) are most naturally interpreted as questions asking for the identity of a person who was fired *as a result of* or at least *after* being reported by a coworker. It is difficult to obtain a reading in which the person reported was fired for a reason that is independent of the coworker reporting them, which would be compatible with the two conjuncts referring to independent events. Both (59a) and (59b) contrast in this respect with (60), in which the two events, the reporting and the firing, are more easily conceptualized as independent of one another—that is, in which the two conjuncts are interpreted as symmetric.

(59) a. Who did John say a coworker reported and the manager fired?
b. Who did John say **that** a coworker reported and the manager fired?

(60) Who did John say **that** a coworker reported and **that** the manager fired?

6.5 Conclusion

In chapter 5, we discussed grammatical cases of ATB extraction—cases where the shared constituent undergoes ATB extraction from parallel positions. We proposed that such examples are exempt from BiCoM because the two parallel positions are *structurally syncretic*. In this chapter, we examined the consequences of structural syncretism. First, we looked at the effects of embedding and showed how our proposal explains why embedding sometimes saves a structure that otherwise violates BiCoM, sometimes does not, and sometimes has no effect at all. Next, we showed how some of the seemingly problematic cases can be explained by the Vacuous Movement Hypothesis for *wh*-subjects and by the raising-to-object analysis of exceptional-case-marking constructions. And finally, we looked at the adverb effect, where the addition of an adverbial improves otherwise ungrammatical extraction from nonparallel positions. We argued that the presence of an adverbial requires adding an extra layer of structure to coordinated clauses, which in turn creates syncretic positions for the movement of the shared *wh*-phrase. We showed that the way ATB extraction interacts with phenomena as diverse as symmetric and asymmetric embedding, raising to object, and the adverb effect can be given a unified analysis, depending on whether the structure makes it possible for the shared constituent to be ATB-extracted without violating BiCoM—that is, whether ATB extraction can proceed from syncretic positions. This we believe provides strong support for our proposal that Merge is constrained by BiCoM and that structural syncretism alleviates BiCoM violations.

7 Conclusion

The central claim of our monograph was that Merge is subject to a binarity constraint operating not on syntactic objects but on the syntactic positions that these objects occupy. We called this constraint, repeated in (1), the Binarity Constraint on Merge (BiCoM).

(1) *Binarity Constraint on Merge*

Merge cannot relate more than two positions at a time within a single derivation, where the position(s) of a syntactic object SO that Merge applies to must overlap with a search path for SO if there is a search path for SO.

While relativizing binarity to syntactic positions is innocuous for structures in which a syntactic object has a single sister, it has significant consequences for multidominant structures, in which a single object may have more than one sister, either as a result of Internal Merge or as a result of Parallel Merge, and thus may occupy multiple positions. With multidominance at play, Merge can relate more than two positions *without* relating more than two objects.

We started by examining the interaction between Parallel Merge and Internal Merge because the effects of BiCoM only become apparent when we look at these two operations in tandem. We took Right Node Raising (RNR) to be an example of Parallel Merge applying in isolation, run-of-the-mill movement to be an example of Internal Merge applying in isolation, and across-the-board (ATB) movement to be an example of *both* Parallel Merge and Internal Merge applying to the same object. We showed that when this happens (i.e., when Internal Merge applies to a syntactic object that has been previously parallel-merged), Merge relates more than two positions within a single derivation. This violates BiCoM. We appealed to BiCoM to account for the well-documented restrictions against ATB extraction from nonparallel positions. We also showed that analogous configurations are well-formed in RNR. This is expected if RNR does not involve movement; there is never a point in the derivation when Merge relates more than two positions. Our proposal thus supports the analyses of RNR in which the shared constituent remains in situ.

The parallelism requirement on ATB extraction has received various explanations in the literature. While previous analyses of the phenomenon all derive (some of) the asymmetries that our system derives, they are construction-specific in that they crucially (explicitly or implicitly) make reference to coordinate structures and/or ATB extraction. Our proposal derives the parallelism requirement in ATB movement from the restriction that Merge in general—not only in coordinate structures and not only in ATB movement—may relate at most two *positions* in a single derivation. In other words, BiCoM is not restricted to multidominant or coordinate structures; we also showed that it captures well-established restrictions on phrase structure such as the restriction against ternary branching.

We further showed that Merge can sometimes relate (or appear to relate) more than two positions at a time, but it can only do so under very restricted circumstances. When two of the three positions involved in a single application of Merge are identical, the computational system can treat them as one. We took this to be an instance of *structural syncretism*. The idea that the grammar can sometimes be "fooled" by appearances is well-known from morphology, where, for example, multiple case requirements can be satisfied by a single constituent if the relevant case forms are identical. Our proposal that BiCoM violations can be obviated by structural syncretism extends the same reasoning to the realm of syntax, offering a unified picture of the role that "identity in form" seems to play in the grammar.

The contrast between RNR and ATB constructions suggests that violations of BiCoM are evaluated relative to a derivation in a workspace that can contain multiple derivations. If other principles of grammar are also evaluated relative to a derivation, which seems to be the null hypothesis, we are a step closer to understanding why, for example, a constituent that undergoes Internal Merge cannot be case-marked twice, but one that undergoes Parallel Merge can: the former is multiply-dominated within a single derivation, whereas the latter participates in two separate derivations and is treated independently in each of them.

We also proposed that in cases of Internal Merge, which operates within a single derivation, BiCoM is not evaluated globally; instead, it is evaluated within a smaller domain: the domain including the probe that initiates Merge and the *closest* position of the goal. This is how we analyzed successive-cyclic movement configurations, where Merge appears to relate more than two positions within a single derivation. The idea that locality plays a role in the evaluation of BiCoM violations is in keeping with the general consensus in the field that syntactic operations are executed and evaluated locally rather than globally.

On an empirical level, the proposal that Merge is constrained by BiCoM and that structural syncretism can obviate BiCoM violations allowed us to unify a range of phenomena that on the surface appear unrelated to each other. In addition to capturing the contrast between ATB extraction and RNR, we explained why the grammaticality of ATB constructions can be affected by embedding one (or both) conjuncts from which the shared *wh*-phrase is extracted. This is because embedding adds new positions for the shared *wh*-phrase to move through prior to undergoing ATB extraction. The result becomes grammatical if the highest of these new positions created by embedding are syncretic across the two conjuncts. If they are syncretic (and they were not before), the ungrammatical cases of ATB extraction become grammatical. If they are nonsyncretic (and they were syncretic before), the grammatical cases of ATB extraction become ungrammatical. The same analysis also captures the adverb effect, where examples of ungrammatical ATB extraction improve if an adverbial is added to the conjunct that contains the subject gap. We again invoked structural syncretism in order to explain the contrast: we proposed that the addition of the adverbial necessarily increases the size of both conjuncts, allowing the shared *wh*-phrase to move through syncretic positions in the two conjuncts before being ATB-extracted. Finally, the analysis correctly predicts that raising-to-object configurations are grammatical in exactly those configurations where the raising of the subject *wh*-phrase from the infinitival clause into the matrix clause results in its occupying a position that is syncretic with its position in the other conjunct, and ungrammatical otherwise.

On a more conceptual level, our monograph contributes to the current debates regarding the existence of multidominance in the grammar, engaging with proposals such as those of Chomsky (2007, 2008, 2019), Larson (2016), and Adger (2017), who argue that the computational system of human language does not generate multidominant representations. By demonstrating some of the empirical and conceptual benefits that can be gained by assuming Parallel Merge and Internal Merge as possible ways in which Merge operates, we hope that our monograph will stimulate further research into the status of multidominance in the grammar. While works with similar empirical focus (i.e., multidominance and multidominant configurations in syntax) do exist, such as Goodall 1987 and Citko 2011b, they tend to focus on arguing for a multidominance approach to a given construction (or a set of constructions) and thus, directly or indirectly, for the existence of multidominance in the grammar. This monograph, we believe, goes a step further by examining the differences between well-established types of multidominant structures and the interaction between them. Thus, it contributes not only to our understanding of configurations involving multidominance, coordination, and/or ATB phenomena, but also (and perhaps more fundamentally) to understanding of the general combinatorial properties underlying the human language faculty.

Notes

Chapter 1

1. The structure in (2b) is a bit of an oversimplification as it ignores intermediate movement steps.

2. For us, Parallel Merge is a two-step process, which preserves the insight that Merge targets two objects at a time; however, nothing crucially hinges on this assumption. We differ in this respect from Johnson (2018), who takes Parallel Merge to be a one-step process yielding (3b) directly, thus allowing Merge to target three objects at a time.

3. Even though we do not exclude the possibility that RNR is not a uniform process, and that some types of RNR (in some languages) involve movement or ellipsis derivations, whereas others involve multidominance (see Barros and Vicente 2011; Larson 2012; Valmala 2013, among others), we will largely abstract away from this issue in the monograph and focus on multidominance accounts. Also, since our focus is primarily on the properties of Merge (rather than on RNR per se), we cannot do justice here to all the research on RNR and the arguments that it has brought forth in favor of (or against) treating RNR in a multidominant way (see Sabbagh 2014 and Citko 2017 and the references therein for a summary of research on RNR).

4. Here and throughout the monograph, we use underscores to indicate the position in each conjunct that is construed with the shared constituent in examples of RNR.

5. In tree diagrams, we use struck-through copies to represent premovement sites of constituents that are not the focus of the discussion. We do this for simplicity's sake, without attaching any theoretical significance to this choice.

6. The examples that we cite from the literature do not always indicate empty categories as traces and/or include coindexation between fronted *wh*-operators and their traces. We add them throughout the monograph for the sake of consistency. This choice does not necessarily imply that the authors we cite analyzed all gaps as traces related to a single operator.

7. We use the term *analogous* to refer to the fact that the shared constituent in RNR occupies positions that are the same as the positions it occupies in ATB constructions and vice versa. In this particular case, these are nonparallel positions in both constructions (e.g., a subject position in one conjunct but an object position in the other conjunct).

8. Two observations are in order here. First, one of the positions is the position of the root, because BiCoM says that the *total* number of positions occupied by *all* the objects that undergo a given instance of Merge cannot exceed two per derivation; it does not say that the number of positions that *a single object* can occupy in a derivation cannot exceed two.

Second, in (10b) the circled root node, which undergoes Merge with the *wh*-phrase, is labeled CP. The same node is labeled C′ in (10c), which represents the structure *after* the *wh*-phrase is internally merged in Spec,CP. We adopt this practice throughout the monograph: we label the node with which the *wh*-phrase merges as C′ in our trees, and we refer to it as C′ in the text.

9. For simplicity's sake, the representation in (12b) ignores intermediate movement steps. If these are taken into consideration, even more positions are involved.

10. We thank an anonymous reviewer for encouraging us to discuss this question.

11. Restricting sideward movement to parallel positions would exclude Zhang's (2007, 2010) derivation for coordinated *wh*-questions, illustrated in (i). Zhang proposes that each *wh*-phrase in (i) sideward-moves from its original position to become either the specifier or the complement of the conjunction head. Since neither the position of the specifier nor the position of the complement of the conjunction head is parallel to the positions that the *wh*-phrases occupy before movement, if sideward movement were restricted to parallel positions, examples like (i) would be impossible to derive.

(i) **What$_i$ and when$_j$** does John normally eat $\boldsymbol{t_i}$ $\boldsymbol{t_j}$?
(Zhang 2007: 2134)

Chapter 2

1. Alternatively, the initial stage of a derivation includes only the lexical array, while the workspace comes into existence only after the first application of Merge.

2. In our system, a lexical array (or numeration) contains only lexical items. See, however, Zwart 2009, 2011 and De Belder and Van Craenenbroeck 2015 for proposals where the numeration itself may contain not only lexical items, but also elements that have already undergone Merge.

3. We take a derivation to be a sequence of stages. However, see (3) and (4) below for specific conditions on how these stages have to relate to one another in order to be part of the same derivation.

4. Collins and Stabler (2016: 47) define sets that are members of the workspace as roots.

(i) For any syntactic object X and any stage S = ⟨LA,W⟩ [where LA is a lexical array] with workspace W [where W is a set of syntactic objects], if X ∈ W,X is a *root* in W.

Collins and Stabler's definition of a stage is as follows:

(ii) A *stage* is a pair S = ⟨LA,W⟩, where LA is a lexical array and W is a set of syntactic objects. We call W the *workspace* of S. (Collins and Stabler 2016: 46)

We thank Karlos Arregi for pointing out to us the importance of being precise about the distinction between sets present in the workspace and sets that are members of the workspace.

5. The reason why it has to be "*exactly* one of the sets^W" is that in a scenario where the workspace contains more than one set^W (more than one root) before Merge, a new application of Merge preserves the number of sets^W only if the newly created set^W contains *not more than one* of the sets^W that existed in the workspace at the previous stage. If the newly created set^W contains as members more than one of the sets^W that existed in the workspace before, the number of sets^W decreases.

6. The insight that the creation of a new root initiates a new derivation is also captured by De Belder and Van Craenenbroeck's (2015: 642) ODWOR principle, given in (i):

(i) *One Derivational Workspace, One Root (ODWOR)*
In every derivational workspace, there is exactly one root, and for every root there is exactly one derivational workspace.

Our proposal differs from theirs in that we allow a single workspace to host multiple derivations.

7. A common way to represent the result of Merge is to include the label as the first member of the set. On this view, the result of merging A and B is (ii), not (i).

(i) Merge A and B = {A, B}
(ii) Merge A and B = {A, {A, B}}

We do not use labels in set notations given in this chapter and throughout the monograph. However, we do use labels in tree representations. This is purely for expository purposes; we do not mean to imply that labels exist in tree representations but not in set representations (see Collins 2002; Chomsky 2008; Citko 2008, 2011b, among others, for a more general discussion of whether labels exist and whether they are necessary).

8. Merge must have access to objects that have undergone a previous Merge operation in order to allow for displacement (i.e., Internal Merge). Johnson (2018) develops a system that does not allow Internal Merge, but derives displacement by Parallel Merge. Our system allows both types of Merge.

9. Following Chomsky (1995: 226), we assume that "[a] derivation converges only if [Merge] has applied often enough to leave us with just a single object, also exhausting the initial [lexical array]." For us, a single syntactic object means a single root, which in turn corresponds to a single set^W; we depart from Van Riemsdijk 2006a, b in this respect.

10. See Partee, ter Meulen, and Wall 1990, Carnie 2008, and the references therein for definitions and a discussion of the role that these definitions play in formalizing and restricting phrase structures. More formal formulations of both the Single Mother Condition (which Carnie refers to as No Multiple Mothers) and the No-Tangling Condition are given in (i)–(ii).

(i) *No Multiple Mothers*
$(\forall xyz \in N)\ [((x \lhd^* z) \,\&\, (y \lhd^* z)) \rightarrow ((x \lhd^* y) \vee (y \lhd^* x))]$
(Carnie 2008: 34)
(ii) *No-Tangling Condition*
$\forall w, x, y, z \in N\ ((\langle w, x\rangle \in P \,\&\, \langle w, y\rangle \in D \,\&\, \langle x, z\rangle \in D) \leftrightarrow \langle y, z\rangle \in P)$
(Partee, ter Meulen, and Wall 1990: 444)

11. Here, sisterhood implies linear ordering between the sister nodes (the left sister precedes the right sister), so this condition prevents any nodes dominated by N from preceding any nodes dominated by M.

12. If these conditions apply to derivations (as seems reasonable to assume), Parallel Merge (as opposed to Internal Merge) does not violate the Single Mother Condition, since in our system there is only one root per derivation, which means that the shared element has a single mother per derivation.

13. A more formal definition of the Extension Condition, due to Chomsky (1993), is given in (i).

(i) *The Extension Condition*
GT [Generalized Transformation] and Move α extend K to K*, which includes K as a proper part.
(Chomsky 1993: 22)

14. If Sub-Merge were possible, it would be the only type of Merge that could apply once the lexical array is depleted, all the instances of Internal Merge have applied, and the workspace contains a single rooted structure. We are unaware of any empirical facts that would suggest the existence of Sub-Merge in a way that certain linguistic phenomena, like RNR, suggest the existence of Parallel Merge. Thus, intuitively speaking, Sub-Merge seems unnecessary, and its existence might be precluded by some form of economy. Such an economy condition, however, would also rule out at least certain instances of Internal Merge, namely, all that apply after the lexical array has been exhausted.

15. As pointed out by a reviewer, our system does not allow Late Merge. This is because for us, every application of Merge creates a set^W (a root), and Late Merge does not create a new root. The fact that our system disallows Late Merge is not necessarily a problem; see, for example, Sportiche 2019 for recent arguments against Late Merge.

16. However, see Hornstein 1999, Boeckx and Hornstein 2006, and Boeckx, Hornstein, and Nunes 2010, among many others, for proposals in which this is possible.

17. Another often-discussed difference between Parallel Merge and Internal Merge structures concerns their behavior with respect to islands. As noted by Wexler and Culicover (1980), RNR constructions allow island violations. However, the lack of island effects in RNR is independent of our proposal that violations of grammatical principles are evaluated relative to a single derivation. Rather, it shows that RNR does not involve movement of the shared constituent and is thus compatible with any nonmovement derivation of RNR, regardless of how many derivations are involved.

18. Paths from terminals to the root are also crucial in the linearization of multidominant constituents in Gračanin-Yuksek 2013 and Johnson 2018.

19. Following the advice of an anonymous reviewer, we define SO_1 in (26) as "the set^W formed by Merge" in order to ensure that the sequence of nodes forming the path that defines the position of a syntactic object SO_n always starts with the root (the set most recently formed by Merge), rather than with any of the other nodes that dominate SO_n. Thus, regardless of how many positions an object occupies, each one is defined by a unique path. Our definition of a syntactic position also ensures that a syntactic object comes to occupy a position only *after* it has undergone Merge (i.e., after it has acquired a sister). This will be crucial in chapter 4, where we show how our proposal excludes ternary branching.

20. A related question, which we do not discuss here, is whether the position of an adjunct can be distinguished from the position of a specifier.

Chapter 3

1. For the sake of simplicity, this derivation ignores the intermediate step, in which the *wh*-pronoun moves to Spec,vP.

2. Larson (2016) argues against a multidominance view of movement on the grounds that it requires Merge to be formulated so "that it can operate on positions instead of or in addition to terms" (pg. 12). This, she states, is "incompatible with a Merge-based approach to structure building" (pg. 1). Her argument proceeds as follows: In successive-cyclic movement, Merge seems to target the most recent copy (crucially, not necessarily the structurally closest copy) created by a previous application of Merge. In a multidominance approach to movement, there are no copies; instead, a multiply-dominated object occupies multiple positions, some of which are inaccessible to higher operations. So, if Merge targeted the object itself, and if in some of its positions the object is inaccessible,

Merge would then, according to Larson, necessarily target an inaccessible object. We agree with Larson that Merge operates on terms/objects rather than positions; however, given that objects targeted by Merge necessarily (come to) occupy positions in a syntactic structure, Merge also necessarily relates their positions. It is thus not implausible to propose that BiCoM makes reference to positions rather than objects.

3. See also Bjorkman's (2016) discussion of the contrast between agreement patterns in the *go get* construction, illustrated in (i) (Zwicky 1969).

(i) a. Every morning I go buy a coffee.
  b. *Every morning he goes buys a coffee.
  (Bjorkman 2016: 54)

4. Williams (1978: 32), following Peters and Ritchie (1973), defines a factor as "any substring of a well-formed labeled bracketing that does not begin with a right bracket or end with a left bracket."

5. (18b) violates the Coordinate Structure Constraint, which Anderson (1983: 5) reduces to the ban against vacuous quantification.

6. Citko (1998) (also 2000, 2011b) develops a multidominance account of free relatives, capitalizing on the parallelism between free relatives and ATB questions with respect to case matching. She notes that free relatives behave differently from ATB questions with respect to the parallelism requirement, as shown in (ia–b).

(i) a. ***Who**$_i$ does Mary t_i like but t_i dislikes her?
  b. Mary dislikes **whoever**$_i$ t_i likes her.
  (Citko 1998: 79)

To explain this difference, she proposes the *Alignment Condition on ATB Merge*, given in (ii). This condition allows C in ATB questions to only merge with TPs that are symmetric in the relevant sense.

(ii) *Alignment Condition on ATB Merge*
  Only symmetric objects can undergo ATB Merge operation.
  (Citko 1998: 80)

This condition faces an issue similar to the one faced by Kasai's proposal (and others discussed in this section); unlike the proposal we advance in this monograph, it is construction-specific.

7. We thank Jason Merchant (pers. comm.) for raising this question.

We abstract away from the more general question of grammatical versus processing accounts of syntactic phenomena (see Hofmeister and Sag 2010; Hofmeister, Casasanto, and Sag 2012, 2013; Sprouse, Wagers, and Phillips 2012a, b, among many others, for processing versus grammatical accounts of syntactic islandhood).

8. Also, even though garden path sentences are hard to process, they are grammatical, which is generally not the intuition native speakers have upon encountering examples like (20a); there is no "I get it" moment that speakers experience once the garden path effect is resolved. We thank Eszter Ronai (pers. comm.) for pointing out this difference.

9. Anderson (1983: 12) states that "the presence of BUT suggests the presence of a new S node," which in current terms would amount to larger conjunct (CP) coordination. Franks (1995: 90) also states that the use of *but* "vastly improve[s] the construction."

10. We thank Anna Szabolcsi for bringing Valmala's paper to our attention. Valmala (2013) reports that ATB extraction from nonparallel positions in Catalan and Spanish is grammatical when the *wh*-phrase is the object of a transitive verb in one conjunct and the subject of an unaccusative or passive verb in the other, as in (ia–b).

(i) a. Quines mostres d'ADN dius que vas portar dilluns i *Catalan*
which samples of+DNA say.2SG that AUX bring Monday and
no van ser analitzades fins dijous?
not AUX be analyzed until Thursday
'Which DNA samples do you say you brought on Monday and were not analyzed until Thursday?'

b. Quines mostres d'ADN dius que et va enviar el jutge el
which samples of+DNA say.2SG that you AUX send the judge the
dimarts i van desaparèixer el dijous?
Tuesday and AUX disappear the Thursday
'Which DNA samples do you say that you sent to the judge on Tuesday and disappeared on Thursday?'
(Valmala 2013: 240)

These examples contrast with the ones in (iia–b), where the *wh*-phrase is the subject of an unergative verb.

(ii) a. ??Quines proves dius que vas trobar tu i van *Catalan*
which evidence say.2SG that AUX find you and AUX
demostrar la seva culpabilitat?
show the his guilt
'Which evidence do you say that you found and showed his guilt?'

b. ??Quines proves dius que demostraven la seva culpabilitat i vas
which evidence say.2SG that showed the his guilt and AUX
destruir tu?
destroy you
'Which evidence do you say that showed his guilt and you destroyed?'
(Valmala 2013: 240)

Valmala accounts for the contrast by proposing that the examples in (ia–b), unlike the ones in (iia–b), do not involve ATB extraction from nonparallel positions. Valmala assumes that in Catalan and Spanish, subjects generally do not raise to Spec,TP, but remain in situ. Thus, in (ia–b), which contain unaccusative verbs, the *wh*-phrase ATB-moves from the original, complement-of-the-verb position in both conjuncts, not violating the parallelism requirement on ATB extraction. In the ungrammatical (iia–b), on the other hand, the *wh*-phrase moves from the object position in the first conjunct and the Spec,vP position in the other conjunct, which is not allowed.

11. Munn (2001: 391) notes the improvement with relative clauses, based on the following contrast:

(i) a. ***Who**$_i$ $\boldsymbol{t_i}$ read the paper but [John thought $\boldsymbol{t_i}$ was biased]?
(Munn 2001: 372)

b. the man **who**$_i$ $\boldsymbol{t_i}$ read the paper and Bob said $\boldsymbol{t_i}$ understood it
(Munn 2001: 391)

He suggests that the improvement seen in (ib) might be due to the fact that it does not involve ATB extraction at all. Instead, it is coordination of CPs with a null relative pronoun in the second conjunct, as shown in (ii).

(ii) the man [$_{CP}$ **who**$_i$ t_i read the paper] and [$_{CP}$ (**who**$_i$) [$_{IP}$ Bob said t_i understood it]]
(Munn 2001: 391)

An alternative way to account for the contrast seen with extraction from nonparallel positions in questions and relative clauses builds on Deal's (2016) proposal that TPs in relative clauses (but not in nonrelative clause enrivonments) are phases, which means that relative pronouns stop in Spec,TP/the phase edge before moving on to Spec,CP. This allows for a derivation of (ib) schematized in (iii), in which ATB movement takes place from parallel positions in the two conjuncts (i.e., Spec,TP positions). We thank an anonymous reviewer for bringing Deal's proposal to our attention. While this is an intriguing possibility, we will not pursue it further as it predicts that ATB extraction from nonparallel positions in relative clauses should always be grammatical, which is not what we find.

(iii) the man [$_{CP}$ **who**$_i$ [$_{TP}$ t_i [$_{TP}$ t_i read the paper]] and [$_{TP}$ t_i [$_{TP}$ Bob said t_i understood it]]]

12. The nonparallelism that Parker focused on, however, was of a different nature; it involved the object of a preposition versus the object of a verb. His sample stimuli are given in (ia–d).

(i) a. The harsh chemicals **which** [$_{IP}$ the technician sprayed the sensitive equipment with __] and [$_{IP}$ the scientist prepared the sterile beakers with __] were manufactured in China. (+ATB, +PARALLEL)
b. The harsh chemicals **which** [$_{IP}$ the technician sprayed __] and [$_{IP}$ the scientist prepared the sterile beakers with __] were manufactured in China. (+ATB, –PARALLEL)
c. The harsh chemicals **which** [$_{IP}$ the technician sprayed the sensitive equipment with __] and **which** [$_{IP}$ the scientist prepared the sterile beakers with __] were manufactured in China. (–ATB, +PARALLEL)
d. The harsh chemicals **which** [$_{IP}$ the technician sprayed __] and **which** [$_{IP}$ the scientist prepared the sterile beakers with __] were manufactured in China. (–ATB, –PARALLEL)
(Parker 2017: 182)

13. The structure in (24b) might conceivably correspond to the string in (i), which would also be ungrammatical on the relevant reading: 'John saw Bill and Bill told a joke'.

(i) *John saw Bill and __ told a joke.

14. Sabbagh's formulation remains agnostic about the analysis of RNR, referring to the three most prominent types of analyses that have been proposed for it: deletion, movement, and multidominance.

15. The term *locative inversion* might be somewhat of a misnomer. Emonds (1976), for example, points out that inversion is not limited to locative PPs.

(i) a. More important has been the establishment of legal services.
b. Just as surprising was his love for clothes.
c. Most embarrassing of all was losing my keys.
d. No less corrupt was the ward boss.
e. Equally difficult would be a solution to Russell's paradox.
(Emonds 1976: 35)

We will nevertheless continue to use this term, following what we take to be the general consensus in the field.

16. Based on the grammaticality of (i), Moltmann (1992: 105) concludes that RNR does not require parallelism. However, the parallelism she is referring to has to do with the depth of embedding and not with the syntactic position of the shared constituent since in (i) the DP *this man* is the object/complement of the verb in both conjuncts.

(i) John saw __, and Mary said she saw __, **this man**.
(Moltmann 1992: 105)

17. We capitalize *Locative Inversion* when the term refers to a syntactic operation, and use lowercase when it refers to the construction.

18. We have encountered some variation in judgments here, with some speakers not finding a strong contrast between the ATB and RNR examples. Some of our consultants found both constructions grammatical. We hypothesize that for such speakers, ATB extraction involves a different structure, with potentially larger conjuncts (perhaps the size of CPs), which would allow the shared *wh*-phrase to be ATB-extracted from parallel Spec,CP positions (see section 5.4 for a discussion of ATB examples in English that display unexpected behavior with respect to the parallelism requirement). On the other hand, some of our consultants found both ATB and RNR examples in the text ungrammatical. The absence of contrast is expected if for these speakers, RNR involves rightward ATB extraction of the shared constituent (Postal 1974; Sabbagh 2007, among others).

19. The genitive in (40b) is the so-called genitive of negation; in Polish, it is obligatory on direct objects in negative sentences and on subjects of the negated verb *być* 'to be' (see Przepiórkowski 2000; Błaszczak 2001; Witkoś 2008a, and references therein). Croatian is different in that existential constructions most commonly take genitive subjects irrespective of whether they are negated or not (Zovko-Dinković 2011).

20. Two points are relevant here. First, following Sekerina (1997), Wiland (2009, 2016), and Slioussar (2011), among others, we assume that postverbal subjects in Slavic languages either occupy Spec,TP (with massive leftward movement of the remaining TP material) or are extraposed to a higher position (e.g., adjoined to TP). The importance of this assumption will become clear in chapter 4, where we present our analysis.

Second, a reviewer asks whether it is possible that the examples in (44) and (45) involve remnant movement of the preverbal *wh*-subject, which the "stranded" NP had already extraposed from (Franks and Progovac 1994). This is unlikely given that in (44a–b) and (45a–b) the verb follows (rather than precedes) the object and the locative PP, which is a typical word order in clauses with postverbal subjects. Also, Bošković (2005) argues against the remnant movement analysis of Left Branch Extraction on the basis that the "stranded" NP must precede postverbal adjuncts, as shown in (ia–b), contrary to what the remnant movement analysis predicts.

(i) a. Crveno je on kupio auto prije tri dana. *Serbo-Croatian*
red is he bought car before three days
'He bought a red car three days ago.'
(Bošković 2005: 11)
b. ?*Crveno je on kupio prije tri dana auto.

Chapter 4

1. We are grateful to an anonymous reviewer for bringing this to our attention and for proposing a solution that we adopt to solve this problem.

2. The one-to-one relationship between syntactic objects and the positions they occupy holds of External Merge only when it combines two objects; only in that situation does each object have a single sister and therefore occupy a single position. If External Merge were to combine more than two objects, the one-to-one relationship between objects and the positions they occupy would be lost because each object would have more than one sister and therefore occupy more than one position.

3. Following the convention established in chapter 2, we do not include labels when we list members of a set.

4. The step in (4b) is independently disallowed by our system for the same reason that Late Merge is disallowed: Merge does not create a new set^{W} (a new root).

5. Parallel Merge results in two different derivations regardless of the order in which it applies. For example, the set {M, Q} might be created before the set {B, Q}, or the two may be built simultaneously (as required in Johnson 2018).

6. The solution we propose in order to solve this problem relies heavily on the solution suggested by the reviewer who pointed out to us the problem with Internal Merge. We are very grateful to the reviewer for the comments and concrete suggestions.

7. If the goal already occupies multiple positions in the structure, the probe's search for the goal ends as soon as it accesses the position of the goal that is closest to the probe. The local search by the probe will also be important for our account of successive-cyclic movement in chapter 5.

8. *Who* also occupies the newly created position ⟨CP, C′⟩, but this one does not enter the calculation because it does not overlap with a search path from the probe C to the goal *who*. Since this is always the case with new positions created by Internal Merge, here and in the rest of the monograph we ignore this position when we discuss Internal Merge.

9. For further discussion of search paths in ATB movement configurations, see section 5.4, where we discuss the differences between successive-cyclic movement and ATB extraction.

10. The matrix Spec,CP position is not taken into consideration for evaluating BiCoM violations for reasons discussed in section 4.1.

11. We will modify the structure in (18b) in section 4.4, where we discuss different views on the position of postverbal subjects in locative inversion structures, including proposals that do not put the locative PP in Spec,TP (see Citko, Germain, and Witkoś 2018 and the references therein for relevant discussion).

12. In diagram (20b), we have omitted vPs and the CP in the last conjunct for reasons of space.

13. See Diercks 2017 for a detailed overview of locative inversion, which we draw on in this section.

14. Similar analyses, which place the postverbal subject in some right-adjoined position associated with focus, have also been proposed by Ndayiragije (1999) and Den Dikken (2006).

15. These authors propose that postverbal subjects in Slavic occupy Spec,TP positions more generally and treat locative inversion as one type of a postverbal subject construction.

16. Hoekstra and Mulder (1990) propose that in the context of locative inversion, unergative verbs become ergativized (become unaccusative) and are interpreted as copular verbs that take a small clause (with the subject in the specifier position) as their complement, just as unaccusatives do.

17. Culicover and Levine (2001: 294n11) also note that "when the verb is unaccusative and the subject is heavy, there is really no way to tell whether the subject is in situ in VP as in the LI [light

inversion] construction, or whether it has moved to the right from [Spec, IP] as in the HI [heavy inversion] construction."

18. The same would be true of RNR constructions if they involved movement of the shared constituent and if this movement proceeded through Spec,vP. If the shared object undergoes successive-cyclic movement to Spec,vP in its conjunct before it is extracted rightward from both conjuncts, it is important for our proposal that in the other conjunct, where it is the subject, the shared constituent occupies a different position.

19. Citko, Germain, and Witkoś (2018), who examine structures involving Locative and Predicate Inversion from the perspective of Chomsky's (2013, 2015) labeling algorithm, also assume that postverbal nominative subjects in these constructions remain in Spec,vP. Their argument is somewhat indirect; the main point of their paper is to show that the fronted nonnominative elements (the PP in locative inversion and the instrumental predicate in predicate inversion) do not occupy Spec,TP. This is because if they did, there would be no way to label the result of DP/PP merging with TP; there is no agreement between the two, and neither is the head. Even though this is not the route Citko, Germain, and Witkoś (2018) take, labeling would not be a problem if the nominative subject were in Spec,TP, since such a subject agrees with T.

20. Slioussar (2007, 2011) argues that in Bailyn's (2003, 2004) anaphor-binding examples, *svoj* 'self's' does not have anaphoric properties, as indicated by the fact that it can be replaced by the nonanaphoric element *sobstvennyj* 'own'. She shows that once we control for the possibility of a nonanaphoric reading of *svoj*, as in (i), the relevant examples become unacceptable (see also Germain 2017 and Pereltsvaig under review for relevant discussion).

(i) *V kvartiru$_i$ vošel svoj$_i$ xozjain. *Russian*
in apartment entered [self's owner].NOM
'The owner of the apartment entered the apartment.'
(Slioussar 2011: 2065)

21. There are also accounts that place the object in Spec,TP and extrapose the subject (e.g., Bailyn 2018 and Pereltsvaig under review; see also Antonyuk under review, where such an analysis is considered to be a possibility). Such accounts are also compatible with our proposal, as they do not take the position of the postverbal subject to be parallel to the position of the object.

22. In Slioussar's original proposal, both the movement of the remnant vP and the movement of the fronted object target the CP layer of the clause. Following Erechko (2003), we assume that these movements target specifiers of a lower projection associated with topics.

23. We thank Julie Anne Legate (pers. comm.) for raising the question of A-movement (see also Goodall 1987, Moltmann 1992, Kasai 2004, and the references therein for discussion).

Another relevant question is whether head movement is subject to BiCoM. Given that the status of head movement (as syntactic versus PF movement) is far from being settled, we do not discuss it here. If it is syntactic, it should be subject to BiCoM. Implicit in our discussion of ATB extraction is the assumption that the auxiliary moves from the T position in each conjunct to a shared C position above the coordination. This movement proceeds from parallel positions and as a result does not violate BiCoM (we discuss grammatical examples of ATB extraction in chapter 5). To examine head movement in relation to BiCoM, we would need to find examples where head movement violates BiCoM. These would have to involve two identical heads (e.g., an auxiliary or a negative head) that occupy different positions in the two conjuncts and are being extracted to a position higher than the coordination. This means that one would have to occupy a higher head and one a lower head (e.g., T and Aux/v). But in such a configuration, the head occupying the lower position would necessarily also violate the Head Movement Constraint (e.g., the auxiliary would move to C without stopping in T).

24. Two observations are in order here. First, examples of this kind were used to argue for the VP-Internal Subject Hypothesis (Burton and Grimshaw 1992; McNally 1992). The alternative in (i), without the vP-internal trace in the first conjunct, would violate the Coordinate Structure Constraint.

(i) $[_{TP}$ **John**$_i$ $[_{\&P}$ [read a book] and [was impressed $\boldsymbol{t}_i$ by it]]].

Second, if coordination were at the vP level instead, the passive auxiliary in the second conjunct would have to remain in v. This is problematic in light of (ii), where negation indicates that the auxiliary has moved to T.

(ii) John read a book but wasn't impressed by it.

This is not an issue if coordination is at the T′ level instead.

25. For Kasai, the exceptional behavior of ATB A-movement with respect to the parallelism requirement follows from the fact that nontransitive predicates provide intermediate landing sites for A-movement. This allows the subject of the passive predicate in the second conjunct to be ATB-extracted from Spec,vP, which is the position the subject of the transitive predicate in the first conjunct is also extracted from.

26. The underlined check marks in (38a–b) indicate possible reconstruction sites, and the underlined asterisks impossible ones.

Chapter 5

1. Recall from chapter 4 that the last position of *who*, defined as the path ⟨CP, C′⟩, does not count for the purposes of BiCoM because it does not overlap with a search path initiated by C.

2. The subscripts on the verbs indicate the cases that these verbs assign.

3. Unlike ATB constructions, RNR constructions improve when the shared element satisfies *only* the case requirements of the verb in the second conjunct (Citko 2011b). For example, (9a–b) improve when the shared element is dative, since the verb in the second conjunct assigns dative case.

4. For the purposes of syncretism, nodes count as "the same" if they have the same label. This raises the question of what information is contained in a label, brought to our attention by Erik Zyman. We remain somewhat agnostic on this question. What matters here is that the categorial features of the two last members of each path are identical, and we take it to be pretty uncontroversial that labels contain categorial features. We do not assume that labels contain all the features of the head, so as to allow, for example, the specifier of an unergative verb to be syncretic with the specifier of a transitive verb (and vice versa).

5. An interesting question, which we already touched upon in section 4.4 and which is somewhat tangential here since it does not arise for ATB extraction from parallel positions, is whether the intermediate Spec,vP position that the moving *wh*-object occupies is syncretic with the thematic position of the subject. According to the definition of syncretic positions we propose, in this particular case they are not: the last two elements in the path defining the position of the *wh*-object are ⟨vP, v′⟩, whereas the last two elements in the path defining the position of the subject are ⟨v′, v′⟩. In Bare Phrase Structure, however, the two *are* syncretic: both occupy a position defined by the path whose last two members are ⟨v, v⟩.

6. We thank anonymous reviewers for raising this question and motivating us to be explicit about it.

7. For reasons of space (and the limitations of our own expertise), we do not attempt to do justice to the vast literature on morphological syncretism and other approaches to it (for more general reviews of research on this topic, see Albright and Fuß 2012, Caha 2019, and the references therein). These include approaches that rely on rules of referral (rules stating that some combinations of features have the same realizations as others; Zwicky 1985b; Stump 1993) or on the interaction of Optimality Theory constraints (Müller 2011).

8. Jakobson's focus is on Russian.

For Jakobson, these features are semantically grounded in ways that are not directly relevant here. For details, see Jakobson 1958 or Franks 1995.

9. Many researchers have pointed out issues with Jakobson's system. For example, it does not capture genitive/accusative syncretism: the feature [−marg] also includes the nominative case (see Neidle 1988; McCreight and Chvany 1991; Franks 1995, among others, for alternative feature decompositions that do not face these issues).

10. This would be an instance of accidental homophony. Albright and Fuß (2012) give a number of diagnostics to distinguish true syncretism from accidental homophony. These include systematicity, syntactic relevance, and psycholinguistic effects. Albright and Fuß illustrate the difference between the two with the German suffix *-en*, which has syncretic 3sg/2pl and 1pl/3pl forms. However, only the 1pl/3pl syncretism is true syncretism. It differs from 3sg/2pl syncretism in that it resolves agreement mismatches. For example:

(i) a. Entweder wir oder sie gewinnen. *German*
either we or they win.1PL/3PL
'Either we or they will win.'
b. Entweder er oder ihr *?gewinnt.
either he or you.PL win.3SG/2PL
'Either he or you will win.'
(Albright and Fuß 2012: 243)

11. This is the so-called *case-matching requirement*, well-known from the literature on free relatives (see Bresnan and Grimshaw 1978; Groos and Van Riemsdijk 1981 and subsequent work).

12. Williams's illustration comes from Latin nominal declension systems, where plural dative and ablative forms are syncretic (see also Harley 2008: 253–255 for relevant data).

13. As Harley (2008) points out, in feature-geometric representations impoverishment can be thought of as a delinking operation (see also Harley 1994). If we were to pursue this analogy and analyze syntactic syncretism as impoverishment and impoverishment as delinking, we could think of one of the syncretic positions/paths in a syntactically syncretic ATB structure as getting deleted/delinked in one of the conjuncts. We choose not to pursue this kind of reasoning because such a delinking operation would delete from the conjunct not only a syntactic position, but also the syntactic object that occupies it, without replacing it with a copy/trace. This would lead to a violation of the Projection Principle (Chomsky 1981).

14. The problem with impoverishment rules that Asarina points out is that they cannot handle the syncretism exhibited by the verb *be*. The fact that it shows no person distinctions in the plural (with all persons being realized as *are* or *were*) suggests an impoverishment rule that would simply

delete person features in the plural. This, however, would not account for singular/plural syncretism in the second person.

15. Recall also our discussion of ternary Merge in chapter 4.

16. This is how we explained why simple (non-successive-cyclic) cases of movement do not violate BiCoM.

17. We draw on Kayne 1981, 1984 and Pesetsky 1982 in making use of paths and path containment. See also Gračanin-Yuksek 2013 for a similar way to compare paths.

18. This might be a bit of an oversimplification; in order for the lengths of multiple available search paths to be compared to one another, the length of each should presumably be known. However, as soon as the paths are compared, only the shortest one, if such exists, matters.

19. Perhaps the easiest way to achieve this is to assume that coordination is symmetric (Gazdar 1981; Goodall 1987; Borsley 2005; Chaves 2012; see Progovac 1998 for a comprehensive overview of symmetric versus asymmetric approaches, and Zoerner 1995 or Johannessen 1998 for representative asymmetric approaches). We do not pursue this possibility here, although we note that our system, which normally does not allow ternary branching because ternary branching violates BiCoM, would allow symmetric coordination. This is because in a structure like (i), two of the three positions that Merge relates to one another are syncretic. The reasoning goes as follows. Since each terminal node in (i) has two sisters, each occupies two positions, defined in terms of paths from the root to each of its sisters. This yields the set of positions {⟨&P, &⟩, ⟨&P, TP$_2$⟩, ⟨&P, TP$_1$⟩, ⟨&P, TP$_2$⟩, ⟨&P, &⟩, ⟨&P, TP$_1$⟩}, which is equivalent to the set {⟨&P, &⟩, ⟨&P, TP$_2$⟩, ⟨&P, TP$_1$⟩}. Crucially, two of these positions—the position occupied by TP$_1$ and the position occupied by TP$_2$—are syncretic, since the last two members of the paths defining these positions have identical labels. Thus, Merge is allowed to relate these two syncretic positions to a third one (the position of the conjunction). This would also derive the Law of the Coordination of Likes (Williams 1981), since the positions of the two conjuncts are syncretic only if they have the same labels, that is, if they are of the same category.

(i)

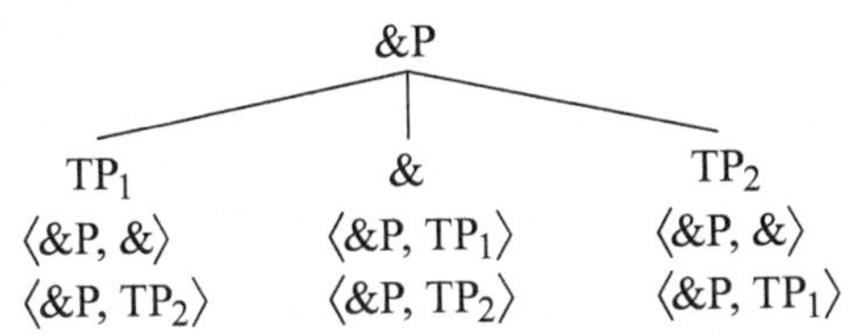

20. In asymmetric coordination, the first conjunct asymmetrically c-commands the second one, but this does not make the search path to the shared goal in the first conjunct shorter than the search path in the second conjunct because neither search path contains the other. We thank David Pesetsky for encouraging us to be explicit about this issue.

21. An alternative way to capture the effects of locality on BiCoM violations is to follow the advice of an anonymous reviewer and build a locality condition into BiCoM itself, as in (i).

(i) *Binarity Constraint on Merge (alternative version, not adopted here)*
Merge cannot relate more than two positions at a time within a single derivation, where the position(s) of a syntactic object SO that Merge applies to must overlap with a shortest search path for SO if there is a search path for SO.

While this is an appealing way to account for the interaction between BiCoM and locality, we would also like to preserve the intuition that locality is a pervasive property of the computational system and is in no way specific to BiCoM. This is why we believe that the reference to shortest path should, in fact, not be part of BiCoM.

22. The translation in example (47b) differs from Valmala's paper. We thank Vidal Valmala (pers. comm.) for providing us with the correct gloss and translation.

23. See also the discussion of A-movement in section 4.5.

24. See also Johnson 2018, where alternative paths from the root to the multiply-dominated constituent are used to derive overt and covert movement.

Larson (2016: 9n3) suggests that a multidominance account of displacement is incompatible with the theory of phases because once a multiply-dominated syntactic item has been spelled out in one position, it stands to reason that it has been spelled out in all positions. However, if Spell-Out is viewed as an operation that severs paths leading from the root of the tree to the sister of syntactic objects contained within the Spell-Out domain, then it only renders inaccessible those syntactic objects that do not have an alternative path available to them, a desired outcome. This implementation of Spell-Out also addresses another concern voiced by Larson (2016): that on the multidominance view of displacement, Merge does not target syntactic objects. If it did, Larson argues, by targeting a syntactic object that occupies an accessible and an inaccessible position, Merge would necessarily target an inaccessible syntactic object. Under our proposal, syntactic objects are accessible or inaccessible (to Merge or other syntactic operations) insofar as the positions that they occupy are accessible or inaccessible. The fact that a syntactic object occupies a position within a domain that is for one reason or another inaccessible to the operations outside of that domain does not make this syntactic object itself inaccessible; what becomes inaccessible is that particular position. We thus believe that the multidominance view of movement, which we have been assuming throughout this monograph, is not incompatible with Merge conceived of as an operation that targets syntactic objects.

25. The fact that all of these positions are specifiers is not sufficient, either. If it were (and if Spec,vP and Spec,TP positions counted as syncretic), ATB extraction in which the extracted shared element occupies Spec,vP in one conjunct and Spec,TP in the other one would be possible, which is not what we find.

26. This was brought to our attention independently by Stefan Keine and Gereon Müller (pers. comm.).

Müller and Sternefeld's original formulation of this principle is given in (i).

(i) *Principle of Unambiguous Binding*
A variable that is α-bound must be β-free in the domain of the head of its chain (where α and β refer to different types of positions).
(Müller and Sternefeld 1993: 461)

27. Müller and Sternefeld limit the domain of the Principle of Unambiguous Binding to Ā-dependencies. One of the many phenomena they examine is the interaction of *wh*-movement and scrambling in German and Russian. The contrast between the ungrammatical examples of scrambling in (ia–b) and the grammatical examples of *wh*-movement in (ic–d) shows that German scrambling, unlike *wh*-movement, is clause-bound.

(i) a. * . . . daß niemand $[_{VP}$ **Pudding**$_i$ $[_{VP}$ sagt $[_{CP}$ t_i' daß sie t_i mag]]]. *German*
that nobody pudding says that she likes
'that nobody says that she likes pudding.'

b. * . . . daß $[_{IP}$ **Pudding**$_i$ $[_{IP}$ niemand sagt $[_{CP}$ t_i' daß sie t_i mag]]].
that pudding nobody says that she likes

c. **Was**$_i$ sagt niemand $[_{CP}$ t_i' daß sie t_i mag]?
what says nobody that she likes

d. **Welchen Pudding**$_i$ sagt niemand $[_{CP}$ t_i' würde sie t_i mögen]?
which pudding says nobody would she like
(Müller and Sternefeld 1993: 465)

This contrast shows that *wh*-movement cannot feed scrambling; if scrambling could proceed through Spec,CP, the examples in (ia–b) should be grammatical. Müller and Sternefeld assume that scrambling in German is Ā-movement and targets adjoined VP or IP positions. The fact that scrambling is Ā-movement makes traces left by scrambling subject to the Principle of Unambiguous Binding: in the ungrammatical examples (ia–b), traces are ambiguously bound (from the VP/IP-adjoined positions and the Spec,CP positions). Russian scrambling, which Müller and Sternefeld also discuss, exhibits the opposite behavior: *wh*-movement is clause-bound (except for movement from subjunctive clauses), whereas scrambling is not. However, the two types of movement interact in the same way in the two types of languages: just as *wh*-movement cannot feed scrambling in German, scrambling cannot feed *wh*-movement in Russian. Müller and Sternefeld capture the difference between Russian and German by allowing scrambled constituents in Russian to adjoin to CP.

28. The derivations are simplified in that they do not include traces in Spec,vP positions. If movement proceeds through Spec,vP, as phase theory dictates, Spec,vP and Spec,CP positions would have to count as the same for the purposes of unambiguous binding.

29. In our system, deriving improper movement from BiCoM would also not be possible for the following reason: in successive-cyclic movement configurations, Merge always accesses only the highest position of the goal probed by the c-commanding probe, so it doesn't matter whether this position of the goal is syncretic with its lower positions or not.

Chapter 6

1. The examples in (7a) and (8a) are the unembedded versions of Goodall's examples in (7b) and (8b). Goodall (1987: 77) also discusses examples like (i), analogous to our (5b), reporting that the contrast between such examples and the ones involving extraction from parallel embedded positions ((7b) and (8b) in the main text) is "not strong, but many speakers find the [sentence in (i) is] worse than those in [(7b)] and [(8b)]."

(i) ?This is the kind of movie **which**$_i$ Tom thinks Americans like t_i and Bill thinks t_i frightens Canadians.
(Goodall 1987: 76)

2. However, as we will show in section 6.1.3, embedding the subject gap instead improves the example.

3. Citko (2000: 48) also discusses asymmetric embedding examples of this kind (i.e., *What will John buy and Mary think Sam should read?*). In her analysis, the *wh*-pronoun moves to Spec,CP in

the second conjunct and only at this point parallel-merges with the verb of the first conjunct. Her analysis is couched in the system that allows Parallel Merge but does not treat movement as Internal Merge/multidominance. Recast in our current system, this proposal would involve Internal Merge followed by Parallel Merge, with both applying to the same object (the *wh*-pronoun). Such a configuration would not violate BiCoM since Parallel Merge initiates a new derivation and relates the position of the shared *wh*-pronoun with a single other position (the position of the verb) in this new derivation.

4. Here, we explain the judgments of speakers who find (15b) ungrammatical. This is the judgment reported by George (1980), Goodall (1987), and Pesetsky (1982), among others.

(i) a. *John, **who**$_i$ Bill thinks $\boldsymbol{t_i}$ will win and $\boldsymbol{t_i}$ likes Mary, . . .
(Pesetsky 1982: 457)
b. *?This is the man **who**$_i$ $\boldsymbol{t_i}$ saw John and Mary thinks $\boldsymbol{t_i}$ is handsome.
(Goodall 1987: 69)
c. *Here is the prisoner **who**$_i$ $\boldsymbol{t_i}$ ratted on the punk and Foley said $\boldsymbol{t_i}$ was torched.
(George 1980: 157)

However, some speakers we consulted found examples involving such configurations to be well-formed. Relative clauses involving this configuration are also reported as grammatical by Munn (2001) (also cited in Hartmann, Konietzko, and Salzmann 2016); see (ii). We turn to these judgments in section 6.2.

(ii) the man **who**$_i$ $\boldsymbol{t_i}$ read the paper and Bob said $\boldsymbol{t_i}$ understood it
(Munn 2001: 391)

5. Since the subject does not move, the term *Vacuous Movement Hypothesis* is a bit of a misnomer, as pointed out to us by a reviewer.

6. A possible problem for the analysis in (17) concerns the linearization of the structure. As we noted in section 4.5, on most algorithms proposed for the linearization of multidominant structures, the shared constituent can only be linearized in a position where it follows all the nonshared material. In (17), by contrast, it would have to be linearized preceding the nonshared material.

7. This movement of the object is followed by V-to-v movement, which restores the original verb –object word order.

8. We thank Benjamin Bruening (pers. comm.) for bringing these facts to our attention.

9. As brought to our attention by a reviewer, there might be some variation in judgments here. The reviewer finds example (33b) degraded, although not ungrammatical. For our purposes, it is important that (33b) is better than (33a).

10. The representation in (36b) is somewhat simplified and will be modified in the course of this chapter.

11. See Pesetsky 2017 for a general overview of existing approaches to the *that*-trace effect, and more generally to complementizer-trace effects.

12. The lexical complementizer *that*, in its derived position (the higher C), agrees with the *wh*-subject in its specifier; and although *that* cannot itself be coindexed with the subject (which is why the *that*-trace effect obtains in the first place), it can transfer the index to its trace in the lower C position, which can then properly govern the trace of the subject *wh*-phrase.

13. Other proposals rely on the same intuition. Rizzi (1997), using the expanded left periphery of the clause, argues that the overt complementizer *that* occupies the highest functional head (the Force head), while the null complementizer occupies the lowest head (the Finiteness (Fin) head) (see also Douglas 2017). He proposes that in the absence of an adverbial, the left periphery is collapsed into a single head—either Force or Fin, depending on whether the complementizer is overt or covert. Rizzi (1997) explains the *that*-trace effect in (37a) by appealing to the analysis in Rizzi 1990: the null complementizer agrees with the subject and thus properly governs its trace after the subject moves, whereas the overt complementizer *that* does not. When the adverbial is present, it occupies the specifier of the intermediate Topic head; consequently, the structure is expanded, with both Force and Fin heads necessarily present. Thus, the presence of the null complementizer in (37b) makes the subject trace properly governed.

Following Pesetsky (1982), Sobin (2002) proposes that both embedded and matrix clauses "prefer" to realize as few positions as possible in the CP layer. One example of this is the prohibition on doubly filled Comp. Sobin proposes to derive this "thinning" effect on the CP layer by the operation *Fuse*, which, among other things, requires a trace in Spec,CP to collapse with C if neither is overt. Since in *that*-trace configurations the complementizer is overt, the trace in Spec,CP fails to fuse with it, leading to ungrammaticality. For Sobin, the presence of an adverbial has an alleviating effect because the adverbial adjoins to the C head, forming a complex complementizer (Carnie 2000). Since this new C involves adjunction of a phrase to a head, the system cannot interpret it as containing true lexical material and regards it instead as phonetically null. As a result, the complex C can fuse with the trace in Spec,CP, and the sentence ends up being grammatical. We remain agnostic as to which analysis outlined here is correct for the *that*-trace effect.

14. See, however, Rizzi and Shlonsky's (2007) proposal that the adverbial is situated in the specifier of ModP, which is higher than the IP field but lower than the CP field.

15. A reviewer notes that our analysis predicts that the addition of an adverbial to the right of the main clause should also alleviate a BiCoM violation. The reviewer offers (i) as a relevant example, finding it improved relative to the variant without the adverbial. We thank the reviewer for the comment and the example.

(i) She is someone that cooking amuses, and hates jogging, according to her personal trainer.

16. Extraction of the shared *wh*-phrase from such coordination also violates BiCoM because the *wh*-phrase occupies nonsyncretic positions in the two conjuncts: Spec,vP in the first conjunct and Spec,CP in the second conjunct.

17. One might wonder whether it is possible for the complementizers that introduce individual conjuncts in this configuration to be overt. The answer seems to be no. Such a possibility would yield (ia) or, if we inverted the two conjuncts, (ib). In both (ia) and (ib), the sequence of two overt complementizers is excluded, probably due to some form of haplology.

(i) a. *She is someone $\mathbf{OP}_i$ that [that cooking amuses t_i] and [that t_i hates jogging].
b. *She is someone $\mathbf{OP}_i$ that [that t_i hates jogging] and [that cooking amuses t_i].

Examples (ia–b) become grammatical if both conjuncts are introduced by an overt complementizer without CP recursion, as in (iia), suggested to us by a reviewer (who finds it perfect). As the reviewer suggests, the grammaticality of (iia) supports the argument that ATB extraction from syncretic Spec,CP positions is grammatical. Note that (iia) cannot involve the structure in (iib) because in (iib) a CP introduced by a null complementizer is coordinated with a CP introduced by an overt *that*, which we have concluded is not allowed.

(ii) a. She is someone that cooking amuses and that hates jogging.
b. She is someone that [$_{CP}$ C$_{\varnothing}$ cooking amuses] and [$_{CP}$ that hates jogging].

18. In (51) and (52b), we place the adverbial in Spec,CP of the second conjunct and allow for multiple CP specifiers in order to also accommodate the moving *wh*-subject. This is not the only possibility, however. We could, for example, assume an articulated CP, so that the adverbial is placed in the specifier of the functional projection that is above the position of the null complementizer (such as Rizzi's [2004] ModP), but below the position the *wh*-phrase moves through before it is ATB-extracted. In that case, the first conjunct would also minimally have to contain the head that hosts the null complementizer and the head through whose specifier the *wh*-phrase moves.

References

Adger, David. 2017. A memory architecture for Merge. Ms., Queen Mary University of London. Downloadable at lingbuzz/003440.

Agbayani, Brian. 2006. Pied-piping, feature movement, and *wh*-subjects. In Wh-*movement: Moving on*, ed. by Lisa Cheng and Norbert Corver, 71–93. Cambridge, MA: MIT Press.

Albright, Adam, and Eric Fuß. 2012. Syncretism. In *The morphology and phonology of exponence*, ed. by Jochen Trommer, 236–288. Oxford: Oxford University Press.

Anderson, Carol. 1983. Generating coordinate structures with asymmetric gaps. In *CLS 19: Papers from the 19th Regional Meeting*, ed. by Amy Chukerman, Mitchell Marks, and John F. Richardson 3–14. Chicago: University of Chicago, Chicago Linguistic Society.

Antonyuk, Svitlana. 2015. Quantifier scope and scope freezing in Russian. PhD dissertation, Stony Brook University.

Antonyuk, Svitlana. Under review. On the syntax of discourse-driven movements: The realization of givenness and focus in OV(PP)S word orders in East Slavic. In *Formal Approaches to Slavic Linguistics: The Second Stony Brook Meeting* 2019, ed. by Andrei Antonenko, John Bailyn, and Anna Melnikova.

Asarina, Alevtina (Alya). 2011. Case in Uyghur and beyond. PhD dissertation, MIT.

Asarina, Alya. 2013. Neutrality vs. ambiguity in resolution by syncretism: Experimental evidence and consequences. In *NELS 41: Proceedings of the forty-first annual meeting of the North East Linguistic Society* , ed. by Yelena Fainleib, Nicholas LaCara, and Yangsook Park, 43–56. Amherst: University of Massachusetts, Graduate Linguistic Student Association.

Babyonyshev, Maria. 1996. Structural connections in syntax and processing: Studies in Russian and Japanese. PhD dissertation, MIT.

Bachrach, Asaf, and Roni Katzir. 2009. Right Node Raising and delayed Spell-Out. In *InterPhases: Phase-theoretic investigations of linguistic interfaces*, ed. by Kleanthes Grohmann, 283–316. Oxford: Oxford University Press.

Bachrach, Asaf, and Roni Katzir. 2017. Linearizing structures. *Syntax* 20: 1–40.

Bailyn, John. 2003. A (purely) derivational account of Russian scrambling. In *Formal Approaches to Slavic Linguistics 11: The Amherst Meeting 2002*, ed. by Wayles Browne, Ji-Yung Kim, Barbara H. Partee, and Robert A. Rothstein, 41–62. Ann Arbor, MI: Michigan Slavic Publications.

Bailyn, John. 2004. Generalized inversion. *Natural Language and Linguistic Theory* 22: 1–50.

Barros, Matthew, and Luis Vicente. 2011. Right Node Raising requires both ellipsis and multidomination. In *Proceedings of the 34th Annual Penn Linguistics Colloquium*, ed. by Lauren Friedman, 1–9. University of Pennsylvania Working Papers in Linguistics 17(1). http://repository.upenn.edu/pwpl/vol17/iss1/2.

Belder, Marijke De, and Jeroen van Craenenbroeck. 2015. How to merge a root. *Linguistic Inquiry* 46: 625–655.

Belletti, Adriana. 1999. "Inversion" as focalization and related questions. *Catalan Working Papers in Linguistics* 7: 9–45.

Belletti, Adriana. 2001. "Inversion" as focalization. In *Inversion in Romance and the theory of Universal Grammar*, ed. by Aafke C. J. Hulk and Jean-Yves Pollock, 60–90. Oxford: Oxford University Press.

Belletti, Adriana. 2004. Aspects of the low IP area. In *The structure of IP and CP: The cartography of syntactic structures (Vol. 2)*, ed. by Luigi Rizzi, 16–52. Oxford: Oxford University Press.

Bhatt, Rajesh, and Shoichi Takahashi. 2011. Reduced and unreduced phrasal comparatives. *Natural Language and Linguistic Theory* 29: 581–620.

Bjorkman, Bronwyn. 2013. A syntactic answer to a pragmatic puzzle: The case of asymmetric *and*. In *Syntax and its limits*, ed. by Raffaella Folli, Christina Sevdali, and Robert Truswell, 391–408. Oxford: Oxford University Press.

Bjorkman, Bronwyn. 2016. Go get, come see. *Natural Language and Linguistic Theory* 34: 53–91.

Błaszczak, Joanna. 2001. *Covert movement and the genitive of negation in Polish.* Potsdam: Universitätsbibliothek.

Blevins, James P. 1990. Syntactic complexity: Evidence for discontinuity and multidomination. PhD dissertation, University of Massachusetts, Amherst.

Bobaljik, Jonathan David. 1995. In terms of Merge: Copy and head-movement. In *Papers on Minimalist syntax*, ed. by Rob Pensalfini and Hiroyuki Ura, 41–64. MIT Working Papers in Linguistics 27. Cambridge, MA: MIT, MIT Working Papers in Linguistics.

Bobaljik, Jonathan David. 2002. Syncretism without paradigms: Remarks on Williams 1981, 1994. In *Yearbook of morphology 2001*, ed. by Geert Booij and Jaap van Marle, 53–85. Dordrecht: Foris.

Boeckx, Cedric, Norbert Hornstein, and Jairo Nunes. 2010. *Control as movement.* Cambridge: Cambridge University Press.

Boeckx, Cedric, and Norbert Hornstein. 2006. The virtues of control as movement. *Syntax* 9: 118–130.

Bondaruk, Anna. 2013. *Copular clauses in English and Polish: Structure, derivation and interpretation.* Lublin: Wydawnictwo KUL.

Borsley, Robert D. 1983. A note on the Generalized Left Branch Condition. *Linguistic Inquiry* 14: 169–174.

Borsley, Robert D. 2005. Against ConjP. *Lingua* 4: 461–482.

Bošković, Željko. 1996. Selection and the categorial status of infinitival complements. *Natural Language and Linguistic Theory* 14: 269–304.

Bošković, Željko. 2005. On the locality of left branch extraction and the structure of NP. *Studia Linguistica* 59: 1–45.

Bresnan, Joan. 1977. Variables in the theory of transformations. In *Formal syntax*, ed. by Peter W. Culicover, Thomas Wasow, and Adrian Akmajian, 157–196. New York: Academic Press.

Bresnan, Joan. 1994. Locative inversion and the architecture of Universal Grammar. *Language* 70: 72–131.

Bresnan, Joan, and Jane Grimshaw. 1978. The syntax of free relatives. *Linguistic Inquiry* 9: 331–391.

Browning, Marguerite Ann. 1996. CP recursion and *that-t* effects. *Linguistic Inquiry* 27: 237–255.

Bruening, Benjamin. 2010. Language-particular syntactic rules and constraints: English locative inversion and *do*-support. *Language* 86: 43–84.

Burton, Strang, and Jane Grimshaw. 1992. Coordination and VP-internal subjects. *Linguistic Inquiry* 23: 305–313.

Caha, Pavel. 2019. Syncretism in morphology. In *Oxford research encyclopedia of linguistics* https://oxfordre.com/linguistics/view/10.1093/acrefore/9780199384655.001.0001/acrefore-9780199384655-e-552. (Accessed November 12, 2019.)

Calabrese, Andrea. 2011. Investigations on markedness, syncretism, and zero exponence in morphology. *Morphology* 21: 283–325.

Carnie, Andrew. 2000. On the definition of X^0 and XP. *Syntax* 3: 59–106.

Carnie, Andrew. 2008. *Constituent structure*. Oxford: Oxford University Press.

Chaves, Rui P. 2012. On the grammar of extraction and coordination. *Natural Language and Linguistic Theory* 30: 465–512.

Chomsky, Noam. 1981. *Lectures on government and binding: The Pisa lectures*. Dordrecht: Foris.

Chomsky, Noam. 1986. *Knowledge of language: Its nature, origin, and use*. New York: Praeger.

Chomsky, Noam. 1991. Some notes on economy of derivation and representation. In *Principles and parameters in comparative grammar*, ed. by Robert Freidin, 417–454. Cambridge, MA: MIT Press.

Chomsky, Noam. 1993. A Minimalist program for linguistic theory. In *The view from Building 20: Essays in linguistics in honor of Sylvain Bromberger*, ed. by Kenneth Hale and Samuel Jay Keyser, 1–52. Cambridge, MA: MIT Press.

Chomsky, Noam. 1994. Bare Phrase Structure. MIT Occasional Papers in Linguistics 5. Cambridge, MA: MIT, MIT Working Papers in Linguistics.

Chomsky, Noam. 1995. *The Minimalist Program*. Cambridge, MA: MIT Press.

Chomsky, Noam. 2000. Minimalist inquiries: The framework. In *Step by step: Essays on Minimalist syntax in honor of Howard Lasnik*, ed. by Roger Martin, David Michaels, and Juan Uriagereka, 89–155. Cambridge, MA: MIT Press.

Chomsky, Noam. 2001. Derivation by phase. In *Ken Hale: A life in language*, ed. by Michael Kenstowicz, 1–52. Cambridge, MA: MIT Press.

Chomsky, Noam. 2004. Beyond explanatory adequacy. In *Structures and beyond: The cartography of syntactic structures (Vol. 3)*, ed. by Adriana Belletti, 104–131. Oxford: Oxford University Press.

Chomsky, Noam. 2007. Approaching UG from below. In *Interfaces + recursion = language?*, ed. by Uli Sauerland and Hans-Martin Gärtner, 1–30. Berlin: Mouton de Gruyter.

Chomsky, Noam. 2008. On phases. In *Foundational issues in linguistic theory*, ed. by Robert Freidin, Carlos P. Otero, and Maria Luisa Zubizarreta, 133–166. Cambridge, MA: MIT Press.

Chomsky, Noam. 2013. Problems of projection. *Lingua* 130: 33–49.

Chomsky, Noam. 2015. Problems of projection: Extensions. In *Structures, strategies and beyond: Studies in honour of Adriana Belletti*, ed. by Elisa di Domenico, Cornelia Hamann, and Simona Matteini, 1–16. Amsterdam: John Benjamins.

Chomsky, Noam. 2019. Some puzzling foundational issues: The Reading program. *Catalan Journal of Linguistics* Special issue: 263–285.

Citko, Barbara. 1998. An ATB analysis of free relative clauses. In *CLS 34: The Main Session*, ed. by M. Catherine Gruber, Derrick Higgins, Kenneth S. Olson, and Tamra Wysocki, 1:69–81. Chicago: University of Chicago, Chicago Linguistic Society.

Citko, Barbara. 2000. Parallel Merge and the syntax of free relatives. PhD dissertation, Stony Brook University.

Citko, Barbara. 2003. ATB *wh*-movement and the nature of Merge. In *NELS 33: Proceedings of the thirty-third annual meeting of the North East Linguistic Society*, ed. by Makoto Kadowaki and Shigeto Kawahara, 87–102. Amherst: University of Massachusetts, Graduate Linguistic Student Association.

Citko, Barbara. 2005. On the nature of Merge: External Merge, Internal Merge, and Parallel Merge. *Linguistic Inquiry* 36: 475–496.

Citko, Barbara. 2008. Missing labels. *Lingua* 118: 907–944.

Citko, Barbara. 2011a. Multidominance. In *The Oxford handbook of linguistic Minimalism*, ed. by Cedric Boeckx, 119–142. Oxford: Oxford University Press.

Citko, Barbara. 2011b. *Symmetry in syntax: Merge, Move, and labels*. Cambridge: Cambridge University Press.

Citko, Barbara. 2017. Right Node Raising. In *The Wiley Blackwell companion to syntax*, ed. by Martin Everaert and Henk C. van Riemsdijk, 3839–3871. 2nd ed. Hoboken, NJ: John Wiley.

Citko, Barbara, Allison Germain, and Jacek Witkoś. 2018. If you cannot agree, move on! On labels and nonnominative subjects. *Glossa* 3(1): 28, 1–46.

Citko, Barbara, and Martina Gračanin-Yuksek. 2013. Towards a new typology of coordinated *wh*-questions. *Journal of Linguistics* 49: 1–32.

Citko, Barbara, and Martina Gračanin-Yuksek. 2016. Multiple (coordinated) (free) relatives. *Natural Language and Linguistic Theory* 42: 393–427.

Collins, Chris. 1997. *Local economy*. Cambridge, MA: MIT Press.

Collins, Chris. 2002. Eliminating labels. In *Derivation and explanation in the Minimalist Program*, ed. by Samuel David Epstein and T. Daniel Seely, 42–64. Malden, MA: Blackwell.

Collins, Chris, and Edward Stabler. 2016. A formalization of Minimalist syntax. *Syntax* 19: 43–78.

Coopmans, Peter. 1989. Where stylistic and syntactic processes meet: Locative inversion in English. *Language* 65: 728–751.

Culicover, Peter W. 1993a. The adverb effect: Evidence against ECP accounts of the *that-t* effect. In *NELS 23: Proceedings of the twenty-third annual meeting of the North East Linguistic Society*, ed. by Amy J. Schafer, 97–111. Amherst: University of Massachusetts, Graduate Linguistic Student Association.

Culicover, Peter W. 1993b. Evidence against ECP accounts of the *that-t* effect. *Linguistic Inquiry* 24: 557–561.

Culicover, Peter W., and Robert D. Levine. 2001. Stylistic inversion in English: A reconsideration. *Natural Language and Linguistic Theory* 19: 283–310.

Deal, Amy Rose. 2016. Cyclicity and connectivity in Nez Perce relative clauses. *Linguistic Inquiry* 47: 427–470.

Diercks, Michael. 2010. Agreement with subjects in Lubukusu. PhD dissertation, Georgetown University.

Diercks, Michael. 2011. The morphosyntax of Lubukusu locative inversion and the parameterization of Agree. *Lingua* 121: 702–720.

Diercks, Michael. 2017. Locative inversion. In *The Wiley Blackwell companion to syntax*, ed. by Martin Everaert and Henk C. van Riemsdijk, 2201–2230. 2nd ed. Hoboken, NJ: John Wiley.

Dikken, Marcel den. 2006. *Relators and linkers: The syntax of predication, predicate inversion, and the copula*. Cambridge, MA: MIT Press.

Doggett, Teal Bissell. 2004. All things being unequal: Locality in movement. PhD dissertation, MIT.

Douglas, Jamie. 2017. Unifying the *that*-trace and anti-*that*-trace effects. *Glossa* 2(1): 60, 1–28.

Dyła, Stefan. 1984. Across-the-board dependencies and case in Polish. *Linguistic Inquiry* 15: 701–705.

Emonds, Joseph E. 1976. *A transformational approach to syntax: Root, structure preserving, and local transformations*. New York: Academic Press.

Engdahl, Elisabet. 1980. The syntax and semantics of questions in Swedish. PhD dissertation, University of Massachusetts, Amherst.

Erechko, Anna. 2003. On subject verb inversion in Russian. In *Proceedings of ConSOLE X*, ed. by Marjo van Koppen, Joanna Sio, and Mark de Vos, 1–14. Leiden: SOLE.

Fox, Danny, and David Pesetsky. 2007. Cyclic linearization of shared material. Ms., MIT.

Franks, Steven. 1995. *Parameters of Slavic morphosyntax*. New York: Oxford University Press.

Franks, Steven, and Ljiljana Progovac. 1994. On the placement of Serbo-Croatian clitics. In *Proceedings of the Biennial Conference on Balkan and South Slavic Linguistics, Literature and Folklore*, 69–78. Indiana Slavic Studies 7. Bloomington: Indiana University Linguistics Club.

Frazier, Lyn, and Janet D. Fodor. 1978. The sausage machine: A new two-stage parsing model. *Cognition* 6: 291–325.

Frazier, Lyn, Alan Munn, and Charles Clifton Jr. 2000. Processing coordinate structures. *Journal of Psycholinguistic Research* 29: 345–370.

Gärtner, Hans-Martin. 2002. *Generalized transformations and beyond: Reflections on Minimalist syntax*. Berlin: Akademie Verlag.

Gazdar, Gerald. 1981. Unbounded dependencies and coordinate structure. *Linguistic Inquiry* 12: 155–184.

George, Leland M. 1980. Analogical generalization in natural language syntax. PhD dissertation, MIT.

Germain, Allison. 2017. Non-nominative subjects in Russian and Lithuanian: Case, argument structure, and anaphor binding. PhD dissertation, University of Washington.

Glushan, Zhanna, and Andrea Calabrese. 2014. Context sensitive unaccusativity in Russian and Italian. In *WCCFL 31: Proceedings of the 31st West Coast Conference on Formal Linguistics*, ed. by Robert E. Santana-LaBarge, 207–217. Somerville, MA: Cascadilla Proceedings Project.

Goodall, Grant. 1987. *Parallel structures in syntax: Coordination, causatives, and restructuring.* Cambridge: Cambridge University Press.

Gračanin-Yuksek, Martina. 2007. About sharing. PhD dissertation, MIT.

Gračanin-Yuksek, Martina. 2013. Linearizing multidominance structures. In *Challenges to linearization*, ed. by Theresa Biberauer and Ian Roberts, 269–294. Berlin: Mouton de Gruyter.

Grimshaw, Jane. 1994. Minimal projection and clause structure. In *Heads, projections, and learnability*, ed. by Barbara Lust, Margarita Suñer, and John Whitman, 75–83. Mahwah, NJ: Lawrence Erlbaum Associates.

Grimshaw, Jane. 1997. Projection, heads, and optimality. *Linguistic Inquiry* 28: 373–422.

Groos, Anneke, and Henk van Riemsdijk. 1981. Matching effects in free relatives: A parameter of core grammar. In *Theory of markedness in generative grammar*, ed. by Adriana Belletti, Luciana Brandi, and Luigi Rizzi, 171–216. Pisa: Scuola Normale Superiore.

Halle, Morris. 1997. Distributed Morphology: Impoverishment and fission. In *Papers at the interface*, ed. by Benjamin Bruening, Yoonjung Kang, and Martha McGinnis, 425–449. MIT Working Papers in Linguistics 30. Cambridge, MA: MIT, MIT Working Papers in Linguistics.

Harley, Heidi. 1994. Hug a tree: Deriving the morphosyntactic feature hierarchy. In *Papers on phonology and morphology*, ed. by Andrew Carnie and Heidi Harley, with Tony Bures, 289–320. MIT Working Papers in Linguistics 21. Cambridge, MA: MIT, MIT Working Papers in Linguistics.

Harley, Heidi. 2008. When is a syncretism more than a syncretism? Impoverishment, metasyncretism, and underspecification. In *Phi theory*, ed. by Daniel Harbour, David Adger, and Susana Béjar, 251–294. Oxford: Oxford University Press.

Hartmann, Jutta, Andreas Konietzko, and Martin Salzmann. 2016. On the limits of non-parallelism in ATB-movement: Experimental evidence for strict syntactic identity. In *Quantitative approaches to grammar and grammatical change*, ed. by Sam Featherston and Yannick Versley, 51–83. Berlin: Mouton de Gruyter.

Harves, Stephanie. 2002. Unaccusative syntax in Russian. PhD dissertation, Princeton University.

Higginbotham, James. 1985. A note on phrase markers. In *Papers in theoretical and applied linguistics*, ed. by Diana Archangeli, Andrew Barss, and Richard Sproat, 87–101. MIT Working Papers in Linguistics 6. Cambridge, MA: MIT, MIT Working Papers in Linguistics.

Hoekstra, Teun, and René Mulder. 1990. Unergatives as copular verbs: Locational and existential predication. *The Linguistic Review* 7: 1–79.

Hofmeister, Philip, and Ivan A. Sag. 2010. Cognitive constraints and island effects. *Language* 86: 366–415.

Hofmeister, Philip, Laura Staum Casasanto, and Ivan A. Sag. 2012. How do individual cognitive differences relate to acceptability judgments? A reply to Sprouse, Wagers, and Phillips. *Language* 88: 390–400.

Hofmeister, Philip, Laura Staum Casasanto, and Ivan A. Sag. 2013. Islands in the grammar? Standards of evidence. In *Experimental syntax and island effects*, ed. by Jon Sprouse and Norbert Hornstein, 42–63. Cambridge: Cambridge University Press.

Hornstein, Norbert. 1999. Movement and control. *Linguistic Inquiry* 30: 69–96.

Jakobson, Roman.1958. Morfologičeskie nabljudenija na slavjanskim skloneniem. In *Selected writings 2*, 154–183. The Hague: Mouton.

Jayaseelan, K. A. 2017. Parallel work spaces in syntax and the inexistence of Internal Merge. In *Perspectives on the architecture and acquisition of syntax: Essays in honor of R. Amritavalli*, ed. by Gautam Sengupta, Shruti Sircar, Madhavi Gayathri Raman, and Rahul Balusu, 115–134. Singapore: Springer Nature.

Johannessen, Janne Bondi. 1998. *Coordination*. Oxford: Oxford University Press.

Johnson, Kyle. 2007. LCA+alignment=RNR. Talk presented at the Workshop on Coordination, Subordination, and Ellipsis, Tübingen, June 2007.

Johnson, Kyle. 2012. Towards deriving differences in how *wh* movement and QR are pronounced. *Lingua* 122: 529–553.

Johnson, Kyle. 2018. Movement as multidominance. Handouts of lectures given at the 2nd Crete Summer School of Linguistics, University of Crete, Rethymno, July 2018.

Kandybowicz, Jason. 2006. Conditions on multiple copy Spell-Out and the syntax-phonology interface. PhD dissertation, UCLA.

Kasai, Hironobu. 2004. Two notes on ATB movement. *Language and Linguistics* 5: 167–188.

Kasai, Hironobu. 2007. Multidominance in syntax. PhD dissertation, Harvard University.

Kayne, Richard S. 1981. Unambiguous paths. In *Levels of syntactic representation*, ed. by Robert May and Jan Koster, 143–183. Dordrecht: Foris.

Kayne, Richard S. 1984. *Connectedness and binary branching*. Dordrecht: Foris.

Kayne, Richard S. 1994. *The antisymmetry of syntax*. Cambridge, MA: MIT Press.

Kramer, Ruth. 2016. Syncretism in paradigm function morphology and Distributed Morphology. In *Morphological metatheory*, ed. by Daniel Siddiqi and Heidi Harley, 95–120. Amsterdam: John Benjamins.

Larson, Bradley. 2012. A dilemma with accounts of Right Node Raising. *Linguistic Inquiry* 43: 143–150.

Larson, Brooke. 2016. The representation of syntactic action at a distance: Multidominance versus the copy theory. *Glossa* 1(1): 39, 1–18.

Lasnik, Howard, and Mamoru Saito. 1984. On the nature of proper government. *Linguistic Inquiry* 15: 235–289.

Lasnik, Howard, and Mamoru Saito. 1992. *Move α: Conditions on its application and output*. Cambridge, MA: MIT Press.

Law, Paul. 1991. Verb movement, expletive replacement, and head government. *The Linguistic Review* 8: 253–285.

Legate, Julie Anne. 2003. Some interface properties of the phase. *Linguistic Inquiry* 34: 506–516.

Levin, Beth, and Malka Rappaport Hovav. 1995. *Unaccusativity: At the syntax–lexical semantics interface*. Cambridge, MA: MIT Press.

McCawley, James D. 1982. Parentheticals and discontinuous constituents. *Linguistic Inquiry* 13: 91–106.

McCreight, Katherine, and Catherine V. Chvany. 1991. Geometric representation of paradigms in a modular theory of grammar. In *Paradigms: The economy of inflection*, ed. by Frans Plank, 91–112. Berlin: Mouton de Gruyter.

McNally, Louise. 1992. VP coordination and the VP-Internal Subject Hypothesis. *Linguistic Inquiry* 23: 336–341.

Moltmann, Friederike. 1992. Coordination and comparatives. PhD dissertation, MIT.

Moro, Andrea. 1997. *The raising of predicates: Predicative noun phrases and the theory of clause structure*. Cambridge: Cambridge University Press.

Muadz, Husni. 1991. Coordinate structures: A planar representation. PhD dissertation, University of Arizona.

Müller, Gereon. 2011. Syncretism without underspecification: The role of leading forms. *Word Structure* 4: 53–103.

Müller, Gereon, and Wolfgang Sternefeld. 1993. Improper movement and unambiguous binding. *Linguistic Inquiry* 24: 461–507.

Munn, Alan. 2001. Explaining parasitic gap restrictions. In *Parasitic gaps*, ed. by Peter W. Culicover and Paul M. Postal, 369–392. Cambridge, MA: MIT Press.

Ndayiragije, Juvénal. 1999. Checking economy. *Linguistic Inquiry* 30: 399–444.

Neidle, Carol. 1988. *The role of case in Russian syntax*. Dordrecht: Kluwer.

Nunes, Jairo. 1995. The Copy Theory of Movement and linearization of chains in the Minimalist Program. PhD dissertation, University of Maryland.

Nunes, Jairo. 2001. Sideward movement. *Linguistic Inquiry* 32: 303–344.

Nunes, Jairo. 2004. *Linearization of chains and sideward movement*. Cambridge, MA: MIT Press.

Nunes, Jairo, and Juan Uriagereka. 2000. Cyclicity and extraction domains. *Syntax* 3: 20–43.

Parker, Dan. 2017. Processing multiple gap dependencies: Forewarned is forearmed. *Journal of Memory and Language* 97: 175–186.

Partee, Barbara H., Alice ter Meulen, and Robert E. Wall. 1990. *Mathematical methods in linguistics*. Dordrecht: Kluwer.

Pereltsvaig, Asya. Under review. Is the OVS order in Russian like that in Hixkaryana? In *Proceedings of FASL 28*, ed. by Andrei Antonenko, John Bailyn, and Anna Melnikova.

Pesetsky, David. 1982. Paths and categories. PhD dissertation, MIT.

Pesetsky, David. 2017. Complementizer-trace effects. In *The Wiley Blackwell companion to syntax*, ed. by Martin Everaert and Henk C. van Riemsdijk, 993–1026. 2nd ed. Hoboken, NJ: John Wiley.

Peters, Stanley, and R. W. Ritchie. 1973. On the generative power of transformational grammars. *Information Sciences* 6: 49–83.

Postal, Paul M. 1974. *On raising: One rule of English grammar and its theoretical implications*. Cambridge, MA: MIT Press.

Postal, Paul M. 1998. *Three investigations of extraction*. Cambridge, MA: MIT Press.

Postal, Paul M. 2004. *Skeptical linguistic essays*. New York: Oxford University Press.

Progovac, Ljiljana. 1998. Structure for coordination. Part I and II. *Glot International* 3.7: 3–6 and 3.8: 3–9.

Przepiórkowski, Adam. 2000. Long distance genitive of negation in Polish. *Journal of Slavic Linguistics* 8: 151–189.

Pullum, Geoffrey K., and Arnold Zwicky. 1986. Phonological resolution of syntactic feature conflict. *Language* 62: 751–775.

Riemsdijk, Henk C. van. 2000. Free relatives inside out: Transparent free relatives as grafts. In *PASE Papers in Language Studies—Proceedings of the 8th Annual Conference of the Polish Association for the Study of English*, ed. by Bożena Rozwadowska, 223–233. University of Wrocław.

Riemsdijk, Henk C. van. 2006a. Free relatives. In *The Blackwell companion to syntax*, ed. by Martin Everaert and Henk C. van Riemsdijk. London: Blackwell.

Riemsdijk, Henk C. van. 2006b. Grafts follow from Merge. In *Phases of interpretation*, ed. by Mara Frascarelli, 17–44. Berlin: Mouton de Gruyter.

Rizzi, Luigi. 1990. *Relativized Minimality*. Cambridge, MA: MIT Press.

Rizzi, Luigi. 1997. The fine structure of the left periphery. In *Elements of grammar*, ed. by Liliane Haegeman, 281–337. Dordrecht: Kluwer.

Rizzi, Luigi. 2004. Locality and left periphery. In *Structures and beyond: The cartography of syntactic structures (Vol. 3)*, ed. by Adriana Belletti, 223–251. New York: Oxford University Press.

Rizzi, Luigi, and Ur Shlonsky. 2007. Strategies of subject extraction. In *Interfaces + recursion = language?*, ed. by Uli Sauerland and Hans-Martin Gärtner, 115–160. Berlin: Mouton de Gruyter.

Ross, John Robert. 1967. Constraints on variables in syntax. PhD dissertation, MIT.

Runner, Jeffrey T. 1998. *Noun phrase licensing*. New York: Garland.

Sabbagh, Joseph. 2007. Ordering and linearizing rightward movement. *Natural Language and Linguistic Theory* 25: 349–401.

Sabbagh, Joseph. 2014. Right Node Raising. *Language and Linguistics Compass* 8: 24–35.

Salzmann, Martin. 2013. Repair-driven verb movement in English locative inversion. In *Repairs: The added value of being wrong*, ed. by Patrick Brandt and Eric Fuß, 155–206. Berlin: Mouton de Gruyter.

Sampson, Geoffrey. 1975. The Single Mother Condition. *Journal of Linguistics* 11: 1–11.

Sekerina, Irina A. 1997. The syntax and processing of Russian scrambled constructions. PhD dissertation, City University of New York.

Slioussar, Natalia. 2007. Mysterious nature of the Russian EPP. In *UiL OTS yearbook 2006*, ed. by Cem Keskin, 113–130. Utrecht: Universiteit Utrecht.

Slioussar, Natalia. 2011. Russian and the EPP requirement in the Tense domain. *Lingua* 121: 2048–2068.

Sobin, Nicholas. 2002. The comp-trace effect, the adverb effect and minimal CP. *Journal of Linguistics* 38: 527–560.

Speas, Margaret. 1994. Null arguments in a theory of economy of projection. In *Functional projections*, ed. by Elena Benedicto and Jeffrey Runner, 179–208. University of Massachusetts Occasional Papers in Linguistics 17. Amherst: University of Massachusetts, Graduate Linguistic Student Association.

Sportiche, Dominique. 2019. Somber prospects for Late Merger. *Linguistic Inquiry* 50: 416–424.

Sprouse, Jon, Matt Wagers, and Colin Phillips. 2012a. A test of the relation between working memory capacity and syntactic island effects. *Language* 88: 82–123.

Sprouse, Jon, Matt Wagers, and Colin Phillips. 2012b. Working memory capacity and island effects: A reminder of the issues and the facts. *Language* 88: 401–407.

Starke, Michal. 2001. Move dissolves into Merge: A theory of locality. PhD dissertation, University of Geneva.

Stroik, Thomas. 2009. *Locality in Minimalist syntax*. Cambridge, MA: MIT Press.

Stump, Gregory T. 1993. On rules of referral. *Language* 69: 449–479.

Sturt, Patrick, and Andrea E. Martin. 2016. Using grammatical features to forecast incoming structure: The processing of across-the-board extraction. Paper presented at the 29th CUNY Human Sentence Processing Conference, Gainesville, FL.

Tajsner, Przemysław. 2008. Inverse binding and the status of the Spec. TP position in Polish. *Studia Anglica Posnaniensia: International Review of English Studies* 44: 409–429.

Valmala, Vidal. 2013. On Right Node Raising in Catalan and Spanish. *Catalan Journal of Linguistics* 12: 219–251.

Vries, Mark de. 2009. On multidominance and linearization. *Biolinguistics* 3: 344–403.

Vries, Mark de. 2013a. Multidominance and locality. *Lingua* 134: 149–169.

Vries, Mark de. 2013b. Unconventional mergers. In *Ways of structure building*, ed. by Vidal Valmala and Myriam Uribe-Etxebarria, 143–166. Oxford: Oxford University Press.

Vries, Mark de. 2017. Across-the-board phenomena. In *The Wiley Blackwell companion to syntax*, ed. by Martin Everaert and Henk C. van Riemsdijk, 20–50. 2nd ed. Hoboken, NJ: John Wiley.

Wall, Robert E. 1972. *Introduction to mathematical linguistics*. Englewood Cliffs, NJ: Prentice-Hall.

Wexler, Kenneth, and Peter Culicover. 1980. *Formal principles of language acquisition*. Cambridge, MA: MIT Press.

Wiland, Bartosz. 2009. Aspects of order preservation in Polish and English. PhD dissertation, Adam Mickiewicz University, Poznań.

Wiland, Bartosz. 2016. Le charme discret of remnant movement: Crossing and nesting in Polish OVS sentences. *Studies in Polish Linguistics* 11: 133–165.

Wilder, Chris. 1999. Right Node Raising and the LCA. In *WCCFL 18: Proceedings of the 18th West Coast Conference on Formal Linguistics*, ed. by Sonya Bird, Andrew Carnie, Jason D. Haugen, and Peter Norquest, 586–598. Somerville, MA: Cascadilla Press.

Wilder, Chris. 2008. Shared constituents and linearization. In *Topics in ellipsis*, ed. by Kyle Johnson, 229–258. New York: Cambridge University Press.

Williams, Edwin. 1978. Across-the-board rule application. *Linguistic Inquiry* 9: 31–43.

Williams, Edwin. 1981. Transformationless grammar. *Linguistic Inquiry* 12: 645–653.

Williams, Edwin. 1994. Remarks on lexical knowledge. *Lingua* 92: 7–34.

Witkoś, Jacek. 2008a. Genitive of negation and single cycle derivations. *Journal of Slavic Linguistics* 16: 247–287.

Witkoś, Jacek. 2008b. On the correlation between A-type scrambling and Weak Crossover effects. *Studia Anglica Posnaniensia: International Review of English Studies* 44: 297–328.

Woolford, Ellen. 1987. An ECP account of constraints on across-the-board extraction. *Linguistic Inquiry* 18: 166–171.

Zhang, Niina. 2004. Move is Remerge. *Language and Linguistics* 5: 189–209.

Zhang, Niina. 2007. The syntactic derivations of two paired dependency constructions. *Lingua* 117: 2134–2158.

Zhang, Niina. 2010. *Coordination in syntax*. Cambridge: Cambridge University Press.

Zoerner, Ed. 1995. Coordination: The syntax of &P. PhD dissertation, University of California, Irvine.

Zovko-Dinković, Irena. 2011. Egzistencijalni glagoli u hrvatskome [Existential verbs in Croatian]. *Suvremena lingvistika* 37: 279–294.

Zwart, Jan-Wouter. 2009. Prospects for top-down derivation. *Catalan Journal of Linguistics* 8: 161–187.

Zwart, Jan-Wouter. 2011. Structure and order: Asymmetric Merge. In *The Oxford handbook of linguistic Minimalism*, ed. by Cedric Boeckx, 96–118. Oxford: Oxford University Press.

Zwicky, Arnold M. 1969. Phonological constraints in syntactic descriptions. *Papers in Linguistics* 1: 411–463.

Zwicky, Arnold M. 1985a. The case against plain vanilla syntax. *Studies in the Linguistic Sciences* 15: 205–225.

Zwicky, Arnold M. 1985b. Rules of allomorphy and phonology-syntax interactions. *Journal of Linguistics* 21: 431–436.

Index

Linguistic Inquiry Monographs

Samuel Jay Keyser, general editor

1. *Word Formation in Generative Grammar*, Mark Aronoff
2. *$\bar{X}$ Syntax: A Study of Phrase Structure*, Ray Jackendoff
3. *Recent Transformational Studies in European Languages*, S. Jay Keyser, editor
4. *Studies in Abstract Phonology*, Edmund Gussmann
5. *An Encyclopedia of AUX: A Study of Cross-Linguistic Equivalence*, Susan Steele
6. *Some Concepts and Consequences of the Theory of Government and Binding*, Noam Chomsky
7. *The Syntax of Words*, Elisabeth O. Selkirk
8. *Syllable Structure and Stress in Spanish: A Nonlinear Analysis*, James W. Harris
9. *CV Phonology: A Generative Theory of the Syllable*, George N. Clements and Samuel Jay Keyser
10. *On the Nature of Grammatical Relations*, Alec P. Marantz
11. *A Grammar of Anaphora*, Joseph Aoun
12. *Logical Form: Its Structure and Derivation*, Robert May
13. *Barriers*, Noam Chomsky
14. *On the Definition of Word*, Anna-Maria Di Sciullo and Edwin Williams
15. *Japanese Tone Structure*, Janet Pierrehumbert and Mary E. Beckman
16. *Relativized Minimality*, Luigi Rizzi
17. *Types of Ā-Dependencies*, Guglielmo Cinque
18. *Argument Structure*, Jane Grimshaw
19. *Locality: A Theory and Some of Its Empirical Consequences*, Maria Rita Manzini
20. *Indefinites*, Molly Diesing
21. *Syntax of Scope*, Joseph Aoun and Yen-hui Audrey Li
22. *Morphology by Itself: Stems and Inflectional Classes*, Mark Aronoff
23. *Thematic Structure in Syntax*, Edwin Williams
24. *Indices and Identity*, Robert Fiengo and Robert May
25. *The Antisymmetry of Syntax*, Richard S. Kayne
26. *Unaccusativity: At the Syntax–Lexical Semantics Interface*, Beth Levin and Malka Rappaport Hovav
27. *Lexico-Logical Form: A Radically Minimalist Theory*, Michael Brody
28. *The Architecture of the Language Faculty*, Ray Jackendoff
29. *Local Economy*, Chris Collins
30. *Surface Structure and Interpretation*, Mark Steedman
31. *Elementary Operations and Optimal Derivations*, Hisatsugu Kitahara
32. *The Syntax of Nonfinite Complementation: An Economy Approach*, Željko Bošković
33. *Prosody, Focus, and Word Order*, Maria Luisa Zubizarreta

34. *The Dependencies of Objects*, Esther Torrego
35. *Economy and Semantic Interpretation*, Danny Fox
36. *What Counts: Focus and Quantification*, Elena Herburger
37. *Phrasal Movement and Its Kin*, David Pesetsky
38. *Dynamic Antisymmetry*, Andrea Moro
39. *Prolegomenon to a Theory of Argument Structure*, Ken Hale and Samuel Jay Keyser
40. *Essays on the Representational and Derivational Nature of Grammar: The Diversity of* Wh-*Constructions*, Joseph Aoun and Yen-hui Audrey Li
41. *Japanese Morphophonemics: Markedness and Word Structure*, Junko Ito and Armin Mester
42. *Restriction and Saturation*, Sandra Chung and William A. Ladusaw
43. *Linearization of Chains and Sideward Movement*, Jairo Nunes
44. *The Syntax of (In)dependence*, Ken Safir
45. *Interface Strategies: Optimal and Costly Computations*, Tanya Reinhart
46. *Asymmetry in Morphology*, Anna Maria Di Sciullo
47. *Relators and Linkers: The Syntax of Predication, Predicate Inversion, and Copulas*, Marcel den Dikken
48. *On the Syntactic Composition of Manner and Motion*, Maria Luisa Zubizarreta and Eunjeong Oh
49. *Introducing Arguments*, Liina Pylkkänen
50. *Where Does Binding Theory Apply?*, David Lebeaux
51. *Locality in Minimalist Syntax*, Thomas S. Stroik
52. *Distributed Reduplication*, John Frampton
53. *The Locative Syntax of Experiencers*, Idan Landau
54. *Why Agree? Why Move?: Unifying Agreement-Based and Discourse-Configurational Languages*, Shigeru Miyagawa
55. *Locality in Vowel Harmony*, Andrew Nevins
56. *Uttering Trees*, Norvin Richards
57. *The Syntax of Adjectives*, Guglielmo Cinque
58. *Arguments as Relations*, John Bowers
59. *Agreement and Head Movement*, Ian Roberts
60. *Localism versus Globalism in Morphology and Phonology*, David Embick
61. *Provocative Syntax*, Phil Branigan
62. *Anaphora and Language Design*, Eric J. Reuland
63. *Indefinite Objects: Scrambling, Choice Functions, and Differential Marking*, Luis López
64. *A Syntax of Substance*, David Adger
65. *Subjunctive Conditionals*, Michela Ippolito
66. *Russian Case Morphology and the Syntactic Categories*, David Pesetsky
67. *Classical NEG Raising: An Essay on the Syntax of Negation*, Chris Collins and Paul M. Postal

68. *Agreement and Its Failures*, Omer Preminger
69. *Voice and v: Lessons from Acehnese*, Julie Anne Legate
70. *(Re)labeling*, Carlo Cecchetto and Caterina Donati
71. *A Two-Tiered Theory of Control*, Idan Landau
72. *Concepts, Syntax, and Their Interface: Tanya Reinhart's Theta System*, Martin Everaert, Marijana Marelj, and Eric Reuland, editors
73. *Contiguity Theory*, Norvin Richards
74. *Impossible Persons*, Daniel Harbour
75. *Agreement Beyond Phi*, Shigeru Miyagawa
76. *The Final-over-Final Condition: A Syntactic Universal*, Michelle Sheehan, Theresa Biberauer, Ian Roberts, and Anders Holmberg
77. *Situations and Syntactic Structures: Rethinking Auxiliaries and Order in English*, Gillian Ramchand
78. *Features of Person: From the Inventory of Persons to Their Morphological Realization*, Peter Ackema and Ad Neeleman
79. *Cardinals: The Syntax and Semantics of Cardinal-Containing Expressions*, Tania Ionin and Ora Matushansky
80. *Composing Questions*, Hadas Kotek
81. *Probes and Their Horizons*, Stefan Keine
82. *A Theory of Indexical Shift: Meaning, Grammar, and Crosslinguistic Variation*, Amy Rose Deal
83. *Merge: Binarity in (Multidominant) Syntax*, Barbara Citko and Martina Gračanin-Yuksek